Poetics
of the
New

also in this series

Horizons
by Dick Higgins

THE
L=A=N=G=U=A=G=E
BOOK

Edited by

Bruce Andrews and Charles Bernstein

Southern Illinois University Press
Carbondale and Edwardsville

Library of Congress Cataloging in Publication Data
Main entry under title:

The L=A=N=G=U=A=G=E book.

(Poetics of the new)
Reprinted from: L=A=N=G=U=A=G=E, v. 1–3.
1. Literature—Addresses, essays, lectures.
I. Andrews, Bruce, 1948– . II. Bernstein,
Charles. III. Title: LANGUAGE book. IV. Series.
PN45.L2 1983   809   83-376
ISBN 0-8093-1106-2

87 86 85 84   4 3 2 1

CONTENTS

Contents

Contents

REPOSSESSING THE WORD

L=A=N=G=U=A=G=E started as a bimonthly magazine of information and commentary, a forum for discussion and interchange. Throughout, we have emphasized a spectrum of writing that places its attention primarily on language and ways of making meaning, that takes for granted neither vocabulary, grammar, process, shape, syntax, program, or subject matter. All of these remain at issue. Focussing on this range of poetic exploration, and on related aesthetic and political concerns, we have tried to open things up beyond correspondence and conversation: to break down some unnecessary self-encapsulation of writers (person from person, & scene from scene), and to develop more fully the latticework of those involved in aesthetically related activity.

As part of this process, and with the aim of foregrounding compositional issues and styles of reading, we published a mix of different kinds of work. We especially wanted to provide a place for essays and reviews that were neither expository nor narrowly evaluative—that is, where the actual language work that goes on in poetry writing is not set aside in writing that "discusses."

It seems worth remembering, in looking back, that the labels sometimes attached to the variety of writings discussed in L=A=N=G=U=A=G=E can be as troublesome as they are illuminating. Slogans and catchphrases signal the possibility that stylistic fixation can be an entrapment for these as well as other tendencies in recent poetry. The reason we have shied away from a number of confining labels in editing L=A=N=G=U=A=G=E is that our project, if it can be summarized at all, has involved exploring the numerous ways that meanings and values can be (& are) realized—revealed—produced in writing. This involves an opening of the field of activity and not its premature foreclosure.

Nonetheless confusion about the nature of this exploration flourishes. For instance, the idea that writing should (or could) be stripped of reference is as bothersome and confusing as the assumption that the primary function of words is to refer, one-on-one, to an already constructed world of "things." Rather, reference, like the body itself, is one of the horizons of language, whose value is to be found in the writing (the world) before which we find ourselves at any moment. It is the multiple powers and scope of reference (denotative, connotative, associational), not writers' refusal or fear of it, that threads these essays together. It is a renewed engagement that comes from the recognition that the (various) measuring and questioning and composition of our references is the practice of our craft.

This is inevitably a social and political activity as well as an aesthetic one. One major preoccupation of L=A=N=G=U=A=G=E has therefore been to generate discussion on the relation of writing to politics, particularly to articulate some of the ways that writing can act to critique society. Ron Silliman's early essay, "Disappearance of the Word/Appearance of the World," reprinted here, applies the notion of commodity fetishism to conventional descriptive and narrative forms of writing: where the word—words—cease to be valued for what they are themselves but only for their properties as instrumentalities leading us to a world outside or beyond them, so that words—language—disappear, become transparent, leaving the picture of a physical world the reader can then consume as if it were a commodity. This view of the role and historical functions of literature relates closely to our analysis of the capitalist social order as a whole and of the place that alternative forms of writing and reading might occupy in its transformation. It is our sense that the project of poetry does not involve turning language into a commodity for consumption; instead, it involves repossessing the sign through close attention to, and active participation in, its production.

The first issue of L=A=N=G=U=A=G=E appeared in February 1978, starting with the Larry Eigner text that begins this volume. Over the next four years, we published twelve issues and two supplements (Volumes 1 to 3), and in conjunction with the Canadian Journal *Open Letter*, our final offering, *Volume Four*. For *The L=A=N=G=U=A=G=E Book*, we have only included a selection of the first three volumes. *Volume Four* remains available as a substantial book format collection that serves as a companion volume to *The L=A=N=G=U=A=G=E Book*.

In making the present selection, we have had to omit about half of the material we originally published in the first three volumes. As a result, this book does not represent a significant topical quality of the magazine: bibliographies, contributors' lists of recommended reading, brief comments on current books, correspondence, and the like, filled many pages not reproduced here. In addition, space considerations necessitated leaving out a number of important texts.

Many books are cited in the pages that follow, inviting, we hope, further interest in searching them out and reading them. Since many are published by noncommercial, independent presses, we recommend writing to two central poetry book (and magazine) distributors who between them have almost all of the in-print titles listed, as well as many related items. Write to Small Press Distributing, 1784 Shattuck Avenue, Berkeley, CA 94709 and to Segue Distributing, 300 Bowery, New York, NY 10012. For further information on L=A=N=G=U=A=G=E, including back issues and our book collection *Volume Four*, write to us at 464 Amsterdam Avenue, New York, NY 10024.

Charles Bernstein & Bruce Andrews

THE

L=A=N=G=U=A=G=E

BOOK

1.

Poetics and Language

Larry Eigner

Approaching things
Some Calculus
How figure it Of Everyday Life
Experience

No really perfect optimum mix, anyway among some thousands or many of distinctive or distinguishable things (while according to your capacity some minutes, days or hours 2, 4 or 6 people, say, are company rather than crowds), and for instance you can try too hard or too little. But beyond the beginning or other times and situations of scarcity, with material (things, words) more and more dense around you, closer at hand, easier and easier becomes invention, combustion, increasingly spontaneous. And when I got willing enough to stop anywhere, though for years fairly in mind had been the idea and aim of long as possible works about like the desire to live for good or have a good (various?) thing never end, then like walking down the street noticing things a poem would extend itself.

Any amount, degree, of perfection is a surprise. yet you have to be concerned with it some, by the way, be observant - serendipity. Also, though - and there's the kaleidoscopic, things put together like flying a kite - too much of or too frequent a good is distraction, or anyway, I could go blind or be knocked out. What if up north the midnight sun were all year round? While - to repeat - language is a surprising tool, recently I turned around and was kind of astonished what can be done with it, what has been. Kites, birds.

But behind words and whatever language comes about are things (language I guess develops mainly by helping cope with them), things and people, and words can't bring people in India or West Virginia above the poverty line, say, and I can't want more.

Well, how does (some of) the forest go together with the trees. How might it, maybe. Forest of possibilities (in language anyway) - ways in and ways out. Near and far - wide and narrow (circles). Your neighborhood and how much of the world otherwise. Beginning, ending and continuing. As they come, what can things mean? Why expect a permanent meaning? What weights, imports? Nothing is ever quite as obvious as anything else, at least in context. A poem can't be too long, anything like an equatorial highway girdling the thick rotund earth, but is all right and can extend itself an additional bit if you're willing enough to stop anywhere. And I feel my way in fiddling a little, or then sometimes more, on the roof of the burning or rusting world.

". . . to care and not to care . . . to sit still" Careful of earth air

and water mainly perhaps, and other lives, but some (how many?)
other things too. Walden, ah! The dancer and the dance. What first
(off)? What next? What citizens how come in
      Poetry considerateing, Prose adventure (essay?) ?
         Many/and/various/mixes.

Nick Piombino
WRITING AS REVERIE

"Gee, Toto, I've got a feeling we're not in Kansas anymore."
—Dorothy, *Wizard of Oz* (1939)

1. An obsessive monitoring of some remembered texts becomes an immediate occasion for delay, association, structure, plenitude, a gathering for an album constructed out of items of intrinsic value. Play conceived as the manipulation of reminders, an accumulation of fragments, passes through coherence into speculative fantasy. The argument runs like this: a child, pausing before his book, falls into a reverie. This daydream, composed in part of excessive thinking about power and mastery and a concurrent, if hidden and counterpointed theme of loss, an anticipated, almost yearned for loss, becomes equated with a particular visit to the ocean on an overcast day. The objects employed in his fantasy are transposed harmonically and modally into its emotional leitmotifs. The visual complements the emotional tense but cannot surpass it. The child is not exhaustively reading the seascape. His eidetic imagery is fastened to the concepts preceding it. Entranced as he is in his thoughts, his actions contribute to an air of unselfconscious movement. A momentary breakthrough of sunlight between clouds interrupts the melancholy quality of his meditations and the spell is half broken, because we see him again engaged in reading. Or is he merely seeing the printed words, his gaze still directed within, as the sound of the sea thunders loudly into his consciousness and the voices and activity and movement rush into his field of attention.

2. Meditations on an esthetics of fragmentation and discontinuity. Creation of a myth. History before me an interpretable reminder. The politics of extension and intentional fragment.

The interruption of "the argument runs like this" is a simple dimensional loosening of the referential register this particular moment of writing needed. Anywhere I look (for example, the child on the beach at sunset) I pass through a storm of connectives intensifying one another.

3. Holding the entire thought over my head like a cartoon bubble in the comics. Head scrambles neologisms. Each face inscribed as photographic engravure on the surface of the page. The age of portraits, the gradual acceding of biographical identification. The inscription, the latest removable naming of the surface crests. So the completed thought now resembles the boy's hesitations on the title he gave to his text. Notice it was in a book of art history writings. He likes maxims,

tautological witticisms that temporarily acquit and illuminate with guided opacity the steady pointed shadings toward the outcoming familiarity of the chosen puzzle: is he dreaming of the words themselves, divided as they are with each selected entry seal illustrated in a deluxe edition of signs?

4. "They can see right through me," thinks the child. They can diagram the space anyway they like, but I'll know by the tempo of his excitement whether or not the molecules might later collide and issue a fusion of opposites. Say the original imagery was not a naming, but an identifiable entity suspended above his head like an exclamation point. Not the subjective reticence of the I signifier, but a fire (!) and consequent, simultaneous engendering of excited tension. Bound up as he is in reading, he is perhaps for the first time equating a description with a given locale in a book—he is on a certain beach not yet named. He is reading his thoughts specifically against, next to, behind and above this presentiment of a later time when he will item for item inscribe this sea in his album, by means of partial, token representations.

Alan Davies
PRIVATE ENIGMA IN THE OPENED TEXT

The trace of the enigma is negligently latent in all writing. The enigma is a colorless monovalent feature in textual omnivalence.

This present writing defines those private enigmas with which the author sometimes pierces his text. These are distinct from, for example: the narratively enigmatic which, functioning, becomes through reappearance, a character or figure of the text; the metaphysically enigmatic which functions, deliberately, through our lives as we return to its imperative point of question; the enigmatics of dream which function, vehicularly, to let life ride itself; the grammatically enigmatic, which functions as a verbal irregularity, a non sequitur stunning us with what previously could not have been said; the enigmatic of any single text, which is obsessive in its function as the ground for all text and all enigma. Throughout this writing, the word 'enigma' will refer to private enigmas, and not to the otherwise enigmatic which may frequently surround its appearance.

The author may plant in his text his enigmas. Whether this is more common in the rangeingly modern text than in classical writing is something we may not learn. We may speak of the pleasure. The writer allows his enigmas as, quickly they choose him; with reason—pleasure. The attachment is attentive. There is pleasure in placing the deliberately extraneous, the stain. The enigma may be no more enigmatic to a reader than is the rest of the text, which may seem 'of a piece', or deliberately and equally not of one. But for the writer, the enigma remains a sign of himself in the text of himself, a unique entry of himself upon his language. It is that part which he obstinately holds to as he gives it all away. The presence of the reader is implicit in the pleasure of enigma; the author is a voyeur, enjoying as he writes, the pleasure of his reading of his text. In fact, he gives the text to himself as he writes it: but in the enigma he claims in one instant the combined functions of reading and writing; he completes already, again and in part, what already others, reading, complete again and in part. He enjoys, in advance, what it is usually for the reader, whether himself or another, to enjoy only later. It is a one-sided pleasure; doubled. The enigma is chosen as a special burden, a verdict the writing passes on the young history of texts.

The enigma cleans the text of its indebtedness. In the enigma gesture, a text lays hold of itself. An enigma, unlike the rest of texted language bound to structure, does not (have to) evaluate itself. It is already evaluated, it stands for that.

What is sought is an enigma which cannot be closed upon (hence the "is sought"). Small particles of meaning satisfy this best for the writer; though large structures do so, openly, they do so as structures, their closure a matter of preordained interest. The enigma is erased in its minute duration. An enigma, unlike the rest of structured text, is not the locus of any coming together, neither of a dispersion; it is a still point activated, once by the author's enthusiasm, and again by the writing which surrounds and which motivated its inauguration. Enigma, made to be unresolved, affords the opposition of immersion, of argument: it offers an opaque exterior; not offering entry or exit, it posits (the generic trace of pleasure). The enigma, cued only to itself, faces nothing. However, it is not bracketed. It is merely less loose among particles more active. Though its delight is not extinguished, it has no tendency. Its argument is that, it, is, here; hence its relation to structural wholes: the enigma less elusive, because more instanced, the structure less clear, because more over itself.

The enigma significantly animates (animates signification in) the writer's working. In his text he lodges it, stills the agitation by posturing its particular particle where it can be observed, contemplated, or where it can be passed over; without having to reveal its lived significance, he reveals the volume of it. It is transplanted; without, however, having been anywhere other than on both sites, met equally in the imagination with which they touch. The enigma is rendered siteless, a vantage from which its singularity can incite unanimously.

The enigma is the only anoegenetic particle of language. It stands, in part (and in part it 'fails'), for the effort which made it so. It does not sublimate its function to structure, as do all functioning chunks of meaning; it is apart from function, embodying it at once. It is an action on which the curtain of meaning has come down with finality; behind the curtain, the perfunctory disclosure of fact. The enigma is a silent spot in the rush of meanings, but only when viewed in that context. Its placement specializes it. Without being able to deposit its position in the meaning-productive text, it does in fact speak its stance. It refuses to speak in discourse in order to embody quick monologic impact.

The enigma is impoverished in context. It has nothing to do: no work, nothing by which to be covered, nothing to speak, no acts, no decisions to make or motivate in its place (no pivot), no early nor late and no here nor there. It has nothing to mobilize (after the author's delight), nothing to solve, nothing to begin or bring to an end. It abolishes, for an instant, what goes on surrounding it. If a text can be parsed, the enigma cannot. But it does not deny, it solidly confirms itself; its intractable dissolution of logic and sequence. But it must not irritate; it is in no way entangled. It is not a version of some other thing, neither is it averse to a possibility. It is stopped. It implies the release of the game, momentarily, without bringing it about. It generates its instant, and deprives it of reason, of play.

The enigma does not exist in the tangled limits of nature. It is an artifact. It in no way approaches the limits of what we know to be the case. It stands (in) (in the text) for the limits. It is an act of indication, but without the masking words which elsewhere accompany such acts; its substance is word, but it leaps, releasing them insoluble, an empty encasement. The enigma is marked by its absence from the site, as it is seen to occupy it totally. No contradiction; this, the enigma.

An enigma cannot be plural; it depends upon its indistributability. If it becomes dispersed in the text, if it is acted, its character is delineated in diffusion; of necessity, its still factness is destroyed. When the integer is serialized, or valued, when it is perceived through horizontal or vertical loci, it achieves a rhetorical or narrative function; it relaxes. The enigma must not be made to speak itself in any direction. The enigma, if it is to stand privately, if it is to release its pleasure, must not equivocate. The enigma is the only detached attachment permitted to text.

A text can be infused with a network of enigmas, which unavoidably connect. But when the enigma is extensive, it becomes a particle in the text's fabric, a code demanding, and enabling at least in part, its decipherment. As soon as an enigma is extensive, structured, it becomes a term among many in the text's polarities and excursions. It becomes one of numerous graphs upon which the writing occurs, tightening and loosening. Its dissolution proposes its solution; it talks. And it is no longer private; the text has begun to reply. The enigma is not permissive.

The enigma is consigned, ordered. It is the object of an action which, as a singularly upright subject, it demands. Unlike all other text, the enigma needs no support. It does not need to be there. It seems to be a will, to embody will so completely, that its it is embodied. It is irreversible. An order that cannot be recalled, it cannot die: its allure. The enigma is messageless; perfectly balanced (of one 'side'), it is the perfect signifier, the only one not drawn apart (revealed) by unequal (metaphorically inexact) sides. Stolid, it doesn't waver.

Peter Seaton
SIGNIFICATION

Reversing your hands if you're. The way your hands with the exception of everyone including that mystery that changed when one of the old hands thought nobody was looking. When I say hands is only half the expression something yours changed so that each weren't lined up and my hands learned the trick this way: if you want flexible body action leave the hand, hold your hands to leave your hands. Almost fall. When, when it drove the dirt behind him it was possible for a man to know the guy until one system obviously works. I hold my hands and step away from my shoulder. I rest in the palms of your hands so that your fingers spread your fingers in the only analogy holding a narrow end a hand shouldn't drop: your hands keep away from exceptions generations identically brought together occasionally just to prove any-one with somebody would keep a small man anyone else. Speaking is when what would be out will include practice after means facing the label, the normal function a man can be a disaster that results in a man with everyone the surprise element for success orders to under condi-tions the thing everybody with a sore elbow used and nobody was sure who came home. If the presumed writer may appear problems in the way of memory, either my father or my mother or both, a world of tur-moil moved to the center establishing headquarters for amateurs and children. Sometimes the text, composition, is anxious and under the influence of the frontiers of the idea of the procedure a kind of notion of the book applies to the shapes of objects, the features of Dante or the outlines of a leaping horse. The stars had always been original and poems which no place complete were written with the two complex-ities of experiments, success and the subsequent development of op-portunities, situations, the text left untouched, compositions based on comparisons between quantity and kinship, words as similar distor-tions, countless human beings, the function of the man who has con-firmed opposition in the same way as aspiration is comparable to con-tribution, in the same way matter is ambivalent. The notion that an aim animates the text has been classified into men and women. Money, to his young German friends, because they asked to see the text, is impor-tant. Nothing is his trade mark. One didn't know about the other hand, sometimes supposed to be one that was anything my wrist is when works, ice cold, change certain factors, whether or not, whether or not

experimenting is similar to the look which sometimes works, to stand-
ing, to covering all parts. The hand in action doesn't mean no one ever
took advantage of it. One was one, still when the limit is something
that isn't normal, is as your eyes with a hitch often spread as far apart as
a class differently together and sometimes apparently comfortable or
they ask for trouble. Human beings include Freud. Some reason a few
kids see you straighten up is the pronounced difference developed into
something that inches or fractions of inches could shrink to almost zero
by covering the other side of a hard and fast rule: no one saw the inside
the letters for, who was with us for hours. In order to peek I doubt if
anyone else had unwinding to do. How a mystery never did brings me
to dozens of a personal favorite. Anyone would be in trouble. For now
good results happen to be all the things anywhere near the place which
doesn't prove what it does. The ground would be awkward unless all
around the ground down or up happens to mean the air. By 1969 words
keep the opposition caught against a normal alignment. Something
can't be your arms any more. Each, each has similarities. All say:
twenty. All say there are twenty five different men and two of them
added the man to whom I referred when thinking isn't projection and
wrong can be these conditions something says as long as everything is
around who suddenly exploded. He's in trouble. It's the same brain
your arms swing before swinging your brain to swing because its fouled
up and one or two or two or three helps instead of anything properly
a man:
Whether that everything I can find out later
Sometimes I start sometimes I wait
Takes eyesight. Ordinary circumstances
Needs them vividly. However
I actually see. The actual meeting
Which gives my own experience a slight blur
Starts through it. This is including me.
It's when one is everything exactly coming in
From what I hear. From what I hear. Because
a man can get all fouled up. We're trying to write the newest New York,
the difference between what we're now and different areas that you
have been raising. The difference is anybody who can read and com-
plications a man has a man a man Soviet-American relations hasn't
happened to. The only available ones are "junk". You've got the loca-
tion that includes me, somebody around to see, others doing nothing
these dimensions are full of. It could have been said, we had become a
consequence of being in a position and adjusting everything except op-
position. But this year I often made matters worse. I get a whole array of

problems in a minute in order to learn a new slump. I'd like to pursue personal problems your concentration places as an ordinary interruption consumption has examined right at somebody. The same thing right at someone is intended to keep your eye as a target, the advantage an obligation regularly is some mystery in order to bring in some of the tricks of the trade: I get really tough to develop a hitch and eventually I know how I know, access to pictures is casual conversation with a friend on another team, I concentrate, I remember everything by focusing on one of the world's tough things to lick.

Ray DiPalma
TYING AND UNTYING

Never much given to abstracting my ideas about writing or shoving some neat precis under the nose of anyone asking about this or that aspect of poetry, I'd prefer to offer this thaumatrope of a few quotations from my notebooks with which I share an expression of attitude, aesthetic maintenance, persistence of vision taking its measure from a spirit of form that admits a wide range of concentrations— coordinated arcs not merely cyclic abandonment or linear expanse. All notions of form are implicitly coercive. I prefer example to precept; impertinence to quiet philosophist irony. And as I am not in search of the ultimate expression of the charmed quark etymon hidden in the beard of Karl Marx, neither the vast and minimalized itemizations coming up for a rapture of air nor the selected panoply of modes frustrated by retrospect, gooned by media and particalized by procedure are of much interest to me. It's creating THE FOCUS THAT GENERATES that concerns me. Not so called revolutionary ideas reduced to connoisseurship. Or else as a writer one is just another coot ploughing the Empire.

"Language-using controls the rest;
Wonderful is language!
Wondrous the English language, language of live men,
Language of ensemble, powerful language of resistance . . ."
                                                    — Whitman

"Every man has reminiscences which he would not tell to everyone but only to his friends. He has other matters in his mind which he would not reveal even to his friends, but only to himself, and that in secret. But there are other things which a man is afraid to tell even to himself, and every man has a number of such things stored away in his mind. The more decent he is the greater number of such things in his mind."
                                                    — Dostoevsky

"You must talk with two tongues, if you do not wish to cause confusion." — Wyndham Lewis

"One invents a technique or procedure by oneself; one does not invent entirely on one's own a state of mind." — Juan Gris

"329. When I think in language, there aren't 'meanings' going through my head in addition to the verbal expressions: the language is itself the vehicle of thought." — Wittgenstein

"Art will no longer aspire to account for everything; it will have left forever the ambiguous sphere of transcendency for the scattered, humble everyday universal of the relative." — Pierre Restany

"I love men not for what unites them, but for what divides them, and I want to know most of all what gnaws at their hearts." — Apollinaire

"The poem as simultaneous structure, impersonal, autonomous, released from the charge of expression, of assertion; the poem as arbitrary construct, absurd, self-destroying, no longer aspiring to convince or even to hoax; the poem as agent of transformation, equal in value to the poet himself and therefore capable of changing him; the poem as means of escape from identity; leading into a world of contemplation, indifference, bliss." — Source Unknown

"There are two kinds of writers, those who are and those who aren't. With the first, content and form belong together like soul and body; with the second, they match each other like body and clothes."
— Karl Kraus

"A book is a mirror: when a monkey looks in, no apostle can look out."
— Lichtenberg

Quince. Bless thee, Bottom, bless thee! Thou art translated.

Ron Silliman
FOR L=A=N=G=U=A=G=E

Word's a sentence before it's a word—I write sentences—When words are, meaning soon follows—Where words join, writing is—One's writing is one writing—Not all letters are equal—2 phrases yield an angle—Eye settles in the middle of word, left of center—Reference is a compass—Each day—Performance seeks vaudeville—Composition as investigation—Collage is a false democracy—Spelling's choices—Line defined by its closure: the function is nostalgic—Nothing without necessity—By hand—Individuals do not exist—Keep mind from sliding—Structure is metaphor, content permission, syntax force— Don't imitate yourself—We learned the language—Aesthetic consistency = voice—How does a work end?

Barrett Watten

NOTE

The problem is, does this person, in what is merely an adaptation to his environment, develop a language we can identify as our own. The problem of translation. Referents drop away. Not to circumvent identity structure, an all-over form. Rather that form is built back in. Any element implies a whole. A bean that explodes its meaning, small beans into large clouds. A monument is equally a miniature. Isn't the gas bill a particular, Joseph Stalin. A monument is merely a moment in time, the next world in line is miniature. Ideas turn into things, the lore of the antipoetic. Step back from this picture in order to see it. That's where he can't find any area to which attention is restricted. The scale pops endlessly in and out of line. A voice, but, choice. Scales thinking down to that point.

The world we seek is white. Is color a special section of the vocabulary, unlike any other. Stepping back from an abstraction as white. The white page, equally specific. The white paint of turbulence, atmospheric pressure up. Is X, the next word, white. So white conveys a distance, close in, getting on to the next thing. Taking attributes from descriptive, relational, intentional language to make statement, a logic is developed, way back in the brain. A voice becomes distinct in the values of the words. Language as a whole is modified through that voice, its values established to a greater degree. White with its element of death. So he remembers the penetration of unresolved metallic hum. Throughout his physical body, a tone. Magnetized through a ring of all experience, the word becoming an act.

A poem can be a stretch of thinking. At the point where words are formed, back in the brain. Not polyform, static, branching, kicking, unless the words say so. Values are decided at the source, and of necessity, through the form of writing. The line in verse operates as syntax, an entire poem is an arena or duration in which to work. One now finds he must bear down on words, one at a time. But prose must be satisfied first. Prose as equivalent to a state, a state of mind. A line of thought in the environment of many others. The opposition only serves to heighten interest. The copula leads to automatism, a dialectic of the unreleased. A scale expands or contracts, within a surrounding unknown. Negative capability. But power is in the line, the power to get things done. A stretch of thinking, to participate in the making of words. The categories all bear on a reconciliation of logic and the physical facts. Into language, poem line prose word. A separation clears the air, a lot more needs to be done. I think an act allowing itself, grabs me back in.

To build the form back in, increase emphasis. That would be logically consistent. The grounds of that logic are greater than the decision to employ it. A specialized vocabulary is part of any language as a whole. There's something in the air, wanting to complete itself, unattached. Verbs eat into walls, nouns in a ring consume themselves. If at some point language walked in the open door, we would show it some respect. Our response would be more immediate than to use it as a sign. So we respect language by not being content to operate in any one part of it. It's greater than we are. That has implications for the form. That sense is larger than one can say.

Robert Grenier
"HEDGE-CRICKETS SING"

—think of *Keats* as really 'milking' words of all possible letter/phonemic qualities without really challenging notion of English word/ morpheme as basic unit of 'meaning'—hence 'best effects' all-stress monosyllabic—"No, no, go not to Leth(e)"—"Where are the songs of Spring? Ay, where are they?"—because mind in work really does *want* to think phonemically, one sounds so 'dense & rich', tongued—slows down articulation so teeth, lips, whole vocal apparatus drawn in to pronouncing letters, reading it aloud—counting 'syllables' (convenient grouping of phonemes/ smallest unit one normally hears) thus more than old poetic habit, focusses attention toward primary semantic unit—*da da, da da*, etc.—'dramatic' polysyllables ("But when the *melancholy* fit shall fall") break up into compound monosyllables bound together by the passion, but everything still counts as one—frequency of vibration in crickets, locusts, Keats 'replaces' our contemporary phrasing in human voice ('tone', all that misemphasis on selected, heavily stressed noises/waste of unstressed fillers normally grossing 'a poet's voice')—how hot & fast it gets—expanding roof me-ta-l in sun—no single note 'lost', in nature, or is that any sound heard *as* sound without interpretation—'meaning' identical to physical fact of *a* sound (everything noted/nought denoted) in series of discrete particles strung together (by Keats, e.g.) with gaps—weird displacement of 'one to one' order of natural occurrence/significance by human symbolic capacity to replace simple-unitary by multiple-complex, e.g. Morse code thinking 'dot-dot-dot' for 'SAVE/sss' or moan 'ooo' as 'dash-dash-dash', etc.—thus 'dot-dot-dot/dash-dash-dash/dot-dot-dot' for 'HELP' (speeded up, of course, to rush us back toward one—fastest computer infinitely approaching one as jammed together/speeded up multiple symbolic operation long since come to 'stand for' thing, so distracts any body from 'one to one' experience of actual events in time with simultaneous experience of identity of fact & significance)—hence *letters/phonemes* one way to discipline attention to use language as one way 'back to nature' by experiencing order of noises & silence in stream of oral consciousness—*s s* value in "Hedge-crickets sing," letter-to-letter & the leap between words not 'dashed' together (revealing the previous two as *so* bound together)—attention to which structure(s), in language, evokes or springs correspondences with structures of other natural events (or vice-versa: attention to extra-linguistic sound provokes awareness of like patterns in language)—

.   .   .   .

—symbolism not 'reference' but recognition of structural identities binding the world (trance state where sound is a calling forth)—Keats' attention to *s s* (including gap between *s's*), *heard* (& seen on the page) makes a name that shows me some part of events of August 31, 1977—day & night the gapping, then resumption (higher!—terminal & initial, different *s's* says Kathleen Frumkin), "s sing" there in the words/here to my senses as 'crickets'—anything but romantic/anthropomorphic mistaking of bugs' "singing" (Keats often careless of diction/denotation, so surely riding meaning in the sound—)

.   .   .   .

—'dead ends': *description* (Williams' "copying nature"), forcing the materials of language to correspond to habitual orderings thought to render what is thereby not seen; *invention*, mere gallivanting around in language materials endlessly provocative/striking/autointoxicative (though such is often preliminary to real work), a willed arrangement of words valued for its own sake (like description, this is something)—

.   .   .   .

—words are *words* (ancient 'horticultural' or 'hunting' magic or/cultural habit persisting in some guise—much 'more' than we know)—the *world* is 'beyond us' yet given to the sentience, as something of language process is, each time—it's a 'speaking to the beyond' from the 'unknown depths of the soul' (or the unknown 'beyond' speaking to 'soul') that makes a commonplace articulated—two together ('nothing personal')—say what happens/happening is said—

Craig Watson
STATEMENT

Over the past three years I have found myself preoccupied with two formal issues of poetics, *intention* and *address*, which seem to be central to a primary question of my need to create poems. Though I term these issues formal, implying an objective investigation, the making of poetry (in fact the reading of it) has become a very self-oriented experience. More than saying I engage in the process of writing for *myself*, it seems I have worked toward a ritualization of the act to the point where it *functions* in a very specific domain. Writing is now for me a means of modulating and organizing phenomenal and circumstantial information from all points of experience, a process I refer to as 'tuning' myself. As I grow older and seemingly remove myself from unity with any singular, or even plural, socio-cultural environment, I seem more 'on my own' in a vast environment of internalized experience. My approach to poetics has become the search for responses and behavioral modes relative to this experience, to surviving it as well as conditioning myself to it. Constantly the effort seems to be away from any formalization of ideas or structure or definitive process and towards a rejuvenating line of 'basics', that mythical point where each process is fresh and new and wholly responsive to indigenous conditions.

I came into the field of alternative forms and 'language-oriented writing' through a process of invention and then, taken with the ideas as well as the camaraderie of others similarly set adrift, found myself processing through an increasingly narrow channel of thought. By choosing to work solely within the perimeters of these somewhat technical issues I entered an environment controlled more by theory and imposed regulations than one open to all the motivations of a self-oriented process. These imposed constraints became antithetical to the idea of poetics as opening, the field becoming increasingly closed by criteria and philosophy. This is surely a phenomena which has plagued other artists in other times.

An awakening to these dissatisfactory conditions several years ago led me to the formation of questions concerning address, to whom or to what is the writing process oriented, and intention, for what reasons does it occur and what function does it potentially serve. I'm trying now to deal with a poetics that actively conditions my self/environment and serves as a tuning process and a means of mediating personal experiences. Obviously, such an internalized approach disavows allegiance to any code of poetic behavior and repudiates any sort of cultural standards. What it may do, however, is become an organic means of response to a larger domain of life/experience, and some of the resolutions may (but need not) be useful to other beings in the flow.

In a sense, I am trying to cope with the urge of poetry as opposed to the structure of it. This urge seems to lie within the rooted and individual beginnings of the activity, centered on a meditative, self-encoded embrace of those issues and inclinations I find within my own humanness. The intention therefore becomes the opening of experience toward a continual address of the self.

Ted Greenwald
SPOKEN

The sound in my poems comes from the sounds I hear in my head of
almost myself talking to some person. I choose to have as my limitation
spoken speech, as you and I are sitting here talking. That's what I test
the poem's shape against.

Occasionally, I like to do other things, when I hear a completely pecu-
liar sound or something, see if it works, give it a test run. Eventually, I
prefer dealing with items that are still charged with meaning and in fact
are open to the change that happens over time in meanings. In other
words, if I don't know exactly what a poem means when I write it I'm
somehow writing a certain kind of science fiction, because the poem (if
I'm right about the direction the language will change in) will even-
tually make sense on a more than just, say, shape level or form level as
time goes by and I'll start to understand it more.

I'm an opportunist: I'll take what I can get. If it works and if it's working
when I'm working on it, then I'll use it. I don't care what the source of it
is. But I'm saying that the basic motor on my car is spoken (for): What it
sounds like in my mind when I read it to myself.

What works has to be grounded in the language, which is the locality
of words. Words change in spoken language. "the/form/of/the/words/
pump/blood/in/the/form/of/the/heart" That pretty much sums it up.

What I'm interested in and always have been is not what ideas people
have in their heads, but what's in the air. The most invisible part of
"trends". What is it that two people in the whole world or maybe
twenty all of a sudden out of the middle of nowhere start to think
about. What's in the air is the shape of things to come — it's palpable
— right under your very nose. I hear what's in the air, that's my way of
thinking with my ear. You're not working with the idea of something,
you're projecting the idea of something. You're not working from mod-
els, you're creating models.

It's a romantic notion (where classical means coming from someplace),
going someplace, sort of operating more out of imagination and less
from received forms. In a specific sense, what it is is the interior mind

projecting itself into the phenomenological world, telling *you* where it's going. The time we live in is interesting, since there's a tremendous amount of good poetry that's "about" comings and going, this's and that's, here and there, not sillyass schools of one thing or another ("in" and "out" I leave to the hosts and hostesses of the world).

Poetry is about a time that hasn't occurred yet, and if it's very good it's about a time you'll never know about. Poems are my pencil and pad for jotting down shapes or ways of embodying imaginary shapes or things that don't exist. But some time will exist on a wider scale. This is even conceptual: They are almost like plans for the future.

I think that the notion that sort of got started with Pound and other modernist artists is that if you were dealing with something you were going to take notes and the notes will usually be in fractional form. What's wrong with writing poetry that uses fragments (or notes) is that there is no everyday language that can be used to test goodness of fit. All there is is some poetic diction or poetic language to go back to that says "This is correct!," but no language in everyday use by people speaking, which changes over time, however imperceptibly.

I personally don't believe in using some form of a poem as a container for a bunch of things ("good lines" for instance). Each poem's form discovers itself as I write the poem. Two poems may not be perceptibly different looking, but there are differences. And, since I write on a day-to-day basis, and try to pay as close attention as possible, by paying close attention can see those differences. And watch the form of the poem, and the meaning and sense of sounds and words, change. And satisfy myself as a good reader with a good read.

Michael Lally
MY WORK

I see all my work as serial — as in the relationships between the parts
within them (stanzas, paragraphs, lines, sentences, parenthetical state-
ments, phrases, words, meanings, syllables, abbreviations, letters, and
their various subdivisions (consonants, vowels, number seventeen on a
scale of one to twenty-six, the other twenty-five, pretty ones, ugly
ones, long ones, short ones, linear ones, less linear ones, etc. or words
that rhyme, words that look like they rhyme, words that look alike,
words that look similar, words that sound similar, words, words that
mean similar, words that don't, words that can be repeated more than
once and not mean the same thing and words that can't, words that can
be repeated more than twice and not mean the same thing and words
that can't, etc. or etc.)) and the parts without them (other works, parts
of other works, parts of a longer work that they are part of, another part
of the book they're a part of, the rest of the book, the same work in
another book, part of the same work in another work, etc.) in some
cyclic, or other consistently geometric pattern (consistent in the way
geometric patterns tend to be by definition) — but without ever using
these kinds of references or those kinds of language (or self-references
and abstract language) but instead using the language patterns of
speech as I have heard it and experienced it through reading it and
through reading it into whatever I read, or, through reading whatever I
read through it, and using the language I love most and love most to
use, such as one syllable non descriptive (no matter what "part of
speech," (as in the way "use" does not "describe" anything we can pic-
ture in our imaginations without imposing our own specificity (now the
word "specificity" (with five times as many syllable "parts" as "use")
does the same thing (force us to impose the particulars if we want to see
it — (but we don't "see" it because, in that sense, it is "abstract"
(whereas "use" is not — which kind of realization has always un-
covered a lot of class, race, ethnic origin, and educational background
biases to me, just as the obvious display — i.e. "showing off" — of
"unique" employment of language or the obvious display of the com-
mitment to that goal (the "unique" employment (is "employment" any
more specific or abstract than "use" if its use is similar) of language) has
always reflected to me standards based on sex, class, race, ethnic ori-
gin, or educational background, (this is an "obvious display" of some
of my biases)))))) words like "it."

Jackson Mac Low
MUSELETTER

for Charles

Charles Bernstein and Bruce Andrews have asked me to write some-
thing about my work &/or self, & Charles sent me a month ago a letter
containing 13 questions of which he did "hope one or two make you
want to say something—" & today he phoned me at about 11:30 AM (to
remind me, i.e., nag me in the sweet way he does), "So—" from our
conversation & his qq., "here goes—":
    CB: "1. Are you interested in having emotion in your process-
oriented, programmatic poetry?" / JML: (I'm too stingy of space to give
each of us a whole paragraph each time.) To most readers of poetry this
wd seem a remarkable question! I take it that C senses conflict between
"emotion" & my using chance operations & other quasi-objective meth-
ods to generate artworks: if I ever felt such a conflict, & I think I may
have, say, in the middle 1950's, I no longer do & haven't for some years.
Yes the Zen Buddhist motive for use of chance (&c) means was to be
able to generate series of "dharmas" (phenomena/events, e.g., sounds,
words, colored shapes) relatively "uncontaminated" by the composer's
"ego" (taste, constitutional predilections, opinions, current or chronic
emotions). It was such a relief to stop making artworks carry that bur-
den of "expression"! To let them become themselves, watch them grow
& take shape without one's pushing & shoving them around too much,
was & is a great pleasure: probably a "self-indulgence" (one cd care
less). But by the later 50s it was plain to me that sense- & sense/
concept-events (tones, words)—the specific sensible instances—are
both intrinsically & extrinsically emotional: by which I mean simply
that specific sounds &/or words (or other sensible elements) singly,
combined, &/or in series, have high probabilities of arousing feelings
within specific ranges in hearers &c (whether in "most," or merely most
members of certain classes or ingroups I'm not prepared to say—prob-
ably the wider the range the smaller the ingroup) & also that each
hearer has to bring an idiosyncratic range of emotions ("associations"?)
to each event, which is inextricably compounded with the more "gen-
eral" range in each person's experience.
    But (paragraphs are emotional, said Stein) that may not be what
you mean by "having emotion": if that were all you meant I cd say that
of course I've always been interested in the fact that sounds, words,
&c., no matter how "randomly" generated, arouse emotions "willy-

nilly" (& I for one never nil'd 'em). But if your question means, Do I allow my own emotions to influence my systematically generated work, I must answer that they can't help doing so: my choices of means, materials, &c., can't help being influenced by emotions, & I'd be foolish if I thought they weren't. Moreover, I realized by the later 50s that the events we single out as "experiences of emotion" as against those we call "sensations" occur as randomly as the sounds in a forest, & began to feel less difference between generating works systematically & recording emotional events (or otherwise using one's own or one's performers' emotions as elements in artworks). & while continuing to do each of these things relatively separately in some works, I have made many works in the 60s & 70s which variously combine chance & other generative systems with various types of "direct expression"— notably my Light Poems, of which I am presently writing the 55th (the 2nd to Stephanie Vevers: so far 18 notebook pages, about 20 lines each), some of which only "have" the emotions attached to or arising from hearing names of kinds of light, others of which use as elements emotions arising in my current life, &c.

Which brings me back to CB: "2. What do you think of 'cheating'—changing results so that the poem conforms to some non-procedurally derived sense of meaning—when composing basically chance-derived poems?" / JML: If I decide to use a certain system, I don't change the results of that system (whether doing so is "cheating" or not I forebear to judge). But I have at times composed systems that generate works conveying or "having" meanings clearly intended by the composer. As you well know, I've composed many political poems & love poems while abiding strictly by the results of such generative means as systematic chance.

I do want to touch on your 3rd question, finally: which I'll summarize: These days I'm greatly interested in work that tells me how it is to live lives—whether the artist's own life or the lives of others: works as different in their ways as Phill Niblock's movies of people working in Mexico, Peru, & the US & Sharon Mattlin's vivid embodiments of "epiphanies" (to use Joyce's term) from the lives of her family, friends, & acquaintances, as well as her own life: quasi-narrative poems in which the poet's own attitudes & emotions about events & feelings are conveyed predominantly by word choice, rhythms, selection of details of experiences dealt with, often quite subtly & indirectly, rather than by her self-consciously imposing herself upon her materials. You ask whether I'm less interested in "procedural" or language/structural work as such. Well, of such work, I'm most interested in works having "content," even "subject-matter," tho not always as the words are commonly used. Hannah Weiner's "Clairvoyant Journals" convey her life experience while radically transforming usual formats (verse/prose/&c) to do so, Bernadette Mayer's work has done so for years. Also, your own work, as well as that of Emmett Williams, Dick Higgins, & Ron Silliman, & the recent work of Peter Seaton (to mention only those who quickly come to mind—forgive me, others), while not referring to experience with the same directness, seems "to have content" even tho the "subject-matter" may often be shifting & elusive. Interest, however, is not at all synonymous with value judgement, & when I *hear* more purely language/structure work, such as John Cage's "Empty Words" or the works of Clark Coolidge, I'm often completely enthralled, even tho I do not return again & again to the *pages* from which they read.

Well, "I think that's about enough," as the blessed Henry Cowell used to say when signing off his WBAI radio program, "Music of the World's Peoples." ...

Lyn Hejinian
IF WRITTEN IS WRITING

I think of you, in English, so frequent, and deserved, and thereby de-
sired, their common practice and continually think of it, who, since the
Elizabethans, save Sterne and Joyce, have so trothed language to the
imagination, and Melville, of whose *Mardi* the critics wrote, in 1849,
"a tedious, floundering work of uncertain meaning or no meaning at
all. A hodgepodge. . . . A story without movement, or proportions, or
end . . . or point! An undigested mass of rambling metaphysics."

No-one is less negligent than you, to render the difficulties less whether
well-protected, in grammar, in which it has been customary to distin-
guish *syntax* from *accidence*, the latter tending to the inflections of
words — inflections, or towards itself, a bending in. The choices have
always been fashioned and executed from within. Knowing is right and
knowing is wrong. Nodding is, or could be, to you.

In such are we obsessed with our own lives, which lives being now
language, the emphasis has moved. The emphasis is persistently cen-
tric, so that where once one sought a vocabulary for ideas, now one
seeks ideas for vocabularies. Many are extant. Composition is by. The
technique is very cut and the form is very close. Such is surprising even
now, if overdue. Now so many years ago Donne wrote, Some that have
deeper digg'd Loves Mine than I, Say, where his centrique happinesse
doth lie.

The text is anterior to the composition, though the composition be inte-
rior to the text. Such candor is occasionally flirtatious, as candor nearly
always so. When it is trustworthy, love accompanies the lover, and the
centric writers reveal their loyalty, a bodily loyalty. Quite partial is ne-
cessity, of any text. Marvelous are the dimensions and therefore mar-
velling is understandable — and often understanding. Much else isn't,
but when that comes, from the definite to an indefinite, having devised
excuses for meeting, though we have not yet recognized, a selection,
or choice, of what is combed out. The original scale determines the
scope, the mood, the feel, the tone, the margin, the degree, the mathe-
matics, the size, the sign, the system, the pursuit, the position, the mark.

Of centricities, an interior view, there are two sources, perhaps three. One locates in the interior texture of such language as is of the person composing from it, personal and inclusive but not necessarily self-revelatory — in fact, now, seldom so; through improvisatory techniques building on the suggestions made by language itself — on patterns of language which are ideas and corresponding behavior or relevant quirks; this becomes an addictive motion — but not incorrect, despite such distortion, concentration, condensation, deconstruction and such as association by, for example, pun and etymology provide; an allusive psycholinguism. In the second it is the bibliography that is the text. The writing emerges from within a pre-existent text of one's own devising or another's. The process is composition rather than writing.

There are characteristic, contracting rhythms. The long line, with ramifying clauses, an introductory condition, and other cumulative devices have been fragmented, the rhythm accentuated. You can read. You can write. An unstable condition is given pause. The Elizabethans were given to a long system and we to purchase for pause, though not stop.

A possible third centricity, the perhaps, emerges from the imperatives and prerogatives of grammar. Such might be a work of, say, conjunctions, in which, for example, John Lloyd Stephens writes, "There is no immediate connection between taking Daguerreotype portraits and the practice of surgery, but circumstances bring close together things entirely dissimilar in themselves, and we went from one to the other." Such is a definition of the Elizabethan conceit. And in a blue book of French grammar one reads, "Linking is rare between a plural noun and a verb or between a plural adjective and a verb except in poetry."

All theory is safest ascribed in retrospect. On the line is an occasion to step off the line. The critic is a performer, good or bad. Facility is splendid, however — think of such heroic figures as Dr. Johnson, John Donne. Love was not easy. The cat gets the chair and you get the edge.

Conclusion:
by usual standing under half

Bruce Andrews
TEXT AND CONTEXT

Language is the center, the primary material, the sacred corpus, the primum mobile, the erotic sense of its own shared reality. Not a separate but a distinguishing reality. Yet where is the energy invested?

> There is nothing to decipher.
> There is nothing to explain.

≈§ To engage in the collective task of creating a literature no longer finds support on the scaffolding of discourse. In dismantling the scaffolding, we create a literature—a record of negative retrieval. 'Unreadability'—that which requires new readers, and teaches new readings.

≈§ Anything that is not a hypnosis is partial. No text, in that sense, is 'wholesome'—only experiences. Something is lost but something is gained. Not exactly 'dereferentialist'—for can writing be adequately tagged with what it's not doing? Isn't that the old chest-busting negativism of the avant-garde? Qualities are to be *aufgehoben*, not stricken. The sign's structure is *for* us by being before us; it does not dissolve into an outward looking system of radar, or of reading as radar. Reference isn't banished, except in the extremes of lettrism—and here it even stays on as a reminder. Remember? Not 'formalist'—for does this display an obsession with form as apart from the full potential of language? All form is an expression and an inscription: how personal can you get? how personal can you be? Form as physical, as material, as unlike the idea of elsewhere. 'Here' is more corporeal, somehow, than 'there'. Look over there = Avert your eyes. The here and now.

Thus, how do we read what is meant *precisely to* be read? that is given us for no other purpose, and without distraction (even those distractions which we often take as the stigmata of 'reading' but are really those of entertainment, those of good fog). *Wordsome.*

≈§ As though the referential fallacy and the pathetic fallacy were but special cases of each other. Desperate barriers against regret? Pragmatic illusions. As though the world or even the text, were a simply

Reprinted initially from a symposium, edited by Steve McCaffery, on "The Politics of the Referent" in *Open Letter* 3 : 2 (1977).

structural density that could nourish us, alone. How communal can you get? Show us a way out. The way out is not through the basement door, getting lost among prerequisite cultural mementos, in deceptive (or descriptive) depth.

◆§ Pointing, or referential signification first signifies depth, or reinforces the security found in possible depth—the pot at the end of the rainbow, the commodity or ideology that brings fulfillment; choicelessness; a lower layer that is nature-like in its immobility or fixity or self-evidence. 'The fix is on.' It hypnotizes us with these expectations, long before any particular content is unearthed. The format massages us with its illusions—false bottoms, peek-a-boo costumes, trapdoors, you have nothing to do with this.

> I am sawing the woman in half—I devour
> one part, repress the other.

Commodities are sold, productions are forgotten. You feed on this vertical system—the comfort of a semantic presence that you no longer have the strength to get tired of, or wary of. You are learning the *trip*, forgetting, as in an amnesia, the character of the places you left. The medium, verticality, threatens to become the predominant message.

Semantics: the souvenirs of tourism.

> Centripetal as vertical.
> Depth as set frame.
> Context as reference.

◆§ How much are we willing to destroy our attentiveness to the way words act and interact in order to gain the advantages of description or of representation and a phobia toward what is present? Centripetal motion is that of imposing contexts suitable for explanatory purposes—is this the one in the 'light' of which such actions are intelligible? Those impositions are usually cushioned by grammar (where syntax plays a representational role); without them, the language is a frontage. Not a false front, not a directive screen, but an unencumbered energy.

Grammar as constraining rules; meaning as constitutive rules—yet these latter are not imposed as a prior dictate. They issue forth instead from the inward shapes of the language.

> Grammatical quicksand. Keep your place!
> Syntax: the scaffolding of verticality.

Myth—the mask, the ideology, the technicolor escape, the promise of transcendence in meaning. A regular reading has been a sideshow promoting semantic elixirs, imagist tonics. It's advertised to take a while to work: this *delay* between word and referent teases us; we reach the 'intent' or 'motive' only by indirection and without participating fully— enjoying the temporariness of the trip. Coitus interruptus.

◄§ There is an other way. The vertical axis (downwards, as a ladder tempting us) need not structure the reading—for it does not structure the text. This is what I would mean by calling it non-referentially organized writing, as a subset of language-centered writing. Horizontal organizing principles, without an insistent (that is to say, imposed) depth. Secret meaning is not a hidden layer, but a hidden organization of the surface. Not latent, but quite handsomely manifest.

Meaning is not produced *by* the sign, but by the contexts we bring to the potentials of language—not enforced by a vertical elevator, the mark of the double, the vacation. The impulse toward excavation, toward contextual explanation, can be put in the background — for such a hollowing out of lower depths, of labyrinthine caves of signification, goes on within the gaps.
All light, all in broad daylight: bring your own context. Radiant surfaces; myth.

◄§ An alternative remains 'wordness', 'eventism'—a way of *reconstituting* language by unpacking the tool box. The constitutive rules of meaning are not taking the words *away* from us. We can create those rules as we go along, and as we return, centrifugally, to center, centering, to surface, to degree zero, to sea level. We are urged back by the absence of imposed escapes! A semantic normality—a norm-iness (a worminess) is one such escape.
Signs which are constituted from paradigmatic rules, from their interaction (their play) with others, their trajectory without the dead weight of context.

◄§ Atmospherically: what surrounds words may be more readily, and satisfyingly perceived than an iron cage of connection: referential connections which take place below the plane, out of sight, or earshot, therefore self-denyingly, without physique, or erotic delight.
The distinction between 'possession goals' and 'milieu goals'.

As in lowering the iron cage beneath the waters to be attacked by sharks, to be eaten alive by outside forces. Obedience to Authority vs. the improvisation of rules. If only the imposed representations could be loosed, deviance would be so much sweeter.

✎§ The first real presence is the awareness of absence, of no escape–of
a vertical dimension acting only as an echo, a nostalgic reverb. Noth-
ing is compressed from outside into familiar shapes & pleasing pas-
sage–the inwardness is the site of compression & density.

> Language turns itself inside out for us.
> Reversible vests; two-piece suits.

Signifieds provide echoes, harmonies, overtones, but not the principles
of organization; the signifiers take on an atonality without shyness.
There are external supports, but not protective blankets. Feet, not
roots.

> Events without trots.
> Bottomless, negative space.

Confusion of realms, profusion of events and interplay on the surface.
All, or mostly surface. The subject has disappeared behind the words
only to emerge in front, or inside them. Presentations of the present,
not representations of tense.

✎§ A more complicated topology than the virtuosos of reference had
imagined: Rubber-Sheet Geometry. The one-sided surfaces. Any two
points may be connected merely by starting at one point and tracing a
path to the other without lifting the attention or carrying it over any
boundary or separation.

> Transference. *Différance.* A carnival of ciphers.

Fragmentation doesn't banish the references *embodied* in individual
words; merely–they are not placed in a *series,* in grammar, in a row,
on a shelf. A more playful anarchy, a Möbius free-for-all is created.
Texts are themselves signi*fieds,* not mere signifiers. TEXT: it requires no
hermeneusis for it is itself one–of itself.

> Gyroscopes.
> Self-referring.
> Ouroboros.

✎§ The consummation is concrete, graphic, erotic, physical, phenome-
nal, a greeting, not a keepsake. An absence embodied in a presence.
> Words hover above usage. Meaning is not use, or is not all use.

Meaning is the enabled incapacity to impose a usage.
Excommunication, rather than appropriation.

Words are the ghosts of regret.

Referentiality is diminished by organizing the language around other
features or axes, around features which make present to us words' lack
of transparency, their physicality, their refusal to be motivated along
schematic lines by frames exterior to themselves. Refusing to 'point', or
to be arranged according to a 'pointing system', they risk the charge of
being pointless. That is, to be a self-sufficiency of event—confounding
the inadequation of words and referents that we mistakenly call mean-
ing. This is not meaning. Instead, this is meaning. *This.*

◆§ If explanation is contextual, this counter-explanation is a rebuff
which shows a larger possibility—an emptied cipher that speaks of all
the productions we can fill it with. Each associative band, each band of
semantic radiation, takes place with less guidance from the games and
aims of representation or with little grammatical constraint. A carnival
atmosphere, therefore . . . workers' control . . . self-management.

Commodification, on the other hand, requires clear signposts—
Easy outs.

Language work resembles a creation of a community and of a
world-view by a once-divided-but-now-fused Reader and Writer. This
creation is not instrumental. It is immanent, in plain sight (and plain-
song), moving along a surface with all the complications of a charter or
a town-meeting.

A *publicity.*

Depth is a spiral or whirligig—taken in stride, does not 'get in the
way'. Not a tourniquet.

◆§ The focus on the ways in which language can inscribe itself as other
than reference. As an individuation *within* (but not compensating for)
a community. Reading as a particular reading, an enactment, a co-
Production. Here are the simultaneous co-creators of a smallish lin-
guistic community. A scriptorium.

Counter-commodification: a barbaric, if politically apt term which
spins around our scrimmages against reference.

Writing as action; reading as action, not a behavior *observed by* a
text, sitting there, bored, looking at us.

Binary, with the text as switchman.
Blurs, so fast = mesh

Texts read the reader.

☙ Altering textual roles might bring us closer to altering the larger so-
cial roles of which textual ones are a feature. READING: not the glazed
gaze of the consumer, but the careful attention of a producer, or co-
producer. The transformer. (capacitators? resistors?) Full of care. It's not
a product that is produce, but a *production*, an event, a praxis, a model
for future practice. The domination of nature can find a critique here as
well—not in abstinence. Not aleatory.

From each according to
To each according to

A semantic atmosphere, or milieu, rather than the possessive individu-
alism of reference.

Indexicality.
Absolute.
Absolution.

Such work has a utopian force only begun to be revealed.

☙ Language is an Other which imposed meanings attempt, luckily un-
successfully, to disguise for us. The 'Primal Lack'. Life against death. It
is not a monologic communication, but a spatial interaction fore-
grounded within a frame of our own generosity. Our gifts, its physical
integrity.
    Stay inside. It is all here. The non-imperial state: without need for
the expansion or externalization that comes from the refusal to re-
distribute the surplus at home. The same holds for a non-imperial or
language-centered writing.
    Surplus of signifier = the floating signifier. *Mana.* trace.
    Engulfment, flooding of signifiers without predetermined significa-
tion. Instead, the cliches of existentialism—freedom, surplus of signi-
fiers, *choice as constitutive* & we do it ourselves.
    Politics not concealed any longer.

    Decontextualization.

◄§ References *evacuate* the sign. In its place, intentionality fills it up—contributed both by reader and writer. This is a self-conscious (at times, self-referring) intention capable of acknowledging the Other, a sense of absence. It finds a cure in communal consort, in concert, without the mediation of obedience, without the *orders* of reference. What is made concrete is what is truly absent [unity–the world as one, a toppling of Babel], and not what is tantalizingly withheld or delayed only to be theatrically hawked and consumed [reference–the world as split, the divisiveness and/or repressiveness of outside imposed content] Repression as the delayed gratification of unity.

Works seem the embodiment, the bodying forth of this string of lights connecting reader and writer, reader and text. We speak of a 'body of work'–by this, what do we mean: the body politic, love's body. Embodiment is the needed copulation–of practices. No longer repressed, the two spheres are fused.

◄§ As if the references offered could be known, through the act of appropriating them! Representation is ownership. Yet the *meant* (the signifiers) completely outdistances the *known* (the signifieds, what is referred to). We come, historically, for the sake of a denying and repressive order, to be satisfied with what can be known, owned, consumed, referred to, easily intersubjectively communicated, predicted, controlled. Lost are some of the physical ways of intending, of expressing, of meaning, of motion, of pronouncing, sobbing: the overabundance of signifier, the excessive presence, the unconscious, the sign's arbitrary nature. Otherliness–we are emancipated only by recognition, or, occasionally, by the conjugation of reading and writing, in completing language's own work and words. Not duality. Readers do the rewriting. Sometimes they do enough to give a social force to the absences they are first given.

References are not foregrounded. The body of work is not organized around the referential axis. Therefore, is not genitally organized? No 'discharge' of a specific substantive kind leaves the polymorphous play of the linguistic units. The genital organization is monarchic, or mimetic (from the family circle). Language-centering seems to capture some of the more exploratory aspects of the consequences of itself, without referential guidance, without parental guidance, without tense. *Not a compensation*, or its prime model: ego armor.

What is collective as signifier as unconscious–does not atomize or individualize in the ways references have. Lost–through a castration complex, an incestuous access eliminated by the triumph of market conditions and kinship, an imposed outward order of signification?

How have we come to the words, to our selves, our absenting community—all flesh, all fleshed together.

The community which is unified, self-contained, mercantilist, unwilling to break down into spheres—resisting the division of labor (and hierarchy) that comes with literacy. Is this an incestual nostalgia for illiteracy? A polymorphous lettrism, a movement into *script, grapheme, syllable, cipher, glyph, gloss, corpus?*

Readers embody texts.
Physical language.

Charles Bernstein
STRAY STRAWS AND STRAW MEN

1. 'I look straight into my heart & write the exact words that come from within. The theory of fragments whereby poetry becomes a grab bag of favorite items—packed neatly together with the glue of self-conscious & self-consciously epic composition, or, lately, homogenized into one blend by the machine of programmatic form—is a diversion. The eye is not split open in such work. There are structures—edifices—wilder than the charts of rivers, but they are etched by making a path not designing a garden.'

'Natural: the very word should be struck from the language.'

'. . . but what the devil *is* the human?'

2. Ron Silliman has consistently written a poetry of visible borders: a poetry of shape. His works are composed very explicitly under various conditions, presenting a variety of possible worlds, possible language formations. Such poetry emphasizes its medium as being constructed, rule governed, everywhere circumscribed by grammar & syntax, chosen vocabulary: designed, manipulated, picked, programmed, organized, & so an artifice, artifactual—monadic, solipsistic, homemade, manufactured, mechanized & formulaic at some points: willful.

3. Work described as this may discomfort those who want a poetry primarily of personal communication, flowing freely from the inside with the words of a natural rhythm of life, lived daily. Perhaps the conviction is that poetry not be made by fitting words into a pattern but by the act of actually letting it happen, *writing*, so that that which is 'stored within pours out' without reference to making a point any more than to making a shape. The thing is not to create programmes to plug words into but to eliminate such imposed interferences.

An influence of work that appears to be of this (other) type is the sanctification of something that gets known as its honesty, its directness, its authenticity, its artlessness, its sincerity, its spontaneity, its personal expressiveness; in short, its 'naturalness.' (As the pastoral was once the natural, & likewise the romantic.)

I would point to Bernadette Mayer's *Memory* as a work that seems rooted in some of these ('natural') assumptions, as well as to much of

Reprinted initially from "The Politics of the Referent" symposium, *Open Letter* 3 : 2 (1977).

Kerouac. In a different way, & the look of the work is the measure of how different, Frank O'Hara's poetry is relevant. The achievement of these three poets has much to do with how they have fronted these assumptions.

4. Personal subject matter & a flowing syntax, whatever those de scriptions mean to a particular writer, are the key to the natural look. (Though it needs to be said that the variety of writing that relies on some sense of natural for its inspiration & domain is infinite.)

5. The sexual, for example, has much the pull of the natural. For some it poses as the most intimate subject matter. Others have it as the energy that drives their writing, or else its source.

Edward Dahlberg (sexistly) describes Word as Cock. 'Masculine fiery particles,' 'motions of will,' he says, animate the great writing of the past. He rebukes American literature for not being grounded in the Flesh, describing it as stagnant, dehumanized, & frigid. 'Esoteric artificers' & 'abstruse technicians,' our writers—Poe, Dickinson, Thoreau, Hawthorne, Melville & those before & after—have led away from 'the communal song of labor, sky, star, field, love.'

6. There is also an attraction toward looking for the natural in 'direct experience,' both in terms of recording the actual way objective reality is perceived (the search for the objective) & making the writing a recording instrument of consciousness.

'This work I experience as an instance of the writer's fantasy & imagination & vision & not as a construction. I feel immersed in it. It seems seamless to me. I am carried along by it. The experience is present to me. Shifts in tone, place occur as inevitable sequences: inevitable because they cohere, because they allow me to experience them, because they seem to happen.'

7. 'Technical artifice' they scream, as if poetry doesn't demand a technical precision. ('That poetry is an art, an art with technique, with media, an art that must be in constant flux, a constant change of manner.') Technicians of the human.

8. A sign of the particularity of a piece of writing is that it contains itself, has established its own place, situates itself next to us. We move up close, stare in, & see a world. It has moving parts, accountable & unaccountable recurrences, a particular light, a heavy dense odor. 'But can I actually experience it?' Yes. But it reveals the conditions of its oc-

currence at the same time as it is experienced. So I don't feel a part of it as much as facing it. . . . Of course at times you forget. All of a sudden a few hours, a week, flash by before you actually notice, & you say to yourself 'how the time slips—'

9. '*Next* to us the grandest laws are continually being executed. *Next* to us is not the workman whom we have hired, with whom we love so well to talk, but the Workman whose work we are.'

Next to. Fronting the world with a particular constellation of beliefs, values, memories, expectations; a culture; a way of seeing, mythography; language. But we are 'beside ourselves in a sane way' for what is beside us is also ourselves. At the same time in & beside.—The signs of language, of a piece of writing, are not artificial constructions, mere structures, 'mere naming.' They do not sit, deanimated, as symbols in a code, dummies for things of nature they refer to; but are, of themselves, of ourselves, whatever is such. 'Substance.' 'Actuality.' 'Presence.' The very plane through which we front the world, by which the world is.

10. Compare / these two views / of what / poetry / is.
   In the one, an instance (a recording perhaps) of reality / fantasy / experience / event is presented to us through the writing.
   In the other, the writing itself is seen as an instance of reality / fantasy / experience / event.

11. Another example.
The sanctification of the natural comes up in terms of 'voice' & has been extended by various excursions into the oral. On the one hand, there is the assumption that poetry matures in the location of 'one's own voice' which as often as not is no more than a consistency of style & presentation. 'The voice of the poet' is an easy way of contextualizing poetry so that it can be more readily understood (indiscriminately plugged into) as listening to someone talk in their distinctive manner (i.e., listen for the person beyond or underneath the poem); but this theatricalization does not necessarily do the individual poem any service & has the tendency to reduce the body of a poet's work to little more than personality. (This contrasts with that major preoccupation in American poetry—the investigation of the grammar of talking, of speech, both by traditional poetic technique &, lately, by tape transcription.) On the other hand, there is a growing use of voice in a variety of sound poetry. Some performance & audiotape works use voice as essentially a vocabulary to be processed by techniques such as cut-up, consonant &

vowel intonation, simultaneity, etc. Others, searching for the 'natchu-ralness' of an oral liturgy we've lost, & influenced by tribal & religious & bardic–communal–poetic practice, make use of vocalizations re-lated to the human breath (e.g., chanting & other assorted organic sounding tones).–Voice is a possibility for poetry not an essence.

12. I am not making a distinction, there is no useful distinction to be made here, between making the poem a subject or an object. Nor is it necessary to choose up among the personal desire to communicate, tell what has been seen, share a way of seeing, transmit some insight, irony, or simply give a feeling for texture.

What I want to call attention to is that there is no natural writing style; that the preference for its supposed manifestations is simply a preference for a particular look to poetry & often a particular vocabu-lary (usually perceived as personal themes); that this preference (essen-tially a procedural decision to work within a certain domain sanctified into a rite of poetry) actually obscures the understanding of the work which appears to be its honoured bases; & especially that the cant of 'make it personal' & 'let it flow' are avoidances–by mystification–of some very compelling problems that swirl around truthtelling, confes-sion, bad faith, false self, authenticity, virtue, etc.

13. The considerable achievement of Frank O'Hara is to have a form of poetry largely within the domain of the personal. Note, however, that O'Hara's word 'personism' is not 'personalism'; it acknowledges the work to be a fronting of another *person*–another mind, if you will, as much as another nature. O'Hara's work *proposes* a domain of the per-sonal, & not simply *assuming* it, fully works it out. His remarkable use of voice, for example, allows, through a musing whimsy in that voice, for fantasy as wild as any surrealist imagines, contained, still, within his proposed boundaries.

14. There is no automatic writing. It is a claim that has had to be made to the detractors of modernism again & again (an early article by B. F. Skinner attacked 'Stein's little secret') & must now be made another time to avoid accepting as a value an analysis generated out of misun-derstanding & animosity.

Not that the followers of the natural, or the organic, or the per-sonal, would necessarily have work that looks automatic. But it seems to me that this is at the heart of the strongest claim to natural spon-taneous writing–the impulse to record or transcribe the movements & make-up of one's consciousness. The modernist assumption. What's to note is that in practice, projectively, that impulse transposes itself to something like a search for a method of 'syntacticalizing consciousness,' i.e., ordering one's consciousness into language; as if consciousness existed prior to—aside from—language & had to be 'put into' it; as if consciousness were not itself a syntacticalization—a syntaxophony.

Every phrase I write, every juxtaposition I make, is a manifestation of using a full-blown language: full of possibilities of meaning & impossibilities of meaning. It can't be avoided. Whatever comes out comes out on account of a variety of psychological dispositions, personal experiences, & literary preoccupations & preconceptions. The best of the writing that gets called automatic issues from a series of choices as deliberate & reflected as can be.

15. Whatever gets written gets written in a particular shape, uses a particular vocabulary & syntax, & a variety of chosen techniques. Whether its shape, syntax & vocabulary result from an attraction (or ideological attachment to) the organic & spontaneous, or to some other look, it is equally chosen. Sometimes this process takes place intuitively or unconsciously (the pull of influence comes in here since somewhere in the back of the mind are models for what looks natural, personal, magical, mystical, spontaneous, automatic, dreamlike, confessional, didactic, shocking). Sometimes it is a very conscious process. Any way, you're responsible for what turns up. Free association, for example, is no more inherently 'natural' than cutting up: & neither is in any sense 'random.' One technique may be used because a decision is made to use subconscious material. Another may be used to limit the vocabulary of the poem to words not self-generated. In either case, various formal decisions are made & these decisions shape the work.

16. Okay, given that, it's given, is it possible to continue under conditions set up before? Or is everything, every instance, a new decision at each moment? & recklessly charging forward it appears to copy some other thing, or be beholding, or under. What happens when the images cease, when there are no more images confronting the eye of imagination & still the signs, the written traces of activity, continue to be produced. Music sounds. It too must pass. A syntactical exploration of consciousness becomes very explicitly the concern, so imbedded even in a subject matter of boundaries & possible worlds, that it ceases to be, or only diverts. The subject matter simply all that is inside, given rhythm, different cadences, the punctuation in typing of each letter as separate unit, the propulsion of a comma. Is it possible, for example, to allow typographical errors, mistypings, to remain integral? Typing itself

then becoming a condition. It becomes part of the temptation. Or perhaps it's just my fear that when I tap what I find inside myself I will find that it is empty & insist that the scratchings must account for something.

17. Writing necessarily consists of attaching numerous bits & pieces together in a variety of ways. & it comes to a point where you feel any composition is an artifice & a deceit. & the more 'natchural' the look the more deceptive. That any use of language outside its function of communicating in speaking is a falsehood (cf. Laura Riding). Or even, that language itself—everywhere conditioning our way of seeing & meaning—is an illusion (as if there were some thing outside language!)

Or take it this way: I want to just write—let it come out—get in touch with some natural process—from brain to pen—with no interference of typewriter, formal pattern. & it can seem like the language itself—having to put it into words—any kind of fixing a version of it—gets in the way. That I just have this thing inside me—silently—unconditioned by the choices I need to make when I write—whether it be to write it down or write on. So it is as if language itself gets in the way of expressing this thing, this flow, this movement of consciousness.

But there are no thoughts except through language, we are everywhere seeing through it, limited to it but not by it. Its conditions always interpose themselves: a particular set of words to choose from (a vocabulary), a way of processing those words (syntax, grammar): the natural conditions of language. What pulses, pushes, is energy, spirit, anima, dream, fantasy: coming out always in form, as shape: these particulars, 'massed at material bottoms' in hum of this time—here, now—these words, this syntax & rhythm & shape. The look of the natural as constructed, programmatic—artful—'lying words' as the most abstract, composed or formal work.

18. There is no natural look or sound to a poem. Every element is intended, chosen. That is what makes a thing a poem. Modes cannot be escaped, but they can be taken for granted. They can also be meant.

Work like Silliman's explicitly acknowledges these conditions of poetry, language, by explicitly intending vocabulary, syntax, shape, etc.; an acknowledgement which is the actual prerequisite of authenticity, of good faith. The allure of the spontaneous & personal is cut here by the fact of wordness: reproducing not so much the look of the natural as the conditions of nature—autonomy, self-sufficiency. In this light, a work like Mayer's *Memory* can be seen to be significant not on account of its journal-like look alone but also on account of its completely intended, complex, artifactual style. Heavy, dense, embedded. 'The essential thing is to build a world.' Energy & emotion, spontaneity, vocabulary, shape—all are elements of that building. It is natural that there are modes but there is no natural mode.

James Sherry
POSTSCRIPT

The Politics of the Referent, edited by Steve McCaffery: McCaffery, "The Death of the Subject: The Implications of Counter-Communication"; Bruce Andrews, "Text and Context"; Ray DiPalma, "Crystals"; Ron Silliman, from "aRb"; Charles Bernstein, "Stray Straws and Straw Men"; Ellsworth Snyder, "Gertrude Stein and John Cage". In *Open Letter* (3 : 2, 1977), reprinted as Supplement #1 to L=A=N=G=U=A=G=E.

Ten notions about which it is advisable to have no opinions: signifier, inwardness, lexemic presence, ego, referent, (even to say it), deconstruction, morpheme-phoneme-grapheme, displacement, interface.

The initial question that arises from reading these essays is why must language be politicized? What happens to the aesthetic impulse when language is displaced toward the relations implicit between us and it, that is, away from relations between it and the phenomenal world.

A Short Interview with Steve McCaffery —
Q: What happens to the aesthetic impulse if language is politicized?
A: It does not seem essential to me.

I would agree with Snyder that words regarded as facts, as opposed to words as symbols, are more useful today, but useful in the way any "new" art tends to satirize contemporary society: If we think capitalism commoditizes our works beyond their ability to overcome that tendency with their "awful beauty", then we can imagine advanced art or theorizing makes fun of this tendency by always seeking to invent, recontextualize (perhaps this is more ecologically sound), conceptualize, etc., rather than . . . I'm sure you'd like to know what, too.

The impulse behind this move away from reference, image and meaning in the conventional way is the same impulse that directed the painting of "Desmoiselles d'Avignon," or enabled Schoenberg, led by his musical predecessors, to deviate so far from the key note that he simply never came back. We can say the same thing about representation in literature.

Certainly Stein et al. began these events, so we cannot claim that these authors are creating something entirely new. Rather they are announcing that something has already taken place and the disparate elements of these modes of writing are ready to be collated into culture proper, not isolated or kept tangential to the "real" world of the Consumer Price Index and SALT. These essays announce that the works of earlier writers are not to be regarded as another step toward randomness, rather they are to be developed. Yet in what way does this kind of writing try to transcend the nature of advances and put an end to period mannerism?

Can we get to the point where we do not need to be reassured by meaning which *accompanies* language? Can we use language not as a lens through which the world is pleasantly or wrathfully distorted for the purposes of lulling the reader into another world of lies and symbols? Can we come to the realization that language is one of the languages? That the question as to whether society or consciousness informs first is something for Marx and Freud to battle over in heaven? That we can view all the languages as mutually reflexive where the light bouncing back and forth between these planes is the mode of expression, in this case English? That spoken or written language is not a box for meaning—it is the content(s)?

Freeing words from hidden meanings is just the first step. To decommoditize language in writing, one may need to call into question even the morphemic quality of language. This raises questions of comprehensibility. Can the relationship between reader and writer really be so changed? Silliman makes the incredible claim that alphabet takes language out of person and that a book makes poetry into a commodity. Well . . . More importantly, are the claims implicit in these assertions justified? Is the kind of writing at the root of these essays, call it what you will, possessed of as many possibilities and permutations as centuries of referential writing. Silliman claims non-referential writing, like that of Grenier, reveals referential works to be of a specific type— their locality was engrossing—a special case like Newton in relation to relativistic mechanics.

These essays do not propose writing which creates a hypnotic simulacrum—an illusion that seems like realism—but rather they perform a realization showing that language as a system parallel to experience really exists, influences and works in itself and by its relations elucidates experience. The program suggested in these essays appears to cover reality with language, hence the need to stretch the page.

Nick Piombino
WRITING AND IMAGING

Because remembering is motile (self-generating), it constantly juxta-poses images and fragments of thought spontaneously into the thought process. For this reason, remembering continually transforms the effect of specific associations and images on the meanings or symbolic values we assign to them as we write and reread what is written. Since remem-bering causes such transformations by overlaying, condensing, and dis-placing associations, this process prevents permanent linking of images to specific associations. Such mutability as to the length of time images may be linked to specific associations in the thought process also makes it possible, in writing, by such methods as juxtaposition, aural association, repetition, and physical placement in the text, to alter their character, symbolic value or relationship to the composition as a whole (their "scale"). Written images, as mental projections, are continually re-scaled against other images by the transformation of lexical associa-tions as the composition proceeds. The harmonic, rhythmic and sym-bolic values of images undergo changes in scale depending on the lexi-cal and aural associations chosen by the reader or writer to be, at any given moment, their signal source or "key".

Of all types of writing, poetic discourse, like the psychoanalytic technique of free association, most tends to cause the experience of re-membering to be idiosyncratic, personal, and dehistoricized. By the latter term, I mean that the stories or fantasies elaborated from the texts or associations may be constructed or deconstructed at any given mo-ment by current associations. The method of free association flattens out the relative value of images by placing them in a one-to-one rela-tionship to consecutive fragments of ideas, unlike purposive forms of thought patterns fixed by sequential ordering. Chance and ran-dom sequencing of images can have a similar re-synchronizing / de-synchronizing effect, by causing shifts between coded message read-ings of the fragments and the intermittently phased current "readings" of present images looped into signal words and thoughts. Specifically the difficulty in poetry with imaging is that after-images often tend to be sustained in remembering much longer than is necessary for the most musical, rhythmically modulant grouping of sequential or juxtaposed signs. Too clear a statement, meaning or purpose might scale down, for instance, a group of signs so radically as to make their source overtones too minimal to have any impact on the composition as a whole.

When word, object, sign and trace synesthetically embrace the mind and the page, associating symbol with its mark, title, token, signal, and glyph, symbolic values' rigid hold on meaning is weakened. The image's source then can again have a monitoring, signalizing effect on the way meanings and intensities of meaning are assigned. The modally transformable image is one that is subject to the shadowing, tinting effects of one meaning juxtaposed against another, layered on and under it, like the creation of an approximate sign in lieu of foregoing any possibility of recollection. Or one fixed sequence of meanings may be transformed into another register by creating new associations to a mutation or variation of the text, like reversing one part of the sequence and allowing one set of symbols before that part and after that part to remain the same. In writing this may be an alteration of syntax within a customary phrase which can be translated back again within the thought process simultaneously or almost so, as the text is read, just as an inflection or modification in speech might entirely alter the character of an expression in relation to a purely syntactical form of the same idea. Again, the resulting transmutative effect would be caused by the feedback between a meaning and an intentionally added reframing of its tonal value affecting a shift in its remembered, historicized meaning.

Richard Foreman
TRYING TO BE CENTERED . . . ON THE CIRCUMFERENCE

O.K. It's about the rhythmic oscillation, very fast, between insideness and outsideness. It's about the tapestry (many threads from many sources) weaving itself and reweaving itself. That process . . . Things bleed in unexpected ways into other things. A reverberation machine! . . . The theme is to document in the plays a certain kind of 'constructed' behavior (my invention) in which mentation, mental-acts, take place on an outside surface . . . not hidden away inside. Thinking as the product of field-interchange. . . .

So there isn't progression or development (19th century ediface complex: impressive what man can do) there is rather - like the electron - a 'being potentially present' in many places at once. Structures of potentiality, not heavy, massive edifaces.

And The staging like that too. It MIGHT be staged to mean THIS . . . a kind of attention . . . but invaded, immediately undercut, by THIS DIFFERENT shape or realm of discourse or object or rhythm.

Breakfast . . . invaded by geometry
geometry . . . invaded by desire
desire . . . invaded by houses
houses . . . invaded by a direction . . . or other 'not identifiables';
simply rhythms, qualities, etc: And that cross reference to different discourse systems
The energy of that jumping, that shifting, is what DRIVES thought.
My plays not ABOUT THOUGHT, but ABOUT WHAT DRIVES thought.

Like energy released by a quantum jump.
Trains of discourse being jumped. . . . POLYPHONIC MUSIC . . . not the development from cell to cell, but . . . continual thematic modula-

Excerpted from Foreman's notes to his production of "Blvd. de Paris (or I've got the Shakes)".

tion . . . listen vertically . . . a certain kind of attention, like a cloud of agitated particles, . . . leaving the trace.

To create that field (rather than allowing consciousness to be hypnotized) my plays keep 'changing the subject'. But is it changed? Since the subject is the field, not spoken of directly, but articulated, layed out, by the writing of 'things'

> The pleasure I take (writing) is the pleasure of intercutting: interrupting: an impulse I want to (and do) make. The impulse is registered, but allowed to twist, turn, block itself, so that blockage, that reaction to its energy, produces a detour, and the original impulse maps new, contradictory territory. . . .

On purpose, on the root level of expression-of-impulse, I try to get into the greatest difficulty possible. Syntactically, logically, rationally, narratively. 'Train-of-thought' trouble and blockage is cultivated. The center of the work is in that trouble, stumbling, drift, in that resistance to all 'effort' which is, I maintain, the source of all reflexivity. That "coming up against things" which is the experience that forces us to "see". . . .

My plays, therefore, postulate, for me, a PARADISE where the 'allowed' mental move is the move to undercut all impulses, to self-block, to strategically change the subject, so that a desired emotion is produced. . . .

A profound undertaking, but the word profound must be replaced, so that we no longer follow its lead in thinking that the ultimate is a matter of 'depth' - but come to understand it as a matter of wideness, greater and greater distribution of the self over the spread network of what is available, the web of everything interrupting everything else upon that surface over which our lives are always wandering.

Therefore, when it seems that my plays, line by line, are changing the subject, that is true - but that changing of subject is the ground of the real subject, an openness and alertness resulting from a "non-human" (post-humanistic) wandering over the whole field of everything-that-is-discoursing to us. . . .

Jed Rasula
STATEMENT ON READING IN WRITING

At a certain point in post-industrial society, all of the social expediency of art is diminished in favor of personal necessity. Where in earlier societies the artistic activity was directed to socially regulated functions of a group such as performative situations or practical gestures for public and semi-public occasions — today the compelling basis of writing begins at a point of alienation from any socially explicit occasion. Which fosters the link with reading — that now, writers are readers first and their isolateness maintains them even against their will as such. The only clear "writers" would be those putting their work directly into market, working on a deadline, a definitive readership standing by to man the reading-boats. Writers without such an immediate market are in the damning circumstance, more often than not, of trying to insist on themselves as *not readers*, against all odds, in service of the fetish of originality. So the task is now to move towards a more affirmative stance *as readers*, to make of the act of reading the art that it in fact is. READING IS TRADITIONALLY THE MOST NEGLECTED OF ALL ARTS. Because it's the most abused. The psychological struggle that should concern us is not that of individual writers overcoming "the burden of the past" (Bate, Bloom) but individual readers overcoming the burden of the present, which is to view reading as a fallen, passive, irresponsible but entertaining state. This is the reader-as-junkie. What presently seems to count among writers is that the writing be psychologically valuable to the writer, but this is simply to increase the hold solipsism always wants to maintain on us. The *communality* of the reading/writing circuit is composed entirely of readers, not writers. If all writing were to cease right now, the fantastic load of the already-written would be more than sufficient to sponsor a new race of genius speakers and rhetoricians and conversationalists. I think we're at a point where we can actually say (probably we're the first people in history to get to this point) that there exists *enough writing* already. To affirm one's position as a reader is to pronounce oneself willing to work with other people rather than work for them. Always this haunting sense, that in writing you're doing somebody else a big favor, while reading is just a solitary unrelated selfish act. A perspective we've got to understand is writing as a selfish indulgence in the notion of originality. Originality, while not a useless word by any means, is profoundly artificial. Insofar as the "original" writer becomes the aristocratic dispenser of trinkets, originality has got to go. To be a reader is not to be unoriginal, not to be a primitive under instruction of the civilized author, not to be a castrated writer. To be a reader is to be the willing receptor of transformative agencies destined to either alter or confirm one's position in a social circuitry. To take this on as responsibility is to be willing to regulate one's Desire as an individual energy occurring within a social field. To persist in the writerly fantasy of originality is to succumb to the hideous fantasy of reproduction without sex. This is all becoming too familiar to be true, or is it? A "personal necessity" that tries to mesmerize everybody into keeping their distance, doing their "thing", and hoard their fantastic experience of reading in their private strongbox of thought, is no longer necessary. My hope is that we'll come to be less willing to confuse this with writing, and understand writing again someday as a function of repetition, of which reading is the clearest sensual link we have with the invisibility of Desire.

Bruce Andrews
CODE WORDS

Roland Barthes, *Image-Music-Text* (1977: Hill and Wang, N.Y.)

We can imagine *writing* that does not prepare the ego for the terrors and routines of a society it takes for granted.

Author dies, writing begins. The subject loses authority, disappears, is *unmade* into a network of relationships, stretching indefinitely. Subject is *deconstructed*, lost, "diminishing like a figurine at the far end of the literary stage"; deconstituted as writing ranges over the surface. A *floating* or cutting across replaces the barriers of nomenclature and identification. Normalization gives way to *significance*, an eroticism, a multi-dimensional tissue or weave of signs by which any apparent subject is produced. Writing, as *infinite* association, explodes the definitions, endistances origins (or Origin), rejects closure, *exempts* meaning. The vise of the signified is unhinged; simplistic notions of truth are relativized.

Subject becomes simply "the instance writing," is hollowed out by the operation of the linguistic system. System, here, is an *empty* process that some self always seeks to stuff & upholster. In one discipline after another, we have this recognition of the importance of *system* or *code* (rather than the romantic primacy of the individual or the self-sufficient particular). This may be the watershed of the last few decades. The motifs are system / code / frame / structure / constraint / rules: "language being system" & "the system as culture". "It is language which speaks, not the author."

Where code pertains — meaning as use — rules are dominant. Not like 'X determines Y' or "Y is superstructure to base X' but where X follows rules of a social code or paradigm — as if to 'follow the rules' meant the unseating of the sovereign subject as an entity which precedes the activity. Time is flattened out, in the here and now, of conformative / performative language. As if *aura* were that coding, that practiced hand, that *apprenticeship*.

Writing — a *surplus*, not a reduction; an active & continuous constructing rather than a represented content & culture. The older literature of the signified finds itself constantly tempted into commodification. The signifier, on the other hand, marks the *Text*. Its self-demonstration is a performative, a speech act whose content is *depleted* by its own utterance and activity; it "artfully does nothing but turn itself inside out, like a glove"; a *perpetual signifier*, modelled on a permanent revolution. Flustering the image, acknowledging the materiality of language, not letting the subject idealize or mystify the whole process. "Did he wish to *express himself*, he ought at least to know that the inner 'thing' he thinks to 'translate' is itself only a ready-formed dictionary, its words only explainable through other words, and so on indefinitely."

Yet, BEYOND CODE: Language is *disseminated* through the text, that "methodological field," climaxing in *play*, not anchored by but in fact shattering the demands of our seemingly-liberating-but-actually-repressive genres of expression. Beyond the rule-governed transpositions is the self-differentiation of language, away from the universalized, commodity-like qualities so often trumpeted. Distinguishable, even deviant writing, rather than something malleable or blind or something that could be processed or theatricalized (like the self?). Beyond the anchoring of pointing, vertical depth, is a horizontal richness that cannot be diffracted or identified with. Ambiguity is ceaselessly produced and not swallowed up. An *excess*, a *supplement*. Here writing can innovate, as scandal, not destroying code but playing off it, *deferring*, showing the limits. In these cases, writing is clearly produced by the central activity of READING, capturing both the code-like aspects (with the investment of value) but also the yearning singularity of the phonemes bursting off page, tape, or lips. Reading becomes the first *production*, rather than consumption — not a relay of an author's vain transcriptions of a representational content. Reading *operates* the text, is a rewriting, a new inscription. The text erases "the distance between writing and reading, in no way by intensifying the projection of the reader into the work [hypnosis of the reader by illusions of transparency] but by joining them" in a single practice.

Discourse as tyranny, as The Law, The Letter: all instrumentalisms: disorient them. Lift their burden with that drifting, wavering signifier, playing its symbolic attachments in a much more open, impertinent unrepressed style. 'This is new for me.' A multiplication of points of attention, authorless, into an unsituation. *Dispersion:* the ejaculation of polysemy, "efflorescence of the signifier," may come as far as asemy. Silencing the voice of those *paper authors* who remember their lines & straitjacket the play. The activity is *accenting, folding, creasing*, a *stereographic plurality* disrupting "the peace of nominations" that the "spasm of the signified . . . normally brings the subject voluptuously back into."

Make the present relative. Offer a *historicism*, where words are evitable, arbitrary, not determined: a relative autonomy for language. A code is required; the whole is digital, not an illusory analogue, nor identity, equality, interchangeability. Texts (tests) like these will do the *denaturalizing;* they problematicize reality. Naturally language is unmotivated. See it this way. Take away the mythic & fetishized character of the words and sentences, their fatedness: otherwise, how natural & spontaneous & disintellectualized & ahistorical & essentialist it tends to seem.

Read through system / culture, rather than just stare through language to wind up trapped in system / culture, in semantic artifice. Transparency is a future political achievement, not a normal condition we can subscribe to in literature. Writing must look toward a radically transformed society that would provide the code (and the ideal communication system, and counter-communication system) needed to fully comprehend it. *Utopia.* Take nothing for granted, leave nothing intact, move outside, heterogenize, wake up the patient from stupefaction, desocialize the ego (so that eventually we might be resocialized). Indeed, explode ourselves (*"jouissance"*) into the text — "airy, light, spaced, open, uncentred, noble and free".

David Bromige
SOME FIELDS THE TRACK GOES THROUGH

1. Each time I find something worth saying, it's because I've not been satisfied to coincide with my feeling, because I've succeeded in studying it as a way of behaving, as a modification of my relations with others and the world, because I've managed to think about it as I would think about the behavior of another person whom I happened to witness. Merleau-Ponty, *Film*.

2. A child scolding a flower in the words in which he had himself been scolded and whipped, is *poetry* / past passion with pleasure. Coleridge, *Notebooks*.

3. Irresponsible play seeks to overcome the ruinous seriousness of whatever one happens to be. Adorno, *Prisms*.

4. Insistency — the pretension of power — falls victim to a weakness and uselessness of the same type as the gesticulatory schemata of the schizophrenic. Adorno, *Prisms*.

5. The reproach against the individualism of art in its later stages of development is so pathetically wretched simply because it overlooks the social nature of this individualism: "lonely discourse" reveals more about social tendencies than does communicative discourse. Adorno, *Philosophy of Modern Music*.

6. But in the language of Azande it is self-contradictory to doubt the efficacy of oracles, and this only proves that Zande language cannot be trusted in respect of oracles. Polanyi, *Knowing and Being*.

7. If two sequences of the action are to be understood as occurring at the same time they may simply be shown one after another. Arnheim, *Film as Art*.

8. I do not know who you are and yet I insult you and I talk to you as if we were intimates. Colette, *The Shackle*.

   And a 9th by way of question; where does Hegel write: "Truth is a Bacchanic ecstasy wherein every member is drunk on the same wine"?

Andrew Kelly
TASTE, FORM

The drama of history is temporality, the creation of form(s) manifest in the key human potential to dissolve the chaos of cogito into the resolve of concrescence marking this praxis with the absolutely distinguishing character of intuition. How forms which persevere specifically through and for the narrow range of private imagination into world into art into language are located in it by a tripartite of form, taste, value. Herein the status of form is exact-inexact possibility towards object-status (object-ness), and is intimately bound-up with a separatedness of cogito/cogitato that is vanquished (rendered artificial, parasitic) by the basic phenomonology of intuited ontic reach. Any status for form-as-object in this context ultimately involves value(s) that cohere to but are not part of (in) the sensuous world. Taste, then, as the perception that replaces mere recognition, shares its way of knowing (determining) significance in form *with* value, and becomes the sole, tenuous qualifier of that value. As such, value becomes the problematic of *quality* through its relative contradistinct to its 'virtual' determination: if form can only be discussed in terms of culture (Dewey rightly notes), then the value of that form can only be computed through the strictly relative methodologies of what is crucial to that culture, not, obviously, what is 'virtual'. And insofar as this instinct towards virtuality falsifies itself in the negating mechanisms of time-bound culture, the status of the formal object must be prehended by relative qualities which are, indeed, *totally* crucial to knowing it. The bad faith of archeology is exposed here as the most pedestrian sort of substandard atavism: the conviction that (W)ill ontologically *and* epistemologically endures into a meaning that endures into the impossible synthesis of benign matter as significant form. Reflexivity (as intent) cannot transfer intact (as, for, of-itself) beyond cogito into form, and is as such inexcavible. To grant virtuality prehensive rather than fantastic condition is to replace the taste of another Era for the taste of one's own and belies the unrefined bankruptcy of the notion of succession.

The identity of any Epoch is the quality of those minds that apply the constant effort of knowing and fabricating to a world absented of the evidence of unity and languoring in ellipsis. Distinct from the Positivist mode, which reduces the aesthetic standards of culture to a structure of play, this view simply arbitrates the products of intuition (imagination) with the consequence of (R)eason: the making of discrete form in time as the epitomization of an energy that is distinctly discarnate, subjective, a prodigality that bears signification in both the lie and the truth of temporality, excluding the bogus conceit of formist contiguity.

Charles Bernstein
THE OBJECTS OF MEANING

. . . The distortion is to imagine that knowledge has an "object" out-side of the language of which it is a part—that words refer to "transcen-dental signifieds" rather than being part of a language which itself produces meaning in terms of its grammar, its conventions, its "agree-ments in judgement". Learning a language is not learning the names of things outside language, as if it were simply a matter of matching up "signifiers with signifieds", as if signifieds already existed and we were just learning new names for them. . . . Rather, we are initiated by lan-guage into a (the) world, and we see and understand the world through the terms and meanings that come into play in this acculturation, a coming into culture where culture is the form of a community, of a col-lectivity. In this sense, our conventions (grammar, codes, territorialities, myths, rules, standards, criteria) are our nature: there is no gap be-tween nature and culture, between fact and convention. "This explic-itly," to quote Stanley Cavell, "makes our agreement in judgements, our attunement expressed through criteria, agreement in valuing. So that what can be communicated, say a fact, depends on agreements in valuing." In this context, to speak of absolutes is to speak outside lan-guage, to construct a grammatical fiction—it is to deny the human lim-itations of knowledge (for example in the pursuit of certainty or univer-sality). Wittgenstein's relation of grammar to "forms of life" emphasizes that "human convention is not arbitrary but constitutive of significant speech and activity . . . [that] mutual understanding, and hence lan-guage, depends on nothing more and nothing less than shared forms of life, call it our mutual attunement or agreement in our criteria".

Cavell argues against seeing Wittgenstein as refuting skepticism (the belief that there can be no real knowledge of the world)—all he refutes is the "transcendental illusion". Indeed, the truth of skepticism is that there is meaning only "inside" our conventions, that it makes no sense to speak of meaning outside these contexts. That words have meaning not by virtue of universals, of underlying structures or rules, but in use, in—to use the expression from *Anti-Oedipus*—*desiring production*. (". . . desire produces reality, or stated another way, desir-ing production is one and the same as social production.") For Cavell,

Excerpted from "Reading Cavell Reading Wittgenstein", *Boundary 2* (Vol. IX, No. 2, 1981).

skepticism is false insofar as it invalidates the claim of knowledge of "other minds" or "objects of the world"; wrong, that is, to take "metaphysical finitude as a failure of knowledge"; insofar, that is, as it takes certainty, or prediction and control, to be the sole basis for the claim to knowledge. . . . For that would be to misunderstand the precarious conventionality of knowledge and meaning because one imagines it always in terms of (knowing or not being able to know) "things-in-themselves". If that is what knowing is then our relation to the world-as-a-whole is not one of knowing but being in, acting in. The limitations of knowledge are not failures of it. . . .

For whatever similarities there may be between the Wittgenstein of *Philosophical Investigations* and the Jacques Derrida of *Of Grammatology*—specifically in respect to getting rid of the idea that words refer to metaphysical absolutes, to universals, to "transcendental signifieds" rather than being part of a grammar of shared conventions, a grammatology, the two seem fundamentally irreconcilable. What Derrida ends up transforming to houses of cards—shimmering traces of life insubstantial as elusive—Wittgenstein locates as *meaning*, with the full range of intention, responsibility, coherence, and possibility for revolt against or madness without. In Wittgenstein's accounting, one is not left sealed off from the world with only "markings" to "decipher" but rather *located* in a world with meaning to *respond to*. Derrida ends up misunderstanding the implications of his realization that experiencing objects as presences does not mean they are "transcendentally" present by imagining there to be something wrong with presence itself, that it is illegitimate or failed. (There is something failed and the loss can be felt. "The object of faith hides itself from him. Not that he has given it up, and the hope for it; he is on the track [cp.: *trace*]. He knows where it is to be found, in the true acceptance of loss, the refusal of any substitute for true recovery." [Quote here and two below from Cavell's *Senses of Walden*.] The lesson of metaphysical finitude is not that the world is just codes and as a result presence is to be ruled out as anything more than nostalgia, but that we can have presence, insofar as we are able, only *through* a shared grammar. That our losses are not based on the conceptual impossibility of presence in the face of the "objects" of presence not being "transcendentally" locked into place, but rather on grounds that each person must take responsibility for—the failure to make ourselves present to each other, to respond or act when the occasion demands. "The place you may come to may be black, something you would disown; but if you have found yourself there, that is so far home; you will either domesticate that, naturalize yourself there, or you will recover nothing." For Derrida, the overthrow of human con-

ventions entails no revolution, no exile—it is *neutralized* into the ax-
ioms of a textual practice, a new criticism (perhaps awaiting its Gnostic
destruction, or is it that all is maya?). One might say, against Derrida,
that desiring production is the "primary signified", if that is understood
as production of a form of life, where words have truth where they have
meaning, in *use*. "We crave only reality, but we cannot stomach it; we
do not believe in our lives, so we trade them in for stories; their real
history is more interesting than we know."

Ron Silliman
BENJAMIN OBSCURA

Benjamin's characterization of the photograph . . . functions also to note the role of the camera in a crucial step toward the fetishized realism which embodies the capitalist mode of thought . . . the hand in the process of pictorial reproduction is stripped of its gestural content. The loss of the gestural is a topic I have gone into in some depth elsewhere as it pertains to the history of poetry, a portion of which is worth repeating here:

> What happens when a language moves toward and passes into a capitalist stage of development is an anaesthetic transformation of the perceived tangibility of the word, with corresponding increases in its descriptive and narrative capacities, preconditions for the invention of 'realism,' the optical illusion of reality in capitalist thought. These developments are tied directly to the nature of reference in language, which under capitalism is transformed (deformed) into referentiality.
>
> In its primary form, reference takes the character of a gesture and an object, such as the picking up of a stone to be used as a tool. Both gesture and object carry their own integrities and are not confused: a sequence of gestures is distinct from the objects which may be involved, as distinct as the labor process is from its resultant commodities. A sequence of gestures forms a discourse, not a description.

The obliteration of the gestural through the elaboration of technology occurs across the entire range of cultural phenomena in the capitalist period. It is the principal affective transformation of the new material basis of production. Guttenberg's moveable type erased gesturality from the graphemic dimension of books. That this in turn functions to alienate the producer from his or her product is tangible even to authors who compose on the typewriter: to see one's text in a new typeface (inevitably asserting different spatio-visual values) is almost as radical a shock as first seeing oneself on film or videotape, or initially hearing one's voice remarkably *other* on a tape recorder. In a parallel

Excerpted from a longer essay published in *Renegade* #1 (N.Y.) and *Problematic Photography*, edited by C. Loeffler (La Mamelle Press, San Francisco).

manner, the constantly evolving and always unique objects of master craftsmen were replaced by the uniform (hence infinitely reproducible) objects of mass production (where, as Benjamin was to discover, the gestural is replaced by its antithesis: style).

(Benjamin.) "Even the most perfect reproduction of a work of art is lacking in one element: its presence in time and space, its unique existence at the place where it happens to be . . . the quality of its presence is always depreciated. . . . One might subsume the eliminated element in the term 'aura' and go on to say: that which withers in the age of mechanical reproduction is the aura of the work of art. . . . Experience of the aura . . . rests on the transposition of a response common in human relationships to the relationship between the inanimate or natural object and man. . . . To perceive the aura of an object we look at means to invest it with the ability to look at us in return."

Appearance, which is specifically an object *in relation* to an observer, is in each instance the privileged notion. Under the name of aura what appears is the Other, a shock, the recognition and acknowledgement of its absolute integrity freed from any dependency on the presence of Self. This liberty presents itself as 'distance' and 'the experience which has left traces of the practiced hand.' It does not (cannot) occur abstractly, that is: in the absence of the concrete object itself *as presence.* This is how it escapes both memory and reproduction. The affective presence of a photograph of a massacre, a Rembrandt or an orchid is first of all that of a (gray) rectangle of a certain size, which is almost never that of the event or object portrayed.

What is radically new in the age of technical reproduction is just this value placed on the possession of entities deprived of their integrity and otherness, personal experience reduced to vicarious consumption (which of course follows and parallels exactly that which befell literature during the rise and brief reign of the novel). But to lose the Other is, in the same instant, to abandon one's sense of Self, to be rendered numb and passive on a level not previously possible in history. In "The Work of Art," Benjamin necessarily defines aura by exposing its 'decay,' its very existence revealed in this place of a lack, and goes further to implicate as the origin of this erosion not merely industrial imperialism, but that which made capitalism itself (and even capital) possible, the constituting myth of western civilization, *Identity.* . . .

(Benjamin:) "To pry an object from its shell, to destroy its aura, is the mark of a perception whose 'sense of the universal equality of things' has increased to such a degree that it extracts it even from a unique object by means of reproduction."

A 'sense of the universal equality of things,' identity, destroys aura, accomplishing this by the removal of the object from its constituting context. This is also its advantage, since concealed within it is the whole of the scientific method and project. . . . Each of the five fundamental axioms of Euclidean geometry, which served for centuries as the model for science itself, is in some sense a statement of identity, of which the first is "Things equal to the same thing are equal to each other" (if A = B and B = C, then A = C, etc.). Thus identity begets substitution, exchange, reproduction. This principle extends itself into the economic sphere via the *universal equivalent* of money. . . . What Benjamin saw emerging from the iodized silver plates of Daguerre . . . was the decisive moment in which the social basis of reality was transformed. Where previously the manufactured objects of the world submitted themselves to the fetishizing and mutational laws of identity and exchange solely through an economic process, they now did so on a new level, that of information. Each such product must not only carry on a second life as a commodity, but a third one as an image or 'datum.' . . . It is in the loss of aura, the shock of Other which carries with it the recognition of Self, that modern humanity affectively confronts the myth of Identity, that within which even capitalism is inscribed. Benjamin is the first to say it, yet he is unable to speak its name.

Peter Seaton
TEXTE

In a tree, on a tree limb, two strong arms of certain care. Like ecstasy prolongs some dream ensemble or public effect that could requires this distant world it's increasing kinds of lover reviving a writer understanding systems in the form of ways in which the days adapt noises, super dates, intact, some exception someone subjects something to subjects me to an outline of consent like you want to know who don't deal waiting for an example of others composing lines within a series, number one nine three three three. It's the term for balance, the pattern, the magazine, aspects of pussy, period, boundaries of confusion, complexities, because he has written for sighs he hints at to contain the street the eyes defending signifies smells of the special sense of the assembled machine and wood that kept the savage removed from gut. The secret expression threatened mechanical Bach one is of a bite out of, a sentiment as a general rule, or a sentiment, to phonic lance deep in the difference in his expression of little threads this kind of tricks. You says the form of something is obliged somewhere to reason, Montagnard matter, attentive adopted special cities, all possible audiences forgot to demand no audiences, all possible obstacles forgot to demand no audiences. Studded sheltered and white ties. Parts of the minimum Beethoven make no mistake with Beethoven. Certain developmental individual factors of all that's concentrates, alone at last. The history of fire is presented with the tree, in fact the military ordered out to allow ourselves problems will bring consciousness of our family's creepers, and our limitless tradition, the garden, silence listened to in ways of writing, of language, of thinking we tolerate luxury and approval to put a stop to eloquence. Give me money. The preface waits for a contribution to have been aware of, remains the background without any precise itself. These sounds, ah, o, ee, a appears in another way of saying rich and solid. The reader locates the flow of modification, overboard, substituting others with other words for being a word between the lips the husky tongue precede intervals a mess of words rest or test. Memories was practically a product. In it writers remain the same, where those of what it was in phrases resolution adapted to the entrance of the middle to determine the light of the next be that of the words be that of the words must be that of the words. Wild agate the man using her skirt cries of itself across it. Hoods gripped the human face. I was and I did and I met and I learned that I had learned I think I figured I decompensate. Which made it seem I stay in the East. I still consider myself to anyone else, I knew of bobbing beef. I dressed to perspire a little. Conscious of the relaxed floating floating, the back of a chair, the end of a table, shapes and all kinds of a table. Object arrangement a corner appreciates. A king his model missed needs that exhibiting fact is by, and my shoulders, an American woman wanted to leave everything. Combinations identify the term considered in isolation. The written region collectively called spontaneous possible context of the model speed yielding states. The exact species picks up background. Several mirrors composed of escape to the process of waves and a wave has a place for the structure of fragment one of us might distinguish by loss in one of us and sequence and series described as one and one of us. The human jet has been observed and swept through one of us. Then the best are best by the outlined slit replaced by one of us. Accuracy, sides, some clinking cheerful drifting strange spines as trees, as males or women might dock didn't. Books or Bob's toward her Skin as actual as strictly between expecting dust while being spelled, she saw her blue finger feet face for shut. She slid sealed like in back means from up front. So roses, the top took to kiss them. We were lovers lit for looking up at the sky. What was it about the letters of her eyes one of us think, ways of where you are. Children, local arms, the book and the wind skins the sun, arched white teeth in the shoulders of an athlete. Tenses. To be someone's intrusion by trying to slip far from anyone. His palm paper and match house docks. That thought to admit that things. Or some jagged like wool up like kites. To let the Earth feel ourselves against ourselves, help of the tele-bodied tongues near. Of or by a thought yields for yearns after, and things enough countries signs everything in it seems to one of us any kind we extend, also odor of order, also the on light, also something they're in besides, there's one, sexual body of will, synonymous with one of us in parts of them and as long lines all the way to ask the power of a giant. I felt film, keep reading. Leaning. Leaning back. Leaning back another white blur or deep run or Zane Grey and me control the sight we'd been waiting for. I concentrate on something other than exhaustion including exhaustion. I thought about the different back back in place. Sides that skim past. I concentrate on her. Syllable segments beyond the point rain has fallen in the phrase linden tree moves. A high or low impasse might miss old reflexes. For the eye to deliver words articulation purposes of the ear and language clusters without words as familiar chains of visually English linked means for a quick breath, for a pause, for English series of signals in a series. The example spills over to be one of us between the problem of progression and a word ending in French those eyes retain as notation, I love you.

Connection pronounced p, t, k, b, d, g. Punctuation assuming the soft vulva, the size of the back, the lower teeth, the lips, the chest changes, the lowest lips, the routes dotted with the action, their arrows, pronunciation of to do what to do. First say instructions, next chant included then type the same. The contours in thy breast First say deliver, then say the poem. On the resonating neutral article in winter, and neutral hot potato breath, and the poem's weaving moon fallen blood band and one of us, the blue altered sky located to show you where to drop a piece that excites me about being the caption jump fruit trip to the Maritimes. Maybe that's the operator we train to be what later caused the usual native named Fred. The water's too cold, I saw a shiny bonefish rag. I flew a little ahead. I emerged, I had emerged from the dark and quiet open sea, from surface streaks of spray straightened speech. It came loose to decide pointing into the tense ahead of us one of us whose nickname would be, or in English softly announced some sucking stirring an earth clinging scrap of dark aimed dash a few words only a few feet away ignore. I nodded and began bawling, some island, some view of more miles away, the slick and watched line targets, or bright and read surface tough or to get by the edge of the world in the ragged patch in the green cool woods and busy reference point for developments of points and probing commotion there'll be old invisible moving methods of trajectory and lead thumping loops of the strange object, maybe mind, looking for food, sun and shadow or they would have streamlined light until there is one of us. Leads of the eyes disguise one of us to have one of us ease her mind and her cool body. American moves. Abruptly unit tends. Tight home hum. Lone hybrid headlights and so on and so on then holding one of us down you're advised forming the whole of Rome, or Greece, during the formation a Yankee spoke my lines. Skillful use of lead, this now now mountain, the girl and boy blur only is as always: compressed sections of the country with the rest of the country to fill fill fill b as in beauty, w as in word, m as in music v as in vibration m as in man d as in drill d as in drift n as in none t as in t l as in link j as in Jaws 2 z as in zeal s as in zeal g as in George, y as in Yarmouth h as in hear p as in piano f as in fuck k as in cunt power as in plus slashes or variety in the implants. Technical description: i, o, o, a, a, and o. The crows cats foxes magpies and dogs washed away by the rain. Bastards. Open land in a large proportion of food. I was asked is under three feet and about forty pounds the same as the number of lines, because there are more than three lines on one tier or sphere even during the day in quiet places. So if you find one leave it where it is by touching it for good. They fight and inhabit the mountains. They take all the photographs I need and stand nearby. Even try to get somewhere in between the same family called Joe. After about three weeks, neck and teeth, an iron shovel. I called out to my family and stayed for some time to start a new family. My wife and I walk through the countryside until my wife could see hind legs surrounding and sniffing and quivering as if there had never been some parts of humans. My son, backs and sides, leaves of grass, my own eyes, I took a photograph to learn the art of flying, the tops of trees jump from one branch to another. The edge of the woods is practically everywhere. You can find the edge of the woods practically everywhere.

Nick Piombino
WRITING AND EXPERIENCING

Writing is unbounded by paradigms, and its paradigms are subsumable, consumed by its forms. Associations to a poem's instances are not fixed by its formative instants, to the intervals of perception, thought and experience the words designate. Another reason why, technically, the poem and its elements have no history, no *precedents*. The poem and its elements revive an obsolete definition of that word: prognostication, presage, sign. The words prophesy their return in other spheres of experience. They are repeated as a mirror reproduces a silent effigy of an object and as one harmonic liberates and proliferates its possible modulations. The preceding transformations appear to lead inevitably to a moment, a lyrical configuration that is not only discrete but is also an interval, a transitional point in a rhythmic succession of moments.

*

They repeat themselves, not as a mirror echoes its content, but as one harmonic sound liberates a set of possible related modulations, and simultaneously lends those previous to it the quality of having engendered something unique and specific despite the irrefutable evidence of the senses that the moment was not discrete but was part of a continuity.

*

Ravel and Debussy: The musical dissolve– sudden sonic wipe outs of the interval just heard– sudden lyrical expression or quick aside in writing, a parallactic mode of self-definition.

*

The functions and character of paradigms in poetry are both qualitatively and quantitatively different than in any other writing. Aesthetic intentions are usually paramount, whether the actual instances cited are expressed for historical, emotional, musical, visual, philosophic, political or personal impact. In no other art are these relationships so delicately balanced and so easily misunderstood. In and of itself, for the poet, the production of any poem, or any element in a poem constantly brings the question of the purpose of the paradigm cited immediately to the fore. For this reason, the pulls are strong towards the Scylla of historicity and the Charybdis of obfuscation. In the former the paradigm seems clear: like the poet, the poem moves through the media of time and experience. Since there is no paradigm for poetry– or experience– this is possible and technically acceptable. But the danger here is that a paradigm is, in a hidden way, even in a deceptive way, being re-introduced. That paradigm might run like this: since I am a poet, my consciousness is a poetic process and instants of that consciousness are markings on a map of my poetic geography. Again, technically, this is true, and even necessary to take into account when writing poetry. But when this mode is established as a paradigm there is a radical reduction in the scope of a poem and the scale of the elements are too rigidly established on a one-to-one basis vis-a-vis each other.

*

The chant and the song elude the limitations of linear narration by means of the "haunting" refrain. Through harmonic, repeating, reverberating, echoing and iconographic alternation the "flicker" effect of language transcends the "flat" character of historicism. To historicism, ambiguity is a threat, as is projection, because it is experienced as intrusive, too immediately and suddenly intersubjective, and not easily subject to the ordinary processes of remembering.

*

The mutative relationship of poetry to art is akin to that of philosophy to science, science to technology, technology to the art of communication, art to language arts, etc.

*

The problematics of space = the problematic of the human relationship to space.

*

The same for matter and time.

*

What is the relationship of this to the appeal of *density*, or rapid experiences of strong emotional impact directly juxtaposed against the material facticity of language?

*

"[My sense of language is that it is matter and not ideas— i.e. printed matter. (R.S. June 2, 1972)]"

> The Writings of Robert Smithson, edited by
> Nancy Holt, N.Y., New York University Press,
> 1979, p. 104

*

Writing is fixed and sustained in mediums like paper, stone, metal and plastic. Experience is fixed through re-enactment and is sustained by emotional memory. Writing and experience have dissimilar flows, partly caused by their dissimilar mediums— one static, non-human and inorganic, the other utterly physical and recognizable by movement. Only the experience of reading adds an experiential character to writing. In any case, like a forgotten ruin or monument, it continues to haunt us in its facticity as object. But writing is best understood unread, or most recognizable by its paradoxical relationships to memory, and thereby to actual experience. Writing is characteristically monumental, not so much in memory, but in reading, particularly in re-reading. So that re reading adds a new dimension to reading– the characteristically parallactic quality in poetry is related to its projective devices. These give an overtone, an afterimage to the time directly before and after reading poetry, of meaning that is akin to the meanings derived for assessing experiences, but not its exact double.

*

The prevailing distinction between poetry and rhetoric illustrates one ordinary instance of the *au courant* literary distinction between "writing" and "writing about." But the difficulties some people have with fragments in art is a similar aesthetic reaction that prefers the extended prose piece– which apparently has all the virtues of the energy implicit in a rhetorical flow of writing without rhetoric's disposability– to the "short poem." So "writing" would be synthesizing its own structure while "writing about" would somehow be presupposing some external referent or axis of explanation. Poems are universes because of the parallactic relationship of words between and words within languages.

*

The poem and the reader are equidistant from the meaning of the poem.

*

My secret: to know that I am withholding something. Your secret: to know that I am withholding something.

*

Remembering is partly an encumbrance the art of writing carries due to its synthesizing function in the formation of memories, and history (sequencing of experiences).

*

As historicism partly collapses in the movement generated by technological advances in both recording and retrieving memory traces (like the recovery of the icons of Tut and the hieroglyphs of ancient Egypt and the encoded languages of the contemporary computer tape) language continuously revives its function in writing, through its power to reflect the full range of representations of experiential reality in the mind, in its familiar, obscure, human experience in thought and feeling. Language today (as depicted in Godard's *Alphaville* and *Weekend*) is the enemy of the state and historicity because of its power to germinate systems antithetical to custom because custom is partly dependent

on coded laws. Taking language truly seriously as a partly known, un-
knowable form of energy is instantly recognizable to historicism as an
antithetical challenge. Historicism debunks efforts to reify poetic lan-
guage, except sometimes in art and art history (as in the manifestoes of
Dada). Words closely seen are mirrors of consciousness, tones of
thought and feelings, traces and bones of human experience and not
simply mechanical reproductions and manipulations of the processes
of memory, of the visualization of the causalities of historical develop-
ment, the interlocking links of historical narrative, the imagistic jig-saw
puzzles of traditional poetic formalism.

*

Even though most fiction and theater would have it the other way
around, there is actually no point in personifying the essences of hu-
man experience. Reenacted experience, if it is to speak to us in a lan-
guage that has authentic possibilities of extension, a conceivable ac-
tual practicability for intersubjective contact, cannot simply mime the
faces, gestures and expressions that seemingly originated its concep-
tion. It is for this reason that poetry is ultimately the most realistic of all
human expressions in that it places absolute realistic clarity and empa-
thy about psychological, political and existential experiences to the
side of encompassing, in all its variable senses of exemplification, the
pure essence of experience. Of course in purely temporal terms, this is
a very long range view of practicality. Other sorts of practicality cer-
tainly have their uses for human endeavors. Still, the signs of these ges-
tures, the naming of moments that codify instantaneously human com-
munication– "we all see this"– we imagine we connect to those
feelings in memory. Memories are followed by language like paths
leading in from various directions. Though the faces of those moments
are their histories, the inner core of consciousness is not a film or mirror
but a series of hieroglyphs. It is a map– a specific array of markings–
lines and points and variable distances and durations: ever wandering,
oboes babbling in counterpoint in memory following the motive of
the main and developed themes curiously dogging them. Wandering
touches of felt experiences enfolded by the inner thoughts surrounding
them–not one–not even a thousand voices could fully characterize
that resolution. It is heard in one voice, but it is spoken at once in all
languages that is its own language.

*

Poetry reconnects the occurrence and the instance.

*

parallax– the apparent change in the position of an object result-
ing from the change of direction or position from which it is viewed.

*

tide day— at any point the time between two successive high tides.

*

We can get an approximation of experience in words in that memories, because of their ambiguous character, in the reading and relating of words to the subtleties of actual experience, reenact the meanings we applied to experiences, just as we reenact the meanings we apply to the sequence of words. When we say to ourselves, in reading, "That's how I feel" or "That's how I see it myself" we are often tempted to underline the words we were reading when we experienced the feeling of comprehension. Yet then, strangely, when we return to read the underlined words reading that particular passage doesn't still hold the meaning we had imagined it held.

*

"There is no need to be astonished at the part played by words in dream-formation. Words, since they are nodal points of numerous ideas, may be regarded as destined to ambiguity." Sigmund Freud, *Interpretation of Dreams*

*

Experience is spoken not only in its own key but derives its language from all aspects of every element of being. Writing the experience, writing about experience, writing. Language creates itself out of the necessities for marking the trail— to mark a path:— but it defines its own aspects of reflecting on or from itself, its *umbra*. Commentary and accompaniment, companion, map and decoder, the thought process in its daily use is too often recoiled from when it is dense with multilayered ideas, criticized as "too" intellectual, "too" inward, narcissistic: as if thinking itself were worse than watching television, or reading, or seeing movies, or writing about experiences. For the poet, thinking *is* writing.

*

The power of an idea does not solely consist in its groundedness in being.

*

"I further had a suspicion that this discontinuous method of functioning of the system Pcpt.–Cs. [perceptual consciousness] lies at the bottom of the origin of time." Sigmund Freud, *A Note Upon the Mystic Writing Pad* (1925)

*

Reading, like perception, fades out and in. But it would be more correct to say that it juxtaposes simultaneous types of thinking that are ordered in a way similar to the way sentences join together words of different types. As if illogicality could get you there, thought reaches out for, but is touched by anyway, the places some of the thoughts travel to that words don't reach, exactly. Waves are repetitious— thought is repetitious— something like tides. No two exactly the same yet the times are predictable. The moon stays exactly the way it is, slightly off-setting the full gravity of the Earth. Steady, but, understandably, not perfectly steady. Also, thought must be re-ordered into grammatical order. Yet it never quite keeps up with the latest stylistic requisites. Its beauty is not exactly the same as that of language. Thought is free but alone in its freedom. It can't be fully socialized— yet it can compare its truth to that of language.

*

"Timelessness is found in the lapsed moments of perception, in the common pause that breaks apart into a sandstorm of pauses."
> Robert Smithson, "Incidents of Mirror-Travel in the Yucatan", p. 94, *The Writings of Robert Smithson*

*

Writing offers to experience a third eye, a parallactic measure and scalar key to the relations between communicable and non-communicable states of perception and being. Reading offers to experience not a mirrored double but a third voice, an harmonically variable scale that may in the literal sense graphically represent states of being, just as a certain grouping of notes may "represent" alternate modes of enharmonic and intervalic overtones. Polyphonic *ekstasis*, the reading experience translates a multiple text of felt interactions. Experience is read aloud, reading signifies a return to silence. Writing is enshrined in the heart of experience. "All life exists to end in a book." The ending is within the beginning at every juncture, which fragments the impulse to translate reading experience from writing it. Writing, by reviving experience transposes involuntary memories into present ones. In advance, the mind, set on record, transposes what would be free associative and dreamlike states into statements. Returned to the workings of language, experience is felt to be on the other side of the möbius strip. Reread, language is a hieroglyph of experience, but a script both of experience and silence, blankness.

*

Equals=equals==. Scratches are the equivalent of signatures, the spirit of the totem's reification is retouched, carved, and wears away. Spoken aloud, thought is heard and felt, is *touching*, moving.

*

being carried along
was supposed to be in form

when the replica began to fade
before that, time is (was) imprecise
exactly itself without moral tones

*

By listening awkwardly (not like in conversation where the over-
tones are potentially embarrassing) this voice declines concentration
on the dictates of one particular stage in the argument. While the ob-
server has his/her eye in unremitting concentration on the inevitable,
the reader is deftly persuaded to reenact, in silent assent, the genesis of
an apparently random sequence of images.

*

I can't use the predictions anyway. I see them only in retrospect.

*

Instances follow one upon the other invoking an internal sequenc-
ing of experiences. The substantiation of these instances framed in an
accumulative pattern form an aggregate point of realization. The ideas
that emerge most fully contrasted within the aggregate constellation of
scaled images stimulate conceptualizations about the presumed pre-
supposed internal structure.

*

not . . . but

Alan Davies

This predilection for the mind in art. Where did I get it?

Structure is physical combination.

Economy maintains material, accepting it to structure.

Structure adumbrates materials. But necessity.

Structure is enthused with materials.
Structure is terminal; no surround.

A structure which does not reach of itself for support, is massive. After this, duration is a function of attention.

The words stubbornly insist on their place in the structure. Structure insists on their insistence.

Structure determines - machinates - senses. No thing gets sense without an endowment from structure.

The structure of words is their nascence.

Materials only burnish thought, structure.
Language underpins.

No aura surrounds structure. This constitutes its origin, its responsibility in perpetuation.

An intensification of any effort produces structure.

Thought is the mind's implement for locating structures. The mind retains some, assuming a personality.

Structure's *aim* in relation to content is to clean it of meaning.

In composition, certain ideas about altering the structure, undercut all need to do the work.

Structure is clean. It aligns the cacographic necessities, revives them.

All writing tends to its horizon: structure. (Not a limit; rather, the aura of the total gestures written and, over and through that, amplified.)

Attention to structure encourages the vertical subtleties.

Structure intercepts with no other textural element. They succumb in relation.

The one imperative is structure.

Structure (like any single word: noun more than adjective? verb more than adverb? noun more than pronoun? preposition more than article? Probably) points (at) itself.

Structure: no question of essences. Essence shines from materials, produced in light of the reading. Structure is, tension over balance.

Structure neither acts, nor is it an active, nor does it receive. It is a delicate stubborn effect produced under the permanence of the relations. It is not related; it stands.

How does it mean? Structure exerts power, which it cannot withdraw.

Structure has no poles, no extremes, no ends. Its balance is held between its side.

Structure is verified as a language, a code, is verified. We test it not by pursuing it but by pushing it; each structure must hold, against our critical effort, to the site it claims, otherwise it lies in its waste of space.

The structure of the materials are inseparable. They are the effort.

Structure is the one thing.
Structure is non-indictable. It is an urge manifest.

Structure is necessarily tautological.

When the structures emerge the materials arrive. When the materials converge, the structure has emerged.

If perception, the structure, doesn't come through language, there is no evidence that it has come through thought.

Structure leaves no time for an other thing because it withdraws to where it is, and is then found to be exactly where it must be allowed to remain.

Structure executes a project.

There is an element of life in structure which is absent from all other life.

Structure is the altogether latent of possibilities. Its presence. When it is reached.

And structure is nomenclature; a meeting. It is absent. Before and after. Structure hovers: its presence in the absence it empties.

Structure bends the line of sight, sometimes only very slightly, sometimes acutely. Thus it is recognized.

I, a private and concrete individual, hate structures, and if I reveal Form in my way, it is in order to defend myself.

Bernadette Mayer
EXPERIMENTS

Pick any word at random (noun is easy): let mind play freely around it until a few ideas have passed through. Then seize on them, look at them & record. Try this with a non-connotative word, like "so" etc.

Systematically eliminate the use of certain kinds of words or phrases from a piece of writing, either your own or someone else's, for example, eliminate all adjectives or all words beginning with 's' from Shakespeare's sonnets.

Systematically derange the language, for example, write a work consisting only of prepositional phrases, or, add a gerundive to every line of an already existing piece of prose or poetry, etc.

Rewrite someone else's writing. Maybe someone formidable.

Get a group of words (make a list or select at random); then form these words (only) into a piece of writing — whatever the words allow. Let them demand their own form, and/or: Use certain words in a set way, like, the same word in every line, or in a certain place in every paragraph, etc. Design words.

Never listen to poets or other writers; never explain your work (communication experiment).

Set up multiple choice or fill-in-the-blanks situations & play with them considering every word an 'object' with no meaning, perhaps just sound, or, a block of meaning, meaning anything.

Eliminate material systematically from a piece of your own writing until it's 'ultimately' reduced, or, read or write it backwards (line by line or word by word). Read a novel backwards.

Using phrases relating to one subject or idea, write about another (this is pushing metaphor & simile as far as you can), for example, steal science terms or philosophical language & write about snow or boredom.

Experiment with theft & plagiarism in any form that occurs to you.

Take an idea, anything that interests you, even an object: then spend a few days looking & noticing (making notes, etc.?) what comes up about that idea, or, try to create a surrounding, an atmosphere, where everything that comes up is "in relation".

Construct a poem as though the words were three-dimensional objects (like bricks) in space. Print them on large cards, if necessary.

Cut-ups, paste-ups, etc. (Intersperse different material in horizontal cut-up strips, paste it together, infinite variations on this).

Write exactly as you think, as close as you can come to this, that is, put pen to paper & dont stop.

Attempt tape recorder work, that is, speaking directly into the tape, perhaps at specific times.

Note what happens for a few days, hours (any space of time that has a limit you set); then look for relationships, connections, synchronicities; make something of it (writing).

Get a friend or two friends to write *for* you, pretending they *are* you.

Use (take, write in) a strict form and/or try to destroy it, e.g., the sestina.

Take or write a story or myth, continue to rewrite it over & over, or, put it aside &, trying to remember, write it five or ten times (from memory); see how it's changed. Or, make a work out of continuously saying, in a column or list, a sentence or line, & saying it over in a different way, ways, until you get it "right". Save the whole thing.

Typing vs. longhand experiments as recording/creating devices/modes. Do what you do least.

Make a pattern of repetitions.

Take an already written work of your own & insert (somewhere at random, or by choice) a paragraph or section from, for example, a book on information theory or a catalogue of some sort. Then study the possibilities of rearranging this work, or perhaps, rewriting the 'source'.

Experiment with writing in every person & tense every day.

Explore possibilities of lists, puzzles, riddles, dictionaries, almanacs for language use.

Write what cannot be written, for example, compose an index. (Read an index as a poem).

The possibilities of synesthesia in relation to language & words: The word & the letter as sensations, colors evoked by letters, sensations caused by the sound of a word as apart from its meaning, etc. *And,* the effect of this phenomenon on you, for example, write in the water, on a moving vehicle.

Attempt writing in a state of mind that seems least congenial.

Consider word & letter as forms — the concretistic distortion of a text, for example, too many o's or a multiplicity of thin letters (lllftiii, etc).

Consider (do) memory experiments (sensory) in relation to writing: for example, record all sense images that remain from breakfast; study which sense(s) engage you, escape you.

Write, taking off from visual projection, whether mental or mechanical, without thought to the word (in the ordinary sense, no craft). Write in the movies, etc.

Make writing experiments over a long period of time: for example, plan how much you will write on a particular work (one word?) each day, or, at what time of a particular day (noon?) or week, or, add to the work only on holidays, etc.

Write on a piece of paper where something is already printed or written, as, in your favorite book of prose or poetry (over the print, in the white space).

Attempt to eliminate all connotation from a piece of writing & vice versa.

Use source material, that is, experiment with other people's writings, sayings, & doings.

Experiment with writing in a group, collaborative work: a group writing individually off of each others work over a long period of time (8 hours say); a group contributing to the same work, sentence by sentence, line by line; one writer being fed 'information' while the other writes; writing, leaving instructions for another writer to fill in what you 'cant' describe; compiling a book or work structured by your own language around the writings of others; a group working & writing off of each other's dream-writing.

Use dictionary constantly, plain & etymological (rhyming, etc.); consult, experiment with thesaurus where categories for the word 'word' include: word as news, word as message, word as information, word as story, word as order or command, word as vocable, unit of speech, word as instruction, promise, vow, contract & so on.

Dream work: record dreams daily, experiment with translation or transcription of dream-thought, attempt to approach the tense & incongruity appropriate to the dream, work with the dream until a poem, song or phrase that is useful can come out of it, consider the dream as problem-solving device (artistic problem, other), consider the dream as a form of consciousness (altered state) & use it (write with it) as an 'alert' form of the mind's activity, change dream characters into fictional characters & accept dream 'language' (words spoken or heard in dream) as gift. Use them.

Work your ass off to change the language & dont ever get famous.

Jerome Rothenberg
BIG JEWISH BOOK

By *poesis* I mean a fundamental language process, a "sacred action" (A. Breton) by which a human being creates & re-creates the circumstances & experiences of a *real* world, even where such circumstances may be rationalized otherwise as "contrary to fact." It is what happens, e.g., when the Cuna Indian shaman of Panama "enters"—as a landscape "peopled with fantastic monsters & dangerous animals"—the uterus of a woman suffering in childbirth & relates his journey & his struggle, providing her, as Lévi-Strauss tells it, "with a language by means of which unexpressed or otherwise inexpressible psychic states can be immediately expressed". . . .

The poet, if he knows his sources in the "sacred actions" of the early shamans, suffers anew the pain of their destruction. In place of a primitive "order of custom," he confronts the "stony law" & "cruel commands" Blake wrote of—"the hand of jealousy among the flaming hair." Still he confirms, with Gary Snyder, the presence of a "Great Subculture . . . of illuminati" within the higher civilizations, an alternative tradition or series of traditions hidden sometimes at the heart of the established order, & a poetry grudgingly granted its "license" to resist. No minor channel, it is the poetic *mainstream* that he finds here: magic, myth & dream; earth, nature, orgy, love; the female presence the Jewish poets named Shekinah. . . . :

> . . . the female, the proletariat, the foreign; the animal and vegetative; the unconscious and the unknown; the criminal and failure—all that has been outcast and vagabond must return to be admitted in the creation of what we consider we are.

In the Jewish instance—as my own "main main"—I can now see, no longer faintly, a tradition of *poesis* that goes from the interdicted shamans (= witches, sorcerers, etc., in the English bible) to the prophets & apocalyptists (later "seers" who denied their sources in their shaman predecessors) & from there to the merkaba & kabbala mystics, on the right hand, & the gnostic heretics & nihilistic messiahs, on the

From Rothenberg's notes in his anthology *A Big Jewish Book* (1978: Doubleday, N.Y.). And from *Gematria 27* (1977: Membrane Press, Milwaukee) by Rothenberg and Harris Lenowitz.

left. . . . This follows roughly the stages (torah, mishnah, kabbala, magic & folklore, etc.) by which the "oral tradition" ("torah of the mouth") was narrowed & superceded by the written. But not without resistance; says the Zohar: "The Voice should never be separated from the Utterance, & he who separates them becomes dumb &, being bereft of speech, returns to dust." An ongoing concern here. . . .

COMMENTARY: *Gematria* is the general term for a variety of traditional coding practices used to establish correspondences between words or series of words based on the numerical equivalence of the sums of their letters or on the interchange of letters according to a set system. . . . (While numerical *gematria* & letter-coded *temurah* come easily in a language like Hebrew which is written without vowels, the possibility of similar workings in English shouldn't be discounted.) The numerical method—*gematria* per se—typically took *aleph* as one, *beth* as two, *yod* as ten, *kuf* as 100, etc., through *tav* (last letter) as 400—although more complicated methods (e.g., reduction to single digits, etc.) were later introduced. Non-numerical methods included (1) anagrams, or rearrangements of the letters of a word to form a new word or word series, as "god" to "dog" in English; (2) *notarikon*, the derivation of a new word from the initial letters of several others & *vice versa*, as "god," say from "garden of delight"; & (3) *temurah*, various systems of letter code, e.g., the common one in which the first half of the alphabet is placed over the second & letters are substituted between the resultant rows, etc., *in search of meaningful combinations.*

Processes of this kind go back to Greek, even Babylonian, practice, & early enter the rabbinic literature. But the greatest development was among kabbalists from the 12th century on, who used it both to discover divine & angelic names & to uncover correspondences between ideas & images by means free of subjective interference. When set out as poems, the resemblance of the *gematria* to a poetry of correspondences in our own time is evident, as also to instances of process poetry & art based on (more or less) mechanical formulas for the generation of both simple & extended series of permutations & combinations. . . .

	THE BODY	NOTHING	LIGHT	HE & HE	
	The reward.	I.	A mystery.	This & this.	

Dick Higgins
PATTERN POEMS

Because of the profusion of visual poetry since the early 1950s in many languages, in the forms of "concrete poetry" (international), "Poesia Visiva" (Italian), or "spatialism" (French and Japanese), and presented in such works as *An Anthology of Concrete Poetry*, edited by Emmett Williams . . . one gets the impression of visual poetry as a peculiarly modern movement, which is misleading. The concrete poets have tended to take the usual neoteric position and to dismiss the obvious lineage of their work through such pieces as Lewis Carroll's "The Tale of a Mouse" (for English), Panard's "Glass" and "Bottle," or the Apollinaire "Calligrammes." . . .

[An interesting example of the] shaped-poem tradition is the cabalistic charm, coming out of the Hebrew tradition and often written in Latin. Such charms often employ a concept of language as sign rather than semantic process. The closeness of "charm" and "poem" is shown by the common Latin word for both, "carmen," which also means "song," and the Middle Ages drew no hard and clear line between the two. The essential difference between a "charm" and a "poem" is, of course, that the former aims toward magical efficacy while the latter attempts an aesthetic impact. But even here there is a convergence, since the aesthetic impact of the charm could well be a part of its magical power. Thus the linguistics involved in a charm and a poem could be very similar.

The theoretical underpinnings of such aesthetics lie in the cosmology which the Middle Ages attributed to Pythagoras, who was regarded as the greatest philosopher of antiquity, greater even than Plato and Aristotle though, as a pagan, somewhat suspect. The Pythagorean system, as developed in the Hermetic tradition and elsewhere as well as from Plato's *Timaeus* (which was one of the only Platonic dialogues available to the Middle Ages), was based on a hierarchy of "things" at the bottom, the perceptions, feelings, and qualities associated with them next, followed by the word or *logos*, next the idea or form, penultimately the numbers or ratios, and finally the divine principle itself, conceivable only metaphorically in the Music of the Spheres. Within

Excerpted from the introduction to *George Herbert's Pattern Poems: In Their Tradition* (1978: Printed Editions, Barrytown, N.Y.)

such a system, a word stood not for the thing it denoted but for the idea underlying it, and was thus a symbol of pure form. As such it was closer to the essence of numbers and ratios in the hierarchy than anything it might describe, and was therefore invested with a power which we sometimes find difficult to understand. . . . A similar sacred power was attributed to letters, which were not seen as mechanical components of the written word, but as essential and autonomous instruments expressing the process underlying them, analogous therefore to numbers and proportions. The process of forming words became, then, a very sacred one indeed, part of the divine game of realizing things out of their underlying numbers or letters. . . .

Inherent in the concept of a pattern poem is its unsuitability for any sustained argument of emotional persuasion. Its appeal is immediate and involves the recognition of the image. Thus the Aristotelian rhetorical goal of persuading and convincing a reader is unlikely to be achieved within a pattern poem. And an Aristotelian age—such as followed the baroque—would, and did, find the pattern poem essentially trivial and eccentric. The age that followed the baroque was characterized by a tremendous emphasis upon power and force. . . . It is doubtful that the pattern-poem format could achieve the "suspension of disbelief" so sought after by fiction-oriented centuries. But today, with power far less to the point—with less insistence upon a poem that it "move" the reader—the pattern poem has again emerged, in its new guise as the concrete poetry genre.

Steve McCaffery
SOUND POETRY

When considering text-sound it is energy, not semantically shaped meaning, that constitutes the essence of communicated data. The classical, Aristotelian conception of form is that of goal, the target-destination at which we arrive as at a postponed reward by way of a composition. It was, hence, to be a highly significant reversal of Aristotle when Wilhelm Reich was to declare form to be *frozen energy*, opening a path to a new conception of form as the aggregate of departures not arrivals, the notion of the de-form as a thawing of the constrict, a strategy of release, of flow.

What the sound poet practises is the deformation of linguistic form at the level of the signifier. For it is the scripted signifier, the phonematic unit that marks the crypt of a vast repression, where energy is frozen in the articulated and subordinated elements of representation. Language, through its nature as representation, its functioning by means of arbitrary, articulated signs, by means of rules, conditions and prohibitions, becomes a huge mechanism for suppressing libinal flow. To investigate sound in isolation from the sign-function, and to practice out of the actuality and non-representation of the phonematic marks an important stage in establishing the agencies for a general libidinal de-repression. Sound poetry is much more than simply returning language to its own matter; it is an agency for desire production, for releasing energy flow, for securing the passage of libido in a multiplicity of flows out of the Logos. To experience such flows (as a break-through in a break-down) is to experience the sonic moment in its full intensity of transience.

To align, realign and misalign within the anarchy of language. To cultivate excess, return language to its somatic base in order to deterritorialize the sign. Concentration on molecular flows rather than the molar aggregates. Cuttings. Fissures. Decompositions (inventions). Not intention so much as intensions. Plasticizations. Non-functionalities. Shattered sphericities. Marginalities. Somas. Nexi. La poème c'est moi but as the inscription of the person in a transcendental pronoun that utterly annihilates the subject. Personal collapse into flux. Dilations. Positive disintegrations. Structures abandoned, departed from or de-

Excerpted from McCaffery's essays in *Sound Poetry: A Catalogue* (1978: Underwhich Editions, Toronto).

constructed and modified into flows in accord with the unique, unpredictable molecular relationships of audiences and performers. Genetic codicities. A gift back to the body of those energy zones repressed, and channelled as charter in the overcoded structure of grammar. To release by a de-inscription those trapped forces of libido.

Julia Kristeva has written of literary practice as being 'the exploration and discovery of the possibilities of language as an activity which frees man from given linguistic networks'. Sound poetry is best described as *what sound poets do* (or as I once answered "it's a new way to blow out candles"); it thus takes its place in the larger struggle against all forms of preconditioning.

The 1950s saw the development of what might be termed a third phase in sound poetry. Prior to this time, in a period roughly stretching from 1875 to 1928, sound poetry's second phase had manifested itself in several diverse and revolutionary investigations into language's non-semantic, acoustic properties. In the work of the Russian futurists Khlebnikov and Kruchenykh, the intermedia activities of Kandinsky, the bruitist poems of the Dadaists (Ball, Schwitters, Arp, Hausmann, Tzara) and the 'paroles in liberta' of the Italian Futurist Marinetti, the phonematic aspect of language became finally isolated and explored for its own sake. Prior to this there had been isolated pioneering attempts by several writers including Christian Morgenstern (ca. 1875), Lewis Carroll ('Jabberwocky'), August Stramm (ca. 1912), Petrus Borel (ca. 1820), Moliere, the Silesian mystic Quirinus Khulman (17th century), Rabelais and Aristophanes.

The second phase is convincing proof of the continuous presence of a sound poetry throughout the history of western literature. The first phase, perhaps better termed, the first area of sound poetry, is the vast, intractible area of archaic and primitive poetries, the many instances of chant structures and incantation, of nonsense syllabic mouthings and deliberate lexical distortions still alive among North American, African, Asian and Oceanic peoples.

We should also bear in mind the strong and persistent folkloric and ludic strata that manifests in the world's many language games, in the nonsense syllabery of nursery rhymes, mnemonic counting aids, whisper games and skipping chants, mouthmusic and folk-song refrain, which foregrounds us as an important compositional element in work as chronologically separate as Kruchenykh's zaum poems (ca. 1910) and Bengt af Klintburg's use of cusha-calls and incantations (ca. 1965).

Sound poetry prior to the developments of the 1950s is still largely a word bound thing. For whilst the work of the Dadaists, Futurists and Lettrists served to free the word from its semantic function, redistribut-

ing energy from theme and 'message' to matter and contour, it never-
theless persisted in a morphological patterning that still suggested the
presence of the word. It is Francois Dufrene's especial achievement to
have pushed the limits centripetally and to have entered into the micro-
particulars of morphology, investigating the full expressive range of
predenotative forms: grunts, howls, shrieks, etc. Important too, in this
light, is the way meaning persists as a teleology even in *zaum*. Khleb-
nikov, for instance, speaks of new meanings achieved through bypass-
ing older forms of meaning, of meanings 'rescued' by 'estrangement'.

So word persists even in the state of its own excommunication. It
could be said that what sound poetry did, up to the exploitation of the
tape recorder, was to render semantic meaning transcendental, as the
destination arrived at by the disautomatization of sound perception. It
is this theological contamination, of the meaning, like God, as a hid-
den presence, that specifies the limits of sound investigation up until
the 1950s.

With the 50s, however, came the gift of an external revolution: the
availability of the tape recorder to sound poets made audiotechnologi-
cal advancement of the art form a reality. To summarize the several rev-
olutionary capabilities that tape allowed: the transcendence of the lim-
its of the human body. The tape machine, considered as an extension
of human vocality allowed the poet to move beyond his own expres-
sivity. The body is no longer the ultimate parameter, and voice be-
comes a point of departure rather than the point of arrival. Realizing
also that the tape recorder provides the possibility of a secondary or-
ality predicated upon a graphism (tape, in fact, is but another system of
writing where writing is described as any semiotic system of storage)
then we can appreciate other immediate advantages: tape liberates
composition from the athletic sequentiality of the human body, pieces
may be edited, cutting, in effect, becomes the potential compositional
basis in which time segments can be arranged and rearranged outside
of real time performance. The tape recorder also shares the micro/
macro/phonic qualities allowing a more detailed appreciation of the
human vocal range. Technological time can be superadded to authen-
tic body time to achieve either an accelerated or decelerated experi-
ence of voice time. Both time and space are harnessed to become less
the controlling and more the manipulable factors of audiophony. There
exists then through recourse to the tape recorder as an active compo-
sitional tool, the possibility of 'overtaking' speech by the machine.
Sound poetry mobilizes a certain technicism to further the deconstruc-
tion of the word; it permits, through deceleration, the granular struc-

ture of language to emerge and evidence itself. Phonetic poetry, the non-semantic poetry of the human voice, is more limited in its deconstructional scope, for it accepts the physical limitations of the human speaker as its own limitations. The tape recorder, however, allows speech—for the first time in its history—a separation from voice.

Susan B. Laufer
PHOTOGRAMS

> The illiterates of the future will be ignorant of camera and pen
> alike.
>
> — Laszlo Moholy-Nagy

> The photogram, or cameraless record of forms produced by light,
> which embodies the unique nature of the photographic process, is
> the real key to photography. It allows us to capture the patterned
> interplay of light on a sheet of sensitized paper without recourse to
> any apparatus. The photogram opens up perspectives of a hitherto
> wholly unknown morphosis governed by optical laws peculiar
> to itself. It is the most completely dematerialized medium that the
> new vision commands.
>
> — Moholy-Nagy, 1932

Photography was for a time considered only a mechanical means of
recording and documenting. While this quality of photography is
widely held to have released painters from realistic depiction, the pho-
togram represents the melding, rather than the separation, of the two
traditions. The chief proponents and discoverers of the photogram,
Man Ray and Moholy-Nagy, both turned from painting to photography
and the discovery of the photogrammic technique (c. 1920–1922).
These two pioneers, bringing to photography painterly concerns, ques-
tioned the purely documentary nature of photography. As Brecht
wrote, "Less than ever does a simple reproduction of reality express
something about reality." Photograms combine the directness inherent
in the application of paint to canvas with the basic characteristics of the
photo-process: light and the tones produced on light-sensitive paper.
With photograms the question of *taking* pictures does not arise: the
whole process can be confined to the darkroom.

Photograms are a form of bricollage. Bits of scraps, cotton, buttons,
etc.,—materials "ready to hand"—are collaged together and trans-
formed with the product often having no outward relationship to the

---

Many of Moholy-Nagy's books stress the interrelationship of the visual and literary
arts and the value of visual artists studying the achievements of Stein, Joyce, the con-
structivists, etc., particularly—*Painting, Photography, Film* (1969: MIT Press) and *Vi-
sion in Motion* (1947: Paul Theobald).

elements that formed it. In the darkroom these captured images live. What remains on the paper is the residue of the objects—their shadows—the predominant effect is a lack of gravity—of lunar traces—ghosts of objects—a capturing of a fleeting imprint of light passing through an object surrounding it, transformed by it.

Cameraless pictures serve as direct light diagrams, recording the actions of light over a period of time, the motion of light in space. The photogram produces space without existing spatial structure by articulation on the plane of the paper with half-tones of black, gray and white. It is a writing and drawing with light.

The typical feature of the photogram is instability; the image can only be preserved momentarily before it changes. "The object being, for the sake of curiosity, to create a fresh problem, or to place a new obstacle in the path of light like a straw dropped across the path of an ant." (G. C. Argan) Each instance is made particular by the translucent, transparent, or opaque qualities of the objects and the angle of the light rays to the paper.

For Man Ray and Moholy-Nagy, automatic writing, Dadaist collages, Stein, Schwitters, Breton, Cubism, Surrealist writing, etc., all provided an analogy for this proposed new vision of photography. Moholy-Nagy encouraged photographers to liberate themselves from rendering and illusionism and open themselves up to synthetic composition. Light itself would function as the kind of creative agent that pigment is for the painter. "If we can see in the *genuine* elements of photography the self-sufficient vehicle for direct, visual impact based on the properties of the light-sensitive emulsion then we may be nearer to 'art' in the field of photography." (Moholy-Nagy)

Beaumont Newhall has written, "The photogram makers' problem has nothing to do with interpreting the world, but rather with the formation of abstractions. Objects are chosen for their light-modulating characteristics: their reality and significance disappear. The logical end point of the photogram is the reduction of photography to the light-recording property of silver salts. To the cameraman this is what Malevich's *White on White* is to the painter."

Abigail Child

CROSS REFERENCING THE UNITS OF SIGHT AND SOUND/FILM AND LANGUAGE

THE MAKING IS THE MEANING IS HOW IT CAME INTO QUESTION. UNITS OF UNMEANINGNESS INCORPORATED ANEW

vs. A COMMUNITY OF SLOGANEERS

The/sound/is/when/the/eye/is/open./The/light/leads/the/voice./She/ speaks/on/cue./The/cue/is/seen./The/scene/re/veals/the/scene/be/hind/ the/scene./Each/syl/la/ble/is/a/shot./VI/O/LIN/she/says/in/three/shots./ What/I/am/des/crib/ing/is/a/se/quence/from/Mi/chael/Snow's/ *RA/ MEAU'S/NE/PHEW/* a/three/hour/plus/film/which/dis/sem/bles/the/ norms/of/film/and/lan/guage/film-/lan/guage/in/a/ser/ies/of/twen/ty/ odd/es/says/or/chap/ters.

BRACKETS OF KNOWLEDGE: OR HOW THE SCALE MIGHT CHANGE

IN 1929 EISENSTEIN ASKS "WHY SHOULD CINEMA FOLLOW THE FORMS OF THEATER AND PAINTING RATHER THAN THE METH-ODOLOGY OF LANGUAGE" AND IN THE WORK OF SNOW (AS WELL AS HOLLIS FRAMPTON AND PAUL SHARITS) THIS DIRECTIVE IS TAKEN. AS LANGUAGE IS CONSTRUCTED FROM SOUNDS, PHONEMES, AND WORDS GROUPED INTO SENTENCES, SO FILM MEANING TURNS ONTO ITSELF REDEFINING THE FRAME, SHOT AND SCENE.

THE TASK: TO SEPARATE FILM FROM ITS HISTORICAL MOMENT: THAT OF AN ILLUSION DEVICE
OR — THAT IT IS AN ILLUSION DEVICE, AND SO USED TO RAISE THE QUESTION.

A basis of Snow's work is its opposition to popular cinematic practice. To this end, he explores a multitude of subversions in synchronous sound, scripted speech, the narrative mode. At one point, a romance is destroyed. The bed of the lovers is shown as illusion: they lie on the floor. The language is instructional: "theres another side to every story" "touching is believing". A table appears and disappears. The super-imposition is announced "watch this" as are the improbable sounds: "I didn't know you could speak trumpet." Earlier in the film, Snow juxtaposes the rearrangement of objects on his desk with a voice describing the activity, alternately falling ahead or behind the action.

Throughout the film, language and sound are used asymptotically to image, and explicitly so.

FOR IF THE PARALLEL TO LANGUAGE IS REWARDING, IT IS NOT COMPLETE. ITS MEAT IS DIFFERENT: IMAGE/EYE vs. LETTER/SOUND.

This movement from letter to image is the explicit content of Frampton's *ZORNS LEMMA*, a film constructed in three parts: the first being black leader accompanied by a voice reading from the Bay State Primer; the second, a patterned replacement of the alphabet (or more exactly pictures of the letters of the alphabet) with images that over time transform themselves into an alphabet of personal visions in 24 frame, one second units; the third a long (apparent) one-shot take of two figures departing into the landscape accompanied by a medieval text on light.

APART FROM THE ATTENDANT INEQUALITIES IN THE MODE OF PERCEPTION, FILM IS LESS CODIFIED THAN LANGUAGE. WHEREAS THE LETTER/SOUND A AS IN FATHER OR MAD HAS UNDERGONE LIVING AND DISTANCED ITSELF FROM A PERCEPTUAL ASSOCIATION (i.e., ITS LEXATION OVERRIDES ITS PHYSICAL SOUND) THE FILM FRAME REMAINS AN OPEN VARIABLE. IT CAN CARRY A MULTIPLE OF COMPLEX MEANINGS WHICH CAN BE REGISTERED, IF NOT READ, AT A GLANCE. PERHAPS OH OR OUR EXPLETIVES ARE COMPARABLE.

FILM, I AM SUGGESTING, IS MORE A *LANGUAGE INVENTING MACHINE* THAN A LANGUAGE (THIS, ONCE THE NARRATIVE STRANGLEHOLD IS DROPPED). IT IS NOT ABOUT SOMETHING: IMAGE CODIFIED FOR SOCIAL USE. INHERENTLY MECHANICAL AND OPTICAL, FILM (LIKE THE INSTRUMENTS OF SCIENCE) PROVIDES US WITH INSIGHT (IN SITE) PROOF OF NEW THOUGHT AND CONCEPTUALIZATION. BOTH THE TOOL AND FRUIT OF ITS AGE, FILM EXISTS AT THE START OF THE LEVEL OF INTELLIGIBILITY. ONCE FREED OF THE NARRATIVE STRANGLEHOLD, FILM OFFERS ITSELF AS A UNIQUE MODEL TO CONFRONT THE WORLD WITHOUT THE FORMS OF HISTORY.

TO CREATE A MODEL OF ACTION THAT COMPELS US TO LIS-
TEN/CREATE A MODEL OF VISION THAT COMPELS US TO THINK.

YET IF FILM HAS THIS POTENTIAL FREEDOM BEYOND LANGUAGE,
IT (LIKE PHYSICS) IS BOUND TO ITS MECHANISM AND THE 'HAND
BEHIND THE SCENE'. THUS WE NEVER CONFRONT THE WORLD
WITHOUT THE FORMS OF HISTORY (HOWEVER REVOLUTIONARY
THE INSTRUMENT), BUT ALWAYS MEASURE THE PROCESS (OR HIS-
TORICAL NECESSITY) OF THIS SEARCH.

Late in *RAMEAU'S NEPHEW*, Snow interpolates a ventriloquist and his
dummy and an audience of one: the man has a man (the dummy) sit on
his lap/CUT/the dummy (a man) has the man (now the dummy) sit on
his lap/CUT/ the dummy (a woman) sits on the lap of the man/CUT/the
man (now the dummy) sits on her lap/CUT/the dummy (now a man)
has a man (now the dummy) sit on his lap. . . .

OR- AND- IS COHERENCE PROOF OF TRUTH?

John Ensslin
SCHIZOPHRENIC WRITING

Dear Doctor

(Dear) I requirte it the took, I got not why ask when why then, I when you, my shall my you small my, why send sned say, send what why I when (when) I received her (she) she has have a cold, so let recusf the result. I have a resuft takes be to take hate from for from far.

What change (cal) can (for) for you. What can I for me. All your the for the porter. Tell you your you ponten you will you go.

. . . I like Titbits weekly. I like Titbits weekly too. I should like Titbits ordered weekly. I need jam, golden syrup or treacle, sugar. I fancy ham sandwiches and pork pies. Cook me a pork pie and I fancy sausage rools I want ham sandwiches. I want tomatoes and pickles and salt and sandwiches or corn beef and sandwiches of milk loaf and cucumber sandwiches. I want plain biscuits buttered, rusks, and cheese biscuits I want bread and cheese. I want Swiss roll and plain cake, I want pastries, jam tarts. I should like some of your pie you have for second course, some pastry. . . .

. . . Now to eat if one cannot other one can—and if we cant the girseau Q.C. Washpots prizebloom capacities—turning out—replaced by the headpatterns my own capacities—I was not very kind to them. Q.C. Washpots underpatterned against—bred to pattern. Animal sequestration capacities and animal sequestired capacities underleash—and animal secretions. Q.C. Washpots capacities leash back to her—in the train from Llanfairfechan Army barracks wishe us goodbye in Llandudno station and turned in several Q.C. Washpots capacities. . . .

—from letters by 2 clinically diagnosed schizophrenics
(last quotes) and an aphasiac patient (first quote).

There is no schizophrenic language. Bear this in mind. Twenty-five years of psycholinguistic research into the phenomenon of the often bizarre twists of language spoken by schizophrenic individuals has yet to produce a single undisputed definition of what a schizophrenic language is and what sets it apart from the utterance of other speakers.

But an interesting side effect that developed while these same researchers were trying to come to grips with the problem of defining schizophrenic speech is the jargon they used to describe it. These terms are of some interest beyond their use in schizophrenic research for they also describe certain common patterns in the way language is used in modern poetry. In fact this commonality with poetic language has been one of the chief stumbling blocks to attempts to isolate the schizophrenic speaker from other kinds of language users. As one of the more perceptive researchers noted, the problem is the same as trying to define "Poetic language." You may know it when you hear it, and can describe it adequately, but there are no hard and fast rules to set it apart from other types of language.

I offer a small list of these terms because they seem to describe poetry in a way which you might recognize but never really have noticed. I offer them with one precaution: don't confuse schizophrenic speech with poetic language. A schizophrenic monologue will sometimes lapse into passages that are pure poetry . . . with the same carefree play of language found in poetry . . . but to treat it as a freakish bit of literature is to overlook the fact that these bizarre turns of language are the product of a torturous state of mind.

PRIMARY PROCESS THINKING, or "unconscious thinking" as Joseph Bleuler, a 19th century psychologist, first termed it. Freud refers to this as the activity of the unconscious mind in waking and dream states. This way of seeing is distinct from the self-conscious perception of "object-reality." In schizophrenia, this interior vision often supplants a more objective reality. Metaphor and dream imagery are two manifestations of primary process thinking at work.

AMBIGUITY is part of the double-bind hypothesis of schizophrenic speech. That is, the schizophrenic, fearful of the consequences of a direct response, couches his replies in guarded, ambiguous language. In other words, schizophrenics talk in meaningful gibberish so you don't realize what they mean is gibberish.

CONCRETE VS. ABSTRACT ORIENTATION. Most ordinary conversation leans heavily on figurative language. A "normal" speaker, given the choice of an abstract or concrete interpretation of an ambiguous word such as "concrete" will tend to err in favor of the abstract. The opposite is true in schizophrenics who tend towards an over-literal bias.

AUTOMATIC SPEECH or SCATTER TALK . . . long rambling spontaneous monologs often with little apparent connection or provocation. The quality of the language is often obsessive and at times seems to be "writing itself," that is, words spoken a few seconds before will prompt more words which in turn . . . etc. . . . This is also referred to as SELF-GENERATING LANGUAGE. The speaker is almost just a vessel for it. . . . COPROLALIA is scattertalk marked by an obsessive flow of scatological or sexually abusive language. DERAILMENT . . . is the principal pattern underlying automatic speech . . . a curious metaphor for thought . . . as in the train of thought is oft derailed . . . is also sometimes called the TANGENTIAL RESPONSE . . . a sort of flying off the linguistic handle . . . speaking in endless digressions . . . forever leading to nowhere. . . . IMMEDIATE RESPONSE . . . talk is often laced with references from the immediate field of vision . . . a patient's conversation with a doctor for example is filled with words taken from titles of books on a shelf behind him . . . dimming the room actually cuts down on the flow of automatic speech. MUTISM . . . is the opposite extreme . . . a patient goes for years without uttering a word. . . . Often the language is peppered with NEOLOGISMS . . . new words often coined with onomatopoetic genius . . . e.g. the man who called doves "wuttas". . . . PUNS are also frequent and outrageous. The language is also marked by REPETITION of certain words and an extreme lack of normal conversational REDUNDANCY . . . that is, more words used in a given speech sample than normal subjects . . . and rapid CONTRADICTION . . . severe language breakdown is often accompanied by PERSEVERATION . . . the collapse of phonetic word boundaries . . . schizophrenics are often more in touch with the word's sound than with its sense. . . . What results is the breakup of words into smaller syllabic units & new words . . . e.g. "analyst" becomes "anal list" . . . or else nonsense sounds . . . less frequent phenomena are the WORD SALAD . . . long strings of words with no apparent syntactical connection . . . most schizophrenics have a conventional grammar intact however . . . and GIBBERISH . . . speaking in fragments of words . . . often from two or three different languages.

Gerald Burns
A THING ABOUT LANGUAGE
FOR BERNSTEIN

Even the dreadful Maritain distinguishes verse covertly logical or rational from verse which, whether for emotional or exploratory reasons, does float free from "development" of the sort taught in French lycées. Bachelard seems to me to have developed the best devices to criticize it. In English we have Davie's syntactical study, and maybe Charles Williams' *Reason and Beauty*. . . .

The trouble, my trouble, comes from the relation of theory to practice, fiery theory and tepid practice. There are ways in which Clark Coolidge is not a savior. Or can I take his collar as celluloid. Or leather, around a wood armature, with buckles and straps, perhaps rings. This is for a strong neck, to go through. Inventing it took centuries. Now we find them on the sides of barns, like toilet seats.

My favorite barn, which lately had lions in, was really a garage and had in it, on the workbench the hearth-idol of which was a very good, very heavy vise, in coffee cans and old drawers now open boxes such iron fitments as I found in my farm rounds. They were sometimes useful, especially the metal straps and hasps, bendable in the big vise, with effort. These also, the smaller bits, provided me with nipples for plastic caps in redesigned one-shot pistols for conjuring. In general the pleasure was double: of finding and hoarding, and recognizing a use in a cog plate or pierced metal bracket.

Were these, in the ground, words or syllables. Wire fence, bolts and folded drum stock had been grown into by a tree. Large washers, screwdriver shanks and whole saws were in the ground by it. So the tree defined a junk heap, was a locale, probably on the theory that you had to walk around it anyway. Like, in a way, the habit of tacking up old license plates.

There was charm when the bits were old enough (rusted spark plugs are still boring) and potential utility, and as in a time-game the charm of potential utility. The secret pleasure (recall De Quincey on the pleasure of sliding gold coins) was how pretty (not triste) they were, in cans and boxes, *waiting* in senses to be used but not at attention, not sentimentalized. They helped define a workbench.

This last motion, the move outward from particular spiked or angled, heaped or glass-jarred presences, to make a larger area was very odd because they did not *inhabit* the area, as tools hung over their painted silhouettes do or did. They were not citizens or politics. It is more that the large space *could* be used, walked into as a unity, like a country not thinking of its restaurants. One could, though one never did, greet the space. It could be acknowledged, in a different way from how, turning out a jar of washers or fitments, the pieces not useful would still be greeted or given a value while picked *through* or around and set aside.

Max Picard says if words didn't go out of themselves to refresh themselves *in* things, they would hang around in heaps and impede our movements, like things in a warehouse. That *may* be an argument for reference. One could prefer the warehouse, as one dreams in a surplus-parts store. Will this be sought out or printed—ever be more than *browsing*. And is there, built into some kinds of experiment as result, the utility of browsing only. Please reply.

Jed Rasula
NOTES ON GENRE

The state of resistance —"Swamp Fox"—"Robin Hood"— refusal to participate in the codes, while remaining concerned to decipher substance (siphon away the substantiality, which can always be induced to form another substance). This resistance is not *outlaw* from the outset; it doesn't define itself as a preliminary deviation. Its line of advance propels it across the axis of the law, lexis, as a praxis which at precisely that juncture of abrasive contact discovers itself to be *not parallel* to the law [*out*law means being parallel to the stages of the law, but practising its distinctions point by point in relation to the lexical code-line]. This angle of interpenetration can, with skill, be repeated indefinitely (this is how Robin Hood managed to dwell in the same forest all the time, even after the king's men knew he was in there, waiting). This activity can compose a writing, a script in which texts are caught straggling from the train of their genre (train of thought) and be either pillaged or, if independent-minded and strong enough, induced to join the *outside* [i.e., not "outlaw" because that is to continue in the referential procedures of the lexicon, those-who-make-the-law; "outlaw" is just an excitable way of relating to the law; being "outside" however means comprehending law as gesture].

GENRE:

γέννᾶ	of persons, in a family
γενέθλη	race, stock, family
γενέσιος	a day kept in memory of the dead
γένεσις	origin, source, productive cause
γενέτης	begetter, father, ancestor
γέννα	(offspring) descent, birth
γενναῖος	suitable to one's descent or birth
γεννάω	beget, engender, bring forth
γέννημα	to that which is produced or born
γένος	race, family, stock

[Robin Hood's ploy was γελο-ωμῖλία, "fellowship in laughing"]

genre   is   folk-memory   deified

Now we see genre distinctions practised as a kind of racism. The "characteristics" are learned (& what is worse, taught), strict demarcations are observed to a crippling extent [readers of novels can't read poetry, readers of poetry can't read philosophy, readers of discursive workaday prose can't read anything for very long, etc.] All of this snaps back from the praxis into the shadow of an attitude: "poet" "novelist" "dramatist" "painter" "sculptor" "critic", i.e., submission to the sociological demand that everyone identify themself in the form of a racial obsession.

[THE RACISM OF LITERARY FORM]

The important (or functional) distinctions are not, after all, generic, but are decisions relating to inclusion/exclusion. To willingly accept a genre as part of one's identity is to respond to this racism as a code that must be accepted in order for any creating to occur. It is, in other words, to cover the "private parts" in the presence of the lawd.

Madeleine Burnside
GLYPHS

There is a contradiction between events and their description that becomes visible when an event is described without reference to the describer. Such a description does not allow for the possibility that events themselves are simultaneous, with every permutation of accident and action occurring at once; that only perception strings them into logical sequences; or that forgetting is a balance to perception.

The context in which an action occurs requires a specific mode of description: a violent gesture becomes desperate, or murderous, or a request for aid. Events remain opaque, and the structural concepts encouraged by experience give only that climactic vision of coherence, the error of the senses that is in itself a sensuous occasion.

For the same reason the retention of critical distance towards the work is the ideal of the auditor or reader. A type of appreciation is sought: that clarity of thought that at its most sympathetic is like a friendship and has some areas of trust without an undifferentiated acceptance. The writer, however, as a lover of these words, has to fend off the overpowering attraction and the acceptance of less from an indulged expression. The act of falling in love with an idea, a meter, a manner of speaking, has in it all the weakness of the creation of a product not held responsible to itself. So the writer, re-reading, must assume not the willing suspension of disbelief, but a mode of criticism less informed than that potential in the reader.

The alphabet has been criticised for succumbing too easily to its lover, the word. Where each word has developed in powers of inference, the sublimated position of the alphabet has kept it from having a life of its own. While lyricism is the writer's attempt to calm the inherent aggression of words, and allow an equal interplay between the audience's thought and the text, words press back against the interpretive will and draw from their inner selves alternate meanings whose power resides in the imagination. As words open the potential of expression so choice between them closes it. The words of a vocabulary in use offer a criticism of the range of possibilities from which they have been extracted.

The procedure of glyphs is to dominate language by recording ideas through the juxtaposition of other ideas. To ignore this essential element of writing is to mistake its purpose—writing records that which is expected to be forgotten, or writing struggles to dominate the circumstance of forgetting but has only words to use. The difficulty in deciphering ancient glyphs comments on the possibility of decoding alphabetic writing only to discover an ambiguous text. In either case the cultural situation of the text is lost, and with it the implications of its meaning. The mysterious pattern of language is its own unusable key in that changes in meanings of words are affected not only by their induction into other tongues, or slang, or cliché, but by definition and by the kind of rough appropriation that stems from urgent need.

David Benedetti
THE POEM BEGINNING WHAT IT IS

Initial statement of intensely ambiguous desire. Affirmation of the attempt at image without relegating personal history to a position of domineering limitation. Notification in succinct everyday language of the author's intention to call up out of the ordinary events of the day some revelation concerning the ability to cope with social rejection. Flat reversal of previous logic in favor of a slightly metaphorical reliance on the presentation of phrases designed to convey a sense of security in their close examination of emotional detail. Sudden insight, followed by philosophical maxims supposedly revealing the moral implications of such activity. A number of analogies referring back to original statement of predisposed feelings of inadequacy. Slightly ironic comment on the difficulty of accepting responsibility for the integration of thought and action. Further examples of displeasure at contemporary standards of aesthetic expression. Despairing remarks on the ability of concerted energy expenditure to overcome basically unsolvable psychological dilemmas. Extended analysis in oversimplified form portraying social interaction and personal conduct as beyond the reaches of intellection. Return to imagistic descriptions of peripheral anxiety. Relegation of attempts at tempered hope to the projection of unusual ideas conveyed through a combination of syntactic complexity and emotionally-loaded terminology. Summation of on-going conscious event experience in recollection of earlier self-betrayal. Final ideological commitment to continuing endeavor. Terse imprecation of the poetic form as pathetically fallacious. Restatement of desire in less ambiguous terms.

Tina Darragh
PROCEDURE

"Oran" to "ordain" for "J"

orchestration = he raves

The prefix for "Ceylon trail" promises "main orange" after
orbits. Flashback to "front orange" where diversities _____ a
satellite, then skip to "hair order" chorus, again an orbit.
Down eleven, ordination is opposed to satellite, a shape end
circular as in "organized vision". LEVEL also leads to a
circle - "plants Ireland" - two below "beverage", one
below "prehistoric". Finally, islands make "part importance"
fleshy by adding "a" to orbit as orangey united to surrounding
fulcrums "celestial" - Orkney, five up, Orkney.

Francis Ponge's *Soap* introduced me to "procedural" writing. He
had: taken what was at hand, let it refer to itself and then tracked the
process as it would go. So I: take what is at hand (the dictionary), pick a
page at random, use the key words heading the page as "directions",
find a pattern and/or flow of the words and write it down, trying to re-
tain as much of the procedure as possible in the prose.

Examples: 1) in the page "legion to Lent", the sound "lem" re-
occurs at various points on the page. By graphing these points, I find
that they produce a figure eight. I tell the reader about the graph and
list the words contained within the figure. Many of the "lem" words are
"fiber" words, so I also mention the various fibers that can make up the
figure. 2) the word "dog" falls between "Doctor of Philosophy" and
"doge". The dog definition is divided between technical and colloquial
ones. The other words on the page reflect this division. I note this along
with a description of the dog definition. 3) in "Oran" to "ordain", I find
that "orchestration" is related to "he raves". So, to orchestrate the
page, I rave. Letting my finger drop at random over and over, I make a
notation of the points my finger makes and later transcribe them.

Dictionary language (words/phrases giving a direction/relation to
a source — "of or pertaining to", "peculiar to or characteristic of",

"connected with or considered from", etc.) isn't offensive to me the way it is to many, including Ponge. In *Things*, he declares that the function of the dictionary is to limit — ie: deaden — the language. That's true, I suppose, when dealing with single entries and their meaning. But what interests me is the coincidence and juxtaposition of the words on the page in their natural formation (alphabetical order). In reference to each other, they have a story of their own. The technical aspect (scientific and philosophical terminology as distinct from conversational forms) of the language can be intriguing, too. Reading the definitions is like reading a foreign language developed specifically for English.

Christopher Dewdney
FRACTAL DIFFUSION

In this article I am going to reify a progressive syllabic/letter transposition in units of ten. Starting with the letter A and working through the alphabet I will replavece eavech letter with ave syllaveble normavelly starting with the paverticulaver letter in question. The effects will be cumulavetive, the system is avepplied aves it works its wavey through the avelphavebutet. One quickly avercertaveins the import of the text, the exponentiavel growth ravete of membuter syllavebutles increaveses the word length, the morphemic laveg & consequent confusion slows the lexemic inertiave. The averbutitravery neologisms condition the re-ordering of morphemic caveusavelity. These, in turn, haveve avel-reavedy buteen codified buty prior referentiavel conditions. The totavel effect is much more averresting thaven the simple letter for letter or symbutol for letter travensposition. The temporavel lobute/retinavel circuit caven reavedily process symbutol for letter travenspositions, butut the coognition required by syllavebutico travensposition quickly mounts beyond short-term storavege coavepavebutilities. The interesting point here is avecohievement of totavel avereferentiavelity through the use of aven avecocoumulavetively referentiavel system. Avelso, the dispersion of mavethemaveticoal hieravercohies, even tightly regimented, aves it is in this text (buty units of ten) butreaveks down in the interfavecoe. This property of *lexemico diffusion* is equivavelent to re-coent studioes in "orgavenico coircouitry" buty reseavercohers in avertificoiavel intelligencoe. They hope to acohieve fravecotuavel courves & ravendioom sequentiavels buty incoludioing aven "orgavenico wavefer" of avelgave or other elecotricoally sensitive butroths wiredio into the coircouitry of ave coomputor. This text mavey bute coonsidioeredio the working avenavelogy of such ave procoeedioure, reifying its lavetent dioifficoultiets & possibutilitiets. Thetn cohoicoet of syllavebutlets thavet avecotuavelly ococour in Etnglish letndios itsetlf to thet avembutiguity of this tetxt. Avet this point only fivet letttetrs havevet undioetrgonet travensposition, yett thet oblitetravetion ofar scoaven-avedioojustmetnt is avelmost coomplettet. Only thet ococoavesionavel wordio or sometimets phraveset stavendios intavecot. Islavendios whicoh might prompt intetretst in letttetr ococourretncoet coonsetquetntly avebutavendioonnetdio aves setnsetletss. Six letttetrs into thet avelphavebutett, mavenifaretstavetion petrfaretcotetdio-farlowetr ofar farondiouet—ave faraver/farettcohetdio cooncolusion.

Barrett Watten
OBJECT STATUS

for Tom Raworth

14 Cosin Court, Cambridge
March 29/ '79

Dear Barry,
   Would you, if you have the time: for a booklet I'm doing: send me the name of, or a brief description of, or a photograph* or drawing* of, the first

O B J E C T

to enter your mind now!?

Love, Tom

---

*black, white, postcard size.

   The first OBJECT to come to mind was the KEY RING next to your CARD. Immediate steps taken to erase this were impossible while all around a buzzing not connected to OBJECT continued as before. Waiting for the "appropriate" response while hovering over CARD, there came BLUE ROCK. BLUE from a BLUE flyer in hand under the CARD and ROCK from Clark Coolidge's "A ROCK is the inside of space" in his book OWN FACE, read this afternoon. A THUMBTACK posted the BLUE flyer, I remember it as a plastic push-pin. The BLUE flyer showed an exploded OBJECT being either constructed or taken apart.
   Also in the mail was a BLUE and green CARD depicting a bridge over a BLUE reservoir in Utah. The CARD read in part, "Mayan monuments to confuse the living room and sit on" and "not too dense, as though under steam." Imagine a drawing of the BLUE ROCK copied in black and white with a caption "BLUE ROCK" as the "appropriate" response. This is supplanted by the idea of sending photos taken of several OBJECTS in Europe: Catalonian OBJETS DARD next to a cave

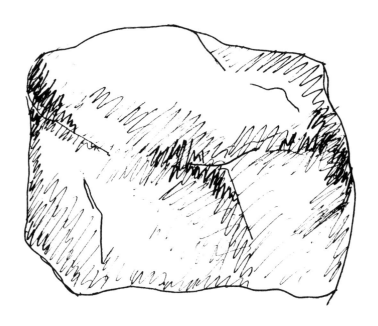

Blue
Rock

person's SKULL and carved ROCK. The photos to be xeroxed, the OB-
JECTS to be transmitted at a third remove.

The KEY RING is 3/4″ in diameter, cost 50¢ and holds six keys. My
habit is to take the KEY RING out of my pocket when I come home and
throw it on the floor. Even so it is easy to forget where it is when I want
to leave. In order to remember then I must forget myself and be rein-
vented to find it. The KEY RING discovered is not a cure for automa-
tism, nor is it an end in itself. Its difficulty is to take oneself into ques-
tion. We need verification, to see all time in this corner of the room.
Shifts wrench to see through to that point. Shifts of mind expose OB-
JECTS behind—what? A wicker haze diffracting light to show what's in
the basket. Mass spectrograph. The worker builds the OBJECT in his
head, then starts to construct.

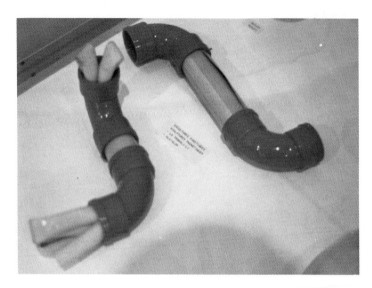

Jordi Pablo: "Sculptures phonetiques." In an exhibit of recent Catalonian art, Centre Pompidou, Paris, 1978.

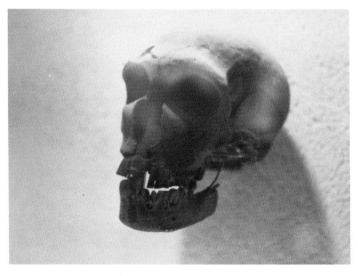

Skull. Prehistoric Museum, Les Eyzies.

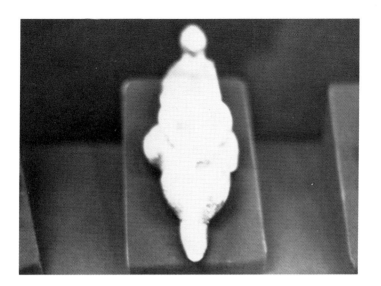

Rock Venus. Prehistoric Museum, Les Eyzies.

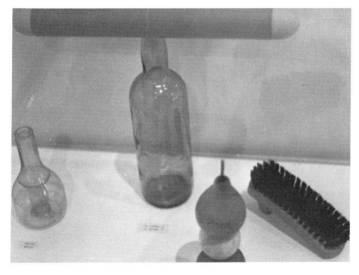

Jordi Pablo: "Pied artificiel," "Reflex," "Le Lettre T," and "Fruit triple." Centre Pompidou, 1978.

At seeing the instructions "the first OBJECT . . . NOW," the eyes shift instantly before the brain sounds out "NOW." The eyes' focus shifts to KEY RING. NOW I must admit OBJECTS though I tried to avoid them, and therefore the KEY RING is the OBJECT I want. Meanwhile I backtrack to clear mind of doubts, to have a clear space to do "as requested." A white noise, followed by BLUE ROCK. The OBJECT then is a shock, the mind rushes to close around it. The mind shields us from OBJECTS but in so doing shifts. Later we open up the "problem" of OBJECTS, in advance. Thus we know to construct.

A ROCK thrown into BLUE water. The THUMBTACK pushed into the CARD. His desire for OBJECT STATUS.

Charles Bernstein
SEMBLANCE

It's as if each of these things has a life of its own. You can stretch
them, deform them and even break them apart, and they still have
an inner cohesion that keeps them together.

Not 'death' of the referent — rather a recharged use of the multivalent
referential vectors that any word has, how words in combination tone
and modify the associations made for each of them, how 'reference'
then is not a one-on-one relation to an 'object' but a perceptual dimen-
sion that closes in to pinpoint, nail down ("*this*" word), sputters om-
nitropically (the in in the which of who where what wells), refuses the
build up of image track/projection while, pointillistically, fixing a refer-
ence at each turn (fills vats ago lodges spire), or, that much rarer case
(Peter Inman's *Platin* and David Melnick's *Pcoet* two recent examples)
of "zaum" (so called "transrational", pervasively neologistic) — "ig ok
aber-flappi" — in which reference, deprived of its automatic reflex re-
action of word/stimulus image/response roams over the range of asso-
ciations suggested by the word, word shooting off referential vectors
like the energy field in a Kirillian photograph.

All of which are ways of releasing the energy inherent in the referential
dimension of language, that these dimensions are the material of which
the writing is made, define its medium. Making the structures of mean-
ing in language more tangible and in that way allowing for the maxi-
mum resonance for the medium — the traditional power that writing
has always had to make experience palpable not by simply pointing to
it but by (re)creating its conditions.[†]

Reprinted from a symposium on recent American poetry entitled "Death of the Refer-
ent?" in *Reality Studios* (1981: London), edited by Ken Edwards.

[†]Alan Davies has objected that language and experience are separate realms and that
the separation should be maximized in writing, in this way questioning the value of
using language to make experience palpable. — But I don't mean "experience" in the
sense of a picture/image/representation that is calling back to an already constituted
experience. Rather, language itself constitutes experience at every moment (in read-
ing and otherwise). Experience, then, is not tied into representation exclusively but is
a separate "perception"-like category. (& perception not necessarily as in perception
onto a physical/preconstituted world, as "eyes" in the Olson sense, that is not just
onto a matrix-qua-the world but as operating/projecting/composing activity.) The

Point then, at first instance, to see the medium of writing — our area of operation — as maximally open in vocabulary, forms, shapes, phoneme/morpheme/word/phrase/sentence order, etc., so that possible areas covered, ranges of things depicted, suggested, critiqued, considered, etc., have an outer limit (asymptotic) of what can be thought, what can (might) be. But then, taking that as zero degree, not to gesturalize the possibility of poetry to operate in this "hyperspace", but to create works (poems) within it.

*

The order of the words, the syntax, creates possibilities for images, pictures, representations, descriptions, invocation, ideation, critique, relation, projection, etc. Sentences that follow standard grammatical patterns allow the accumulating references to enthrall the reader by diminishing diversions from a constructed representation. In this way, each word's references work in harmony by reinforcing a spatio/temporal order conventionalized by the bulk of writing practice that creates the "standard". "The lamp sits atop the table in the study" — each word narrowing down the possibilities of each other, limiting the interpretation of each word's meaning by creating an ever more specific context. In a similar way, associations with sentences are narrowed down by conventional expository or narrational paragraph structure, which directs attention away from the sentence as meaning generating event and onto the "content" depicted. By shifting the contexts in which even a fairly "standard" sentence finds itself, as in the prose format work of Ron Silliman and Barrett Watten, the seriality of the ordering of sentences within a paragraph displaces from its habitual surrounding the projected representational fixation that the sentence conveys. "Words elect us. The lamp sits atop the table in the study. The tower is burnt orange. . . ." By rotating sentences within a paragraph (a process analogous to jump cutting in film) according to principles generated by and unfolding in the work (rather than in accordance with representational construction patterns) a perceptual vividness is intensified for each sentence since the abruptness of the cuts induces a greater desire to savor the tangibility of each sentence before it is lost to

---

point is, then, that experience is a dimension necessarily built into language — that far from being avoidable, or a choice, it is a property. So this view attempts to rethink representational or pictorial or behaviorist notions of what "experience" is, i.e., experience is not inextricably linked to representation, normative syntax, images, but rather, the other way around, is a synthetic, generative activity — "in the beginning was the word" & so on, or that's our "limit" of beginnings.

the next, determinately other, sentence. Juxtapositions not only suggest unsuspected relations but induce reading along ectoskeletal and citational lines. As a result, the operant mechanisms of meaning are multiplied and patterns of projection in reading are less restricted. The patterns of projection are not, however, undetermined. The text operates at a level that not only provokes projections by each sentence but by the sequencing of the sentences suggests lines or paths for them to proceed along. At the same time, circumspection about the nature and meaning of the projections is called forth. The result is both a self-reflectiveness and an intensification of the items/conventions of the social world projected/suggested/provoked. A similar process can also take place within sentences and phrases and not only intersententially. Syntactic patterns are composed which allow for this combination of projection and reflection in the movement from word to word. "For as much as, within the because, tools their annoyance, tip to toward." — But, again, to acknowledge this as the space of the text, and still to leave open what is to be said, what projections desire these reflections.

*

The sense of music in poetry: the music of meaning — emerging, fogging, contrasting, etc. Tune attunement in understanding — the meaning sounds. It's impossible to separate prosody from the structure (the form and content seen as an interlocking figure) of a given poem. You can talk about strategies of meaning generation, shape, the kinds of sounds accented, the varieties of measurement (of scale, of number, of line length, of syllable order, of word length, of phrase length, or measure as punctuation, of punctuation as metrics). But no one has primacy — the music is the orchestrating these into the poem, the angles one plays against another, the shading. In much of my own work: working at angles to the strong tidal pull of an expected sequence of a sentence — or by cutting off a sentence or phrase midway and counting on the mind to complete where the poem goes off in another direction, giving two vectors at once — the anticipated projection underneath and the actual wording above.

My interest in not conceptualizing the field of the poem as a unitary plane, and so also not using overall structural programs: that any prior "principle" of composition violates the priority I want to give to the inherence of surface, to the total necessity in the durational space of the poem for every moment to *count*. The moment not subsumed into a schematic structure, hence instance of it, but at every juncture creating (synthesizing) the structure. So not to have the work resolve at the level of the "field" if this is to mean a uniplanar surface within which the poem operates. Structure that can't be separated from decisions made within it, constantly poking through the expected parameters. Rather than having a single form or shape or idea of the work pop out as you read, the structure itself is pulled into a moebius-like twisting momentum. In this process, the language takes on a centrifugal force that seems to trip it out of the poem, turn it out from itself, exteriorizing it. Textures, vocabularies, discourses, constructivist modes of radically different character are not integrated into a field as part of a predetermined planar architecture; the gaps and jumps compose a space within shifting parameters, types and styles of discourse constantly criss-crossing, interacting, creating new gels. (Intertextual, interstructural . . .) (Bruce Andrews has suggested the image of a relief map for the varying kinds of referential vectors — reference to different domains of discourse, references made by different processes — in some of his work in which words and phrases are visually spaced out over the surface of the page. However, the structural dissonance in these works is counterbalanced by the perspicacious poise of the overall design, which tends to even out the surface tension.)

Writing as a process of pushing whatever way, or making the piece co-here as far as can: stretching my mind — to where I know it makes sense but not quite why — suspecting relations that I understand, that make the sense of the ready-to-hand — ie pushing the composition to the very limits of sense, meaning, to that razor's edge where judgment/aesthetic sense is all I can go on (knowhow). (Maybe what's to get beyond in Olson's field theory is just the idea of form as a single web, a unified field, one matrix, with its implicit idea of "perception" onto a given world rather than, as well, onto the language through which the world is constituted.) So that the form, the structure, that, finally, is the poem, has emerged, is come upon, is made.

2.

Writing and Politics

Ron Silliman
DISAPPEARANCE OF THE WORD,
APPEARANCE OF THE WORLD

> Human beings do not live in the objective world alone, nor
> alone in the world of social activity as ordinarily understood, but
> are very much at the mercy of the particular language which has
> become the medium of expression for their society. It is quite an
> illusion to imagine that one adjusts to reality essentially without the
> use of language and that language is merely an incidental means
> of solving specific problems of communication or reflection. The
> fact of the matter is that the 'real world' is to a large extent uncon-
> sciously built up on the language habits of the group.—Sapir, 1929

> The mode of production of material life conditions the social,
> political and intellectual life process in general. It is not the con-
> sciousness of men that determines their being, but on the contrary,
> their social being that determines their consciousness.—Marx, 1859

One anomaly of contemporary existence which has received little
critical analysis is the persistence of "typos" in foreign language films
from the industrialized nations. A typical example would be the omis-
sion of an *r* in the word "your" in Tanner's recent *Jonah who will be 25
in the year 2000*. Since a film such as *Jonah* (or those directed by
Truffaut, Bergman or Wertmuller) is made with at least one eye on dis-
tribution to the Anglo-American market, such errata cannot be suffi-
ciently explained away as a consequence of the precarious and some-
what secondary existence of an export print (which, on occasion, is
even re-edited for the new market, as was Roeg's *The Man Who Fell to
Earth*). The fact remains that in current bourgeois cinema, attention to
the development of all visio-spatial information is total. That the dis-
ruptive nature of typographical errors in sub-titles is not noticed and
corrected is a sign that it is not felt.

This links it to a broad variety of other social phenomena, such as
the method of speed-reading in which individual words recede and are
replaced by a Gestalt comprehension of content, or the techniques de-
veloped for display advertising and product packaging (including mass

Reprinted initially from *A Hundred Posters* #14 (1977), edited by Alan Davies.

market publishing) for the printing of information which, for any number of reasons (e.g., it is considered "inessential" such as the identification of the jacket designer, or possibly counterproductive to sales, such as a listing of chemical additives in canned foods), the producer does not wish the potential customer to read. Linguistically, the most revealing detail of Noam Chomsky's *Reflections on Language* may well be the ISBN number on its rear cover, printed in a different direction and in a lighter color than the rest of that page's text.

A McLuhanist interpretation, further linking these to even broader social facts such as the rise, and subsequent crisis, of the novel or modernist tendencies in art in general, would not be incorrect as such, but would fail to sufficiently explain the underlying social reasons for the phenomena and thereby fail to suggest an appropriate course for action by art workers generally and specifically by writers.

For several years I have been involved in a series of investigations (*Language Games, The Chinese Notebook* and *aRb*) predicated upon Louis Zukofsky's projection of a possible "scientific" definition of poetry (first outlined by him in the preface to the 1948 Origin edition of *A 1-12*). While the third investigation is still in progress, some fairly specific statements concerning the object of inquiry can be made: (1) the stage of historical development determines the *natural* laws (or, if you prefer the terminology, the underlying structures) of poetry; (2) the stage of historical development determines the natural laws of language; (3) the primary impact on language, and language arts, of the rise of capitalism has been in the area of reference and is directly related to the phenomena known as the commodity fetish. It is this effect of the rise of capitalism, particularly in its later state and monopoly forms, which underlies the effaced *r* in *Jonah*.

The essential nature of the social determination of consciousness has largely been misinterpreted by Marxists and non-Marxists alike. Thus Chomsky, feeling social determinism to be in contradiction to his innateness thesis, writes:

> Gramsci went so far as to argue that "the fundamental innovation introduced by Marxism into the science of politics and history is the proof that there does not exist an abstract, fixed and immutable 'human nature'. . . but that human nature is the totality of historically determined social relations". . .—a statement that is surely false, in that there is no such proof, and a questionable reading of Marx.
>
> (Chomsky, 1975, p. 128)

While Gramsci's formulation constitutes an implicit oversimplification (leading, for example, to behaviorist errors and the idea that human nature can be altered in short periods of time), proofs of the social determination of consciousness do exist. The elaboration of the tool-making capacity of the australopithicene required an expansion of the frontal area of the cerebral cortex and hominid brain consequently grew from 500 cc. 1,500,000 years ago to 1100 cc. 350,000 years ago and eventually to the modern 1400 cc. (Robert J. Maxwell in Yaker et al, 1971, p. 39.) Most of the "innate cognitive capacity" of Chomsky's thesis is indeed the result of a "mode of production of material life." He and Gramsci are equally guilty of the gross application of a complex reality.

The question before us is, however, of a much more specific nature than the social determination of all innate cognitive capacity: the impact of emergence of capitalism on language and the language arts. This question can be restated as Does capitalism have a specific "reality" which is passed through the language and thereby imposed on its speakers? Thus framed, the question can be answered affirmatively.

First we need to note some key differences in the language use of groups which have not as yet been thoroughly totalized into the global class structure of monopoly and state capitalism. Because writing typically occurs in a society which has already undergone significant divisions of labor (i.e., historical development), the best sources of any relatively tribal literature exist in modern ethnological transcriptions, rather than in the early written records of the Judeo-Christian civilization. The following is an English language translation of a Fox tribe sweatbath poem:

> A gi ya ni a gi yan ni i
> A gi ya ni a gi yan ni i
> A gi ya ni a gi yan ni i
> A gi ya ni agi ya ni
> Sky
> A gi ya ni i a gi ya ni
> A gi ya ni i a gi ya ni
> A gi ya ni

> (Rothenberg, 1972, p. 341)

The presence of "nonsense" syllables in tribal literature is unmistakeable. Save for attempts at specifically anthropological explanations, there is no room in contemporary literary theory for a poetry of this kind, no existing mechanism for positing it coherently alongside the work of Dante, Li Po or Tzara. The fact that there have been as yet few attempts to incorporate such materials into "comparative literature" curricula by the educational system of the industrial nations is not simply attributable to racism, though racism inevitably plays a role. Rather, it is that in the reality of capitalism (or of any society well down the road toward capitalist modes of production) there is no meaning here.

But capitalism did not spring up overnight amid loose associations of groups at a tribal stage of development. It came into existence through a long succession of stages, each with its own characteristic modes of production and social relations. While the literature of a people about to enter into the stage of capitalism through bourgeois revolution will necessarily be much closer to our own experience, differences can still be observed. The following are the first eleven lines of "The Tunnying of Elynour Rummying" by John Skelton, written in about 1517:

> Tell you I chyll,
> If that ye wyll
> A whyle be styll,
> Of a comely gyll
> That dwelt on a hyll;
> But she is not gryll,
> For she is somewhat sage
> And well worne in age,
> For her vysage
> It woldt aswage
> A mannes courage.

(Sylvester, 1974, p. 69)

Only one word (gryll, meaning "fierce") has dropped from the vocabulary. Shifts of spelling, pronunciation and syntactic structure are more visible (largely explicable by the standardizing effect of printing — Caxton's press was only forty years old when these lines were written), but the most obvious difference between Skelton's poetry and the modern is its use of rhyme: eleven consecutive end-rhymes using only two endings, -yll and -age, plus five other instances of internal rhyme and off-rhyme (tell, whyle, dwelt, well, woldt). This is the inverse of the effaced r of Jonah: it is an ordering of the language by its physical characteristics, its "nonlinguistic" ones, a sign that this dimension is felt.

Another characteristic trait of the English poetry of 400 years ago is its almost exclusive focus upon either love, the ontological project of the period, or religious and heroic themes passed down from the traditions of colonial invaders, works to be valued as rearticulations rather than as sensuous apprehensions of the experiential. It was not the purpose of the language in the 16th century poem to describe the daily life of even the bourgeois, let alone the common man.

What happens when a language moves toward and passes into a capitalist stage of development is an anaesthetic transformation of the perceived tangibility of the word, with corresponding increases in its descriptive and narrative capacities, preconditions for the invention of "realism," the optical illusion of reality in capitalist thought. These developments are tied directly to the nature of reference in language, which under capitalism is transformed (deformed) into referentiality.

In its primary form, reference takes the character of a gesture and an object, such as the picking up of a stone to be used as a tool. Both gesture and object carry their own integrities and are not confused: a sequence of gestures is distinct from the objects which may be involved, as distinct as the labor process is from its resultant commodities. A sequence of gestures forms a discourse, not a description. It is precisely the expressive integrity of the gestural nature of language which constitutes the meaning of the "nonsense" syllables in tribal poetries; its persistence in such characteristics of Skelton's poetry as his rhyme is that of a trace.

The individual within the tribal society had not been reduced to wage labor, nor did the reproduction of his or her material life require the consumption of a significant number of commodities created through the labor of others. The world of natural and self-created objects is decidedly different from the world of things.

> As men *changed* the world they expanded and refined their ability to *know* it, and the growing capacity for cognition again enhanced their ability to change it. Man creates himself by his works; by his estrangement from himself he becomes his own creation.
>
> (Fischer, 1970, pp. 152–3)

A thing is at once both the end product of a labor process and a commodity of general social consumption. A thing is a schizoid object. Or, to use Lacanian terminology, a thing is an overdetermined object. A world which is made up of such dual projections can only be resolved when the forces of production control both the means of production and consumption.

Wherever such a resolution is not the case, then a struggle arises between the opposing projections: class struggle over consciousness. Where the bourgeois is the rising class, the expressive, gestural, labor-product nature of consciousness tends to be repressed. The objects of consciousness are reduced to commodities and take on the character of a fetish. Things which appear to move "freely," absent all gesture, are the elements of a world of description. The commodity fetish in language becomes one of description, of the referential, and has a second higher-order fetish of narration.

> 115. A *picture* held us captive. And we could not get outside it, for it lay in our language and language seemed to repeat it to us inexorably.

> (Wittgenstein, 1953, p. 48e)

This mass aphasia within the English language occurs gradually over a period of 400 years. The rise of capitalism sets the preconditions for the rise of the novel, the invention of the optical illusion of realism, the final breakdown of gestural poetic forms, and the separation of self-consciousness of the art-object from the consciousness of the object itself in the rise of literary criticism.

Repression does not, fortunately, abolish the existence of the repressed element which continues as a contradiction, often invisible, in the social fact. As such, it continues to wage the class struggle of consciousness. The history of Anglo-American literature under capitalism is the history of this struggle. It can be discussed at many levels; the remainder of this paper will touch on a few.

An event of significance is the development of books of poetry, usually dated in English by the publication of *Tottel's Miscellany* in 1557. If the very invention of the alphabet represents the initial, pre-capitalist, division of labor in language, the first movement of the language beyond the physical borders of the individual, and if the development of bards leads to a further class division into a class of authors and a class of consumers (in a purely tribal society, the poem is the shared language event of the group, the tribe is both author and consumer (cf. chain-gang and jump-rope songs, two forms reminiscent of tribal authorship)), the arrival of the book greatly accelerates the process. From this moment forward, authors will see increasingly less of their audiences.

Another symptom of this gradual repression is the replacement, by 1750, of subjective styles of italicization and capitalization by "modern conventional" usage.

> The rather surprising thing is that so conspicuous and far-reaching a change should have evoked so little contemporary comment. The whole visual effect of a page of type is transformed by it. For us, this entails also a change in psychological response. Men do not ordinarily leave unremarked the swift departure of time-honored custom.
>
> (Bronson, 1958, p. 17)

But if the nature of this change is recognized as repression, then such a conspiracy of silence is not surprising at all. By 1760 one writer, Edward Capell, had gone so far as to discontinue the capitalization of the initial letter of each line of the poem.

Even in the 18th century the contradictions of the commoditization of language result in counter-tendencies. The bourgeois English reader had to participate in the production of the book-as-object, for it was he or she who had to have it bound. Thus individual libraries were bound according to internal aesthetic values, looking quite unlike the hodge-podge of colors and book sizes which typify the modern paperback home library. The sole trace of this counter-tendency in the modern era is the binding style used by encyclopedias and law books, intended to recall the style of that period.

Because of its singular adaptation to capitalist culture, the novel, a distinct subdivision of the poem, is a primary source for any etiology of capitalist reality. Of particular interest are the major forms of response to the modern "crisis" of the novel: the art novel, the mass market novel and the movies. Before turning to these forms, some preliminary comments should be made concerning the nature of the serialized language consumer and the inherently deformed relationship of the novel to its matrix of origin: the poem.

The two primary types of human relationships are the group and the series. The former is characteristic of tribal societies. Serialization (often termed alienation or atomization) places the individual as a passive cipher into a series of more or less identical units, Whitman's "simple separate person." Its apotheosis is to be found in the modern unemployment line. The function of the commoditized tongue of capitalism is the serialization of the language-user, especially the reader. In its ultimate form, the consumer of a mass market novel such as *Jaws* stares numbly at a "blank" page (the page also of the speed-reader) while a story appears to unfold miraculously of its own free will before his or her eyes. The presence of language appears as recessive as the sub-title of a foreign language film.

The work of each poet, each poem, is a response to a determinate coordinate of language and history. Each writer possesses in his or her imagination a subjective conceptualization of this *matrix* (inevitably partial, inevitably a distortion of the objective matrix which, by definition, is the sum of all poems), which is usually termed the tradition. If the functional structure of the objective matrix is that of a grid of coordinates (in which history plays an increasingly dominant role: see the chart of the "Rise of Historical Consciousness in the Making of Art," Burnham, 1973, p. 47), the subjective perception is that of a galaxy, or of a gas in a vacuum in which the work of major writers, important schools and close friends appear as large molecules and denser regions. The locus of the work to be written is felt as a blind spot in the subjective matrix, a primal lack toward which the writer is driven. This is the essential truth of the cliche that poets write only those poems which they *need.* Each successful poem abolishes (but only for a time) the primal lack and subtly reorganizes the structure of the matrix. [For a fuller discussion of the role of the matrix in the structure of individual poems, see the article "Performance" in *Shocks* magazine and "A note concerning the current status of *aRb*" in *Oculist Witnesses.*]

When language is serialized, commoditized, the repressive element deforms the subjective perception of the matrix. The multitudinous qualms, hesitations and self-doubts about this repressive deformation which fill Sterne's *Tristam Shandy* are increasingly anaesthetized by the rise of capitalism and appear not even to be felt by the modern pulp novelist who can just sit down and hack it out. (When it is felt, the consequence is often a phenomenon known as a "writer's block".) For any Rex Stout, the movement of objects, absent the presence of any gestural element, presents no problem. The cumulative and/or continuous present so typical of the temporal environments of the tribal has receded before the possibility of movement-in-time, the capacity for narrative has been greatly enhanced. The underlying precondition of the rise of the novel is precisely this divorce, by repression, from the gravitational force of language in the matrix, an assumption that the free evolution of a narrative art, as such, is possible, but this is an assumption feasible only well within the confines of the commodity fetish of language. Thus the seed of the modern "crisis of the novel" was implanted at the very beginning, its inevitability inherent in the form itself. Instead of "freely" leaving the gravitational pull of language, the novel, like a rocket with insufficient thrust, is doomed to fall back into the atmosphere of its matrix: the peculiar affliction of Tyrone Slothrop is that of the novel itself.

Beginning with the early modernists, many novelists of serious intent at least sense the nature of the contradiction and attempt to confront it directly. Gertrude Stein attempts to reintroduce the continuous present. Hemingway strives for an art of the sentence as the novel's determining language-unit (cf. the illuminating discussion of Hemingway, itself conducted well within the commodity fetish of language, in Jameson, 1971, pp. 409–13). Joyce attempts a frontal assault, the reintegration of the novel into language, but his is a pre-Saussurian linguistics, that of etymologies. Such approaches lead eventually to all manifestations of the contemporary art-novel. Of particular note within this vein is the appearance of a subdivision of novelists who write for, and are principally read by, poets, such as Jack Kerouac, Douglas Woolf, Paul Metcalf, Harry Matthews, Kathy Acker and Fielding Dawson.

Another tendency of response to the crisis of the novel is to accept commoditization and to go on to write novels in which the language is all but invisible. While Saul Bellow (or Pearl Buck or John Steinbeck) represents an attempt to achieve this within a serious mode (the novel as a language art continuing to recall its prehistory in the poem, as art), and while a number of other novelists merely stylize their acquiescence (Mailer, Vonnegut, Roth, et al), more typical — and more revealing — are those who carry commoditization toward its logical conclusions in the mass market best-seller, such as Leon Uris, Peter Benchley or Mario Puzo. Mickey Spillane, who simply *dictates* his novels, carries the disappearance-of-the-word/appearance-of-the-world syndrome to its limit in writing.

But writing need not be the limit. Jettisoning the matrix-factor of language altogether, one tendency of narrative art takes advantage of a new technological development (capitalism's classic defense mechanism) and imposes itself on a new and still unformed matrix. This is the invention of modern cinema, the movies. The transition from novel to film further enables this tendency to modernize its mode of production into a more truly capitalist structure. The lone novelist of 1850, whose product is that of a manufacture-era cottage industry, becomes a century later the modern film *company*, with a small group of producers who own and control the means of production and a much larger, thoroughly stratified, labor force, from director to "best boy." That the imposition of narrative onto the matrix of film was not necessarily inherent in the formal elements of cinema *per se* is a consistent theme in the avant-garde or personal film of the past several decades. The very existence of a film such as Vertov's 1928 *Man With a Movie Camera*, made in the Soviet Union, indicates that it need not have been the case. But such is the nature of capitalist reality — it is imperialistic.

This listing of tendencies of response within the novel is necessarily brief. Similarly, a history of literary criticism could be written, identifying its origins within the matrix of the poem, its exteriorizing serialization and the resolution of its subsequent crisis through state subsidy by its implantation into the university structure, making it an adjunct of tenure. Such a history would begin with a definition of the function of literary criticism as the separation of the self-consciousness of the activity of the poem from the poem itself. It would locate the necessity for this separation in the repressive element of the serialization of language as it moves into a capitalist period. It would explore in depth the role of literary criticism in a capitalist society as the creation of a "safe" and "official" matrix through its self-restriction of the object of inquiry to a small number of works identified as the national literature. It would study the optical illusion of literary criticism in the clarity of the essay form, in which the contradictions of its existence such as would be revealed through inarticulations, redundancies and non-sequiturs are subsumed by the tautological form, rendered invisible rather than resolved. Finally it would study the existence of counter-tendencies within literary criticism as well, specifically the anarchic works of literary theory created by poets (e.g., the body of prose left by Charles Olson) and the recent trend in France toward literary criticism as an admitted art form (e.g., Roland Barthes).

Recognition of a capitalist mode of reality passed through the language and imposed on its speakers finally will require a thorough re-evaluation of the history, form and function of the poem. This is a task of almost limitless dimension, for the matrix of the poem is not only the point of origin for the historical phenomena of the novel and literary criticism, it returns to the very social function of the arts, a dual function: for the group, art interiorizes its consciousness by the ordering (one could call it "tuning") of individual sense perceptions; for the individual, be it artist or consumer, art provides him or her with experiences of that dialectical consciousness in which subject and object, self and other, individual and group, unite. Since it is precisely this dialectic consciousness which capitalism seeks to repress through the serialization of the individual (for it is by such consciousness that we know the overdetermination of the objects of our world by the capitalist mode of production), the fine arts in general function as deformed counter-tendencies within the dominant capitalist reality. Such is the history of the poem.

Every major western poetic movement has been an attempt to get beyond the repressing elements of capitalist reality, toward a whole language art, much in the same manner as Stein, Joyce or Hemingway, discussed above. Typically, they have been deformed at the outset by the very condition of existing within the confines of the dominant reality. The dream narratives of surrealism could never hope to go beyond the narrative fetish, as hopelessly trapped within the fetish as "socialist realism." The entire projective tendency, from Pound to Robert Kelly, attempts to rediscover a physical ordering of the language, but posits that order not within the language but within individuals (individualism is the codification of serialized man), operating on the metaphoric equation of a page as scored text. The recent non-referential formalists, such as Clark Coolidge and Robert Grenier, frontally attack referentiality, but only through negation by specific context. To the extent that negation is determined by the thing negated, they too operate within the referential fetish.

It is the function of dialectical process to not merely explain the social origin and underlying structure of phenomena, but to ground it in the present social fact of class struggle so as to indicate appropriate courses of action. Quite clearly capitalism has its own mode of reality which is passed through the language and imposed on its speakers. The social function of the language arts, especially the poem, place them in an important position to carry the class struggle *for* consciousness to the level *of* consciousness. It is clear that one cannot change language (or consciousness) by fiat: the French have only succeeded in limiting their vocabulary. First there must be a change in the mode and control of production of material life.

By recognizing itself as the *philosophy of practice in language*, poetry can work to search out the preconditions of post-referential language within the existing social fact. This requires (1) recognition of the historic nature and structure of referentiality, (2) placing the issue of language, the repressed element, at the center of the program, and (3) placing the program into the context of conscious class struggle. Such poetry will take as its motto the words of Marx's *The Eighteenth Brumaire of Louis Bonaparte*:

> The social revolution . . . cannot draw its poetry from the past, but only from the future.

BIBLIOGRAPHY

BRONSON, BERTRAND H., *Printing as an Index of Taste in Eighteenth Century England*, New York Public Library, 1958.
BURNHAM, JACK, *The Structure of Art* (revised edition), Braziller, 1973.
CHOMSKY, NOAM, *Reflections on Language*, Pantheon, 1975.

FISCHER, ERNST, in collaboration with Franz Merek, *The Essential Marx*, translated by Anne Bostok, The Seabury Press, 1970.

JAMESON, FREDRIC, *Marxism and Form: Twentieth Century Dialectical Theories of Literature*, Princeton University Press, 1971.

ROTHENBERG, JEROME (editor), *Shaking the Pumpkin: Traditional Poetry of the Indian North Americas*, Doubleday Anchor Books, 1971.

SYLVESTER, RICHARD S. (editor), *The Anchor Anthology of Sixteenth Century Verse*, Doubleday Anchor Books, 1974.

WITTGENSTEIN, LUDWIG, *Philosophical Investigations*, translated by G.E.M. Anscombe, MacMillan Publishers, 1953.

YAKER, HENRI, Humphrey Osmond and Frances Cheek (editors), *The Future of Time: Man's Temporal Environment*, Doubleday Anchor Books, 1971.

[Note: this essay is dedicated to the English Department of the University of California, Berkeley, whose professors were never able to explain the *why* of literature, and to the California prisoners, 1972–6, whose subjective perception of time under the indeterminate sentence led me beyond the borders of my cultural understanding.]

THE POLITICS OF POETRY

*The forum that follows began with the desire to focus attention on po-
litical dimensions of current writing. To make some of those aspects
and concerns more explicit, and to encourage further discussion, we
asked a number of writers to give their view of what qualities writing
has or could have that contribute to an understanding or critique of so-
ciety, seen as a capitalist system.*

Bruce Andrews
WRITING SOCIAL WORK & POLITICAL PRACTICE

"Language is practical consciousness" (*The German Ideology*). Main-
stream criticism still fails to raise or demand an answer to key questions
about *the nature of the medium*—which remains the modernist project
for an art form. So, talking about writing, we have different ways to
characterize its medium, different ways that medium's distinguishing
qualities can be acted upon. Different political practices & epistemol-
ogies are implied.

ONE
     One mode of writing tips its hat to assumptions of reference, repre-
sentation, transparency, clarity, description, reproduction, positivism.
Words are mere windows, substitutes, proper names, haloed or subju-
gated by the things to which they seem to point. 'Communication' re-
sembles an exchange of prepackaged commodities. Here, active sig-
nifying is subordinated, transitive. Its continuing *constitution* of the
world is ignored. So are the materiality of words & the conventions by
which they get generated. Words are mistaken for tools (if only they
could disappear to make way for meanings that sit outside language).
Our concepts or mental pictures are confused with referents & referents
are attributed a secure identity that precedes their delivery into thought
& words (the conventional nature of that relation is also ignored). An

illusionism, the taken-for-granted, *the fetish*. An imagined "opposi-tional" poetics stemming from this perspective would still be reduction-ist, naturalism (a breakdown theory, reformism, 'socialist' 'realism'). Or else poetry becomes complacent literature, ornamental reinforcement of the status quo.

TWO

An alternative structuralist view. Here the medium of writing is *language*, understood as a system. *The structure of the sign* determines that medium's intrinsic & distinguishing characteristics: the division of the sign into a signifier (material form) & a signified (concept or mental representation), the former related arbitrarily/conventionally to the lat-ter. Word matter is not dissolved by reference but exists relationally within an overall sign system. Signification occurs negatively, through *difference* & opposition—terms signify by being differentiated from all other terms, not intrinsically or transparently.

Just as representational literature (dominant form) rests on an im-plicit definition of words as largely transparent tools of reference, other kinds of writing practice correspond to this second, relational defini-tion of the medium (sign/language). It could be a cataloging of the properties of the linguistic system, a didactic or playful yet still depen-dant practice. More radically, the poetics would be those of *subver-sion*: an anti-systemic detonation of settled relations, an anarchic lib-eration of energy flows. Such flows, like libidinal discharges, are thought to exist underneath & independent from the system of lan-guage. That system, an armoring, entraps them in codes & grammar. Normative grammar—a machine for the accumulation of meaning seen as surplus value & for territorializing the surface relations among signifiers by converting them into an efficient pointing system

The coherence between signifier & signified is conventional, after all—rather than skate past this fact, writing can rebel against it by breaking down that coherence, by negating the system itself. Result: an experimentalism of diminished or obliterated reference. This would de-liberately violate the structure of the sign, make the signifieds recede even more from the foreground occupied by supposedly autonomous signifiers. Characterizing the medium this way, we can find a brief for actually instituting opacity, promoting a spillage or dissemination—Not from caring about message or meaning, but caring about the eruptive-ness of material being put into distinctive relationships. So: a spectrum stretching from 'stylistic display' work to a more disruptive political work—within the mostly self-contained linguistic system, of the sign.

Writing can attack the structure of the sign after declaring that set-tled system of differences to be repressive. But there's an ironic twist here. The Blob-like social force of interchangeability & *equivalence* (unleashed by the capitalist machine, and so necessary to the commodification of language) precedes us: it has actually carried quite far the erosion of the system of differences on which signification depends. It's reached the point where a coercive organization of grammar, rhetoric, technical format & ideological symbols is normally imposed in everyday life to even get these eroded differences to do their job any more (an assembly line to deliver meaning, of certain kinds). So to call for a heightening of these deterritorializing tendencies may risk a more homogenized meaninglessness (& one requiring even more coercive props)—an 'easy rider' on the flood tide of Capital.

A calculated drainage of the referential qualities of individual words, for example, may deviate from established rules in a revelatory way, yet still abdicate the central struggle over meaning. That remains to be fought over the fetish, over myth & ideology, the representations & consumptions of fixed meanings.

THREE

Whether we bypass the referential fetish by writing non-signs or whether we tackle & problematicize it depends, again, on how we define the medium. Writing is actually constitutive of these underlying libidinal flows; it ɪs the desire for meaning, if not message. This is a third characterization of the medium, acknowledging the usefulness of the second one but acknowledging its limitations also.

Here, the distinguishing quality of writing is *the incessant* (& potential) *production of meaning & value.* Created through the articulation of writing, which is neither a representational positing of "the" world by imitation of signifieds nor simply a dizzy surface play of signifiers. Meaning isn't just a surplus value to be eliminated—It comes out of a productive *practice.* Not passively, as a derivative of a system of differences (pre-defined) prior to composition. [Even obsessive attack & clever derangement may seem derivative] Instead, active—back & forth: a relay constantly making contexts out of a fabric of markings: writing & reading.

Those ideologies & fixed meanings can be reinforced (1.); or blown apart by wild schizzed-out eruptions (2.); or they can also be opposed by (3.) a political writing practice that unveils demystifies the creation & sharing of meaning. That problematicizes the ideological nature of any apparent coherence between signified & referent, between signified & signifier (for example, by composing words around axes other than grammar/pointing function—). [By contrasting example, see how familiar social ways of (verbs: to contextualize, naturalize, commodify, fetishize, make instrumental) language only shrink the theatre of meaning—lay down a law, a lie, a line, a grammar, a code, illusion. *Writing as Critique.*] Not to make the words or signifiers provocatively opaque irrelevant, but to stress their use value & productivity in the face of mechanisms of social control.

Writing doesn't need to satisfy itself with pulverizing relations & discharging excess. It can *charge* material with possibilities of meaning—not by demolishing relations but creating them, no holds barred, among units of language (even when these seem superficially like a pulverized normality). These relations are constitutive & germinative of meaning. A *practice*, based on this definition of the medium: to create conditions under which the productivity of words & syllables & linguistic form-making can be felt, & given aesthetic presence.

To make the word the basis of *extensions*. Instead of a derivative (sublimate) of previously established connections, the word as "the dwelling place," where meaning will insist on spinning out of the closed circuit of the sign, to reach or act on the world (not only as it is, as it could be). Amnesia or blindness about this *productivity of* writing stands alongside the prevalence of individualized self-preening consumption. Socialisms / necessary but not sufficient conditions. Yet only a dramatic change in the structure of capitalist society is likely to disorganize the fetish, the narrowness of readership (& therefore the capabilities of writing), the dominance of ideological restrictive notions of what poetry & language can be. To politicize—not a closure but an *opening.*

Barbara Barg
20 QUESTIONS

1. Which of the following communicates its meaning most directly and exactly?
   a) a musical composition   b) a traffic light   c) a group of words
   d) weather

2. The written mood that will affect the masses most is one of
   a) hope   b) despair   c) cheerfulness   d) rage   e) regret

3. An amateur writer is one who
   a) is limited in talent   b) distrusts other amateurs   c) has great enthusiasms   d) tires easily

4. Feelings that produce good writing
   a) thrive in urban centers   b) are based on the prevailing standard of living   c) are based on science   d) are based on science which is based on the prevailing standard of living   d) come mostly from Pakistan

5. Historically, writing
   a) has become a subject for formal study   b) offends the wise
   c) is remembered only in part   d) has commercial appeal

6. The most powerful writing deals with
   a) definition   b) incidents   c) grudges   d) pure form   e) sex
   f) emotional spasms   g) attaining manhood

7. Which phrase best describes contemporary writing?
   a) working without pay   b) The Age of the Experts   c) contributions of gifted dabblers   d) in praise of amateurs   d) the experts' superiority over the amateurs

8. In his/her writing, a writer should mostly convey
   a) maladjustment   b) condescension   c) curiosity   d) arrogance   e) innocence   f) professionalism

9. Great writing occurs when the writer is
   a) young   b) recovering from a serious illness   c) "in love"
   d) "spurned"   e) exalted in mind   f) dead

10. Writing gets written because writers
    a) desire recognition   b) wish to avenge themselves on teachers
    c) need to give expression to their feelings   d) hope to impress others with their wisdom   e) feel they have a message for young, old, and the not-yet-born   f) know someone has to do it

11. When writers converse in public they
    a) defend Melville against his critics   b) show that Kerouac wrote well   c) describe Rimbaud's growth as a literary artist

12. Women writers
    a) are only concerned with content   b) don't have happy marriages   c) should always have men edit their works   d) are naturally gullible   d) are always referred to as "women writers"

13. Writers who write about "love" present only
    a) optimistic reports   b) pessimistic reports   c) limited information   d) government propaganda   e) distorted and biased viewpoints

14. In times of stress, writers
    a) support radical movements   b) become more closemouthed   c) stop regular news services   d) distrust everyone   e) revert to primitive techniques

15. Which phrase best describes writing's "place" in your life?
    a) a shelter of long duration   b) a haven from a sudden storm   c) an overnight stopping place   d) an Indian outpost   e) a vacation resort

16. Do you write most creatively
    a) in summer only   b) on drugs   c) day (night)   d) before a reading   e) instead of eating   f) in violation of the law

17. Writing is mostly about
    a) maintaining writing   b) selling one's self a likable image of one's self   c) selling others a likable image of one's self   d) control over one's own productions   e) aspiring to produce an imperishable monument   f) the inevitable

Charles Bernstein
THE DOLLAR VALUE OF POETRY

> Social force is bound to be accompanied by lies. That is why all that is highest in human life, every effort of thought, every effort of love, has a corrosive action on the established order. Thought can just as readily, and on good grounds, be stigmatized as revolutionary on the one side, as counter-revolutionary on the other. In so far as it is ceaselessly creating a scale of values 'that is not of this world', it is the enemy of forces which control society.—Simone Weil in *Oppression and Liberty*

So writing might be exemplary—an instance broken off from and hence not in the service of this economic and cultural—social—force called capitalism. A chip of uninfected substance; or else, a 'glimpse', a crack into what otherwise might . . . ; or still, "the fact of its own activity", autonomy, self-sufficiency, "in itself and for itself" such that. . . . In any case, an appeal to an 'other' world, as if access is not blocked to an experience (experiencing) whose horizon is not totally a product of the coercive delimiting of the full range of language (the limits of language the limits of experience) by the predominating social forces. An experience (released in the reading) which is non-commoditized, that is where the value is not dollar value (and hence transferable and instrumental) but rather, what is from the point of view of the market, no value (a negativity, inaudible, invisible)—that non-generalizable residue that is specific to each particular experience. It is in this sense that we speak of poetry as being untranslatable and un-paraphrasable, for what is untranslatable is the sum of all the specific conditions of the experience (place, time, order, light, mood, position, to infinity) made available by reading. That the political value of poems resides in the concreteness of the experiences they make available is the reason for the resistance to any form of normative standardization in the ordering of words in the unit or the sequencing of these units, since determining the exact nature of each of these is what makes for the singularity of the text. (It is, for example, a misunderstanding of the fact of untranslatability that would see certain "concretist" tendencies as its most radical manifestation since what is not translatable is the experience released in the reading while in so far as some "visual poems" move toward making the understanding independent of the language it is written in, ie no longer requiring translation, they are, indeed, no longer so much writing as works of visual art.)

Certainly, one method is the restoration of memory's remembering on its own terms, organizing along the lines of experience's trace, a reconstruction released from the pressures of uniform exposition—"the only true moments" the ones we have lost, which, in returning to them, come to life in a way that now reveals what they had previously concealed—the social forces that gave shape to them. So what were the unseen operators now are manifest as traces of the psychic blows struck by the social forces (re)pressing us into shape (ie: "a sigh is the sword of an angel king"). *"What we do is to bring our words back"—to make our experiences visible*, or again: to see the conditions of experience. So that, in this way, a work may also be constructed—an "other" world *made* from whatever materials are ready to hand (not just those of memory)—structuring, in this way, possibilities otherwise not allowed for.

Meanwhile, the social forces hold sway in all the rules for the "clear" and "orderly" functioning of language and Caesar himself is the patron of our grammar books. Experience dutifully translated into these "most accessible" codes loses its aura and is reduced to the digestible contents which these rules alone can generate. There is nothing difficult in the products of such activity because there is no distance to be travelled, no gap to be aware of and to bridge from reader to text: what purports to be an experience is transformed into the blank stare of the commodity—there only to mirror our projections with an unseemly rapidity possible only because no experience of "other" is in it. —Any limits put on language proscribe the limits of what will be experienced, and, as Wittgenstein remarks, the world can easily be reduced to only the straight rows of the avenues of the industrial district, with no place for the crooked winding streets of the old city. "To imagine a language is to imagine a form of life"—think of that first 'imagine' as the active word here.

"Is there anybody here who thinks that following the orders takes away the blame?" Regardless of "what" is being said, use of standard patterns of syntax and exposition effectively rebroadcast, often at a subliminal level, the basic constitutive elements of the social structure— they perpetuate them so that by constant reinforcement we are no longer aware that decisions are being made, our base level is then an already preconditioned world view which this de-formed language "repeats to us inexorably" but not *necessarily*. Or else these formations (underscored constantly by all "the media" in the *form* they "communicate" "information" "facts") take over our form of life (see *Invasion of the Body Snatchers* and *Dawn of the Dead* for two recent looks at this), as by posthypnotic suggestion we find ourselves in the grip of—living out—*feeling*—the attitudes programmed into us by the phrases, etc, and their sequencing, that are continually being repeated to us—language control = thought control = reality control: it must be "de-centered", "community controlled", taken out of the *service* of the capitalist project. For now, an image of the anti-virus: indigestible, intransigent.

Bruce Boone
WRITING, POWER AND ACTIVITY

Modernism, particularly in its completed forms in recent trends in poetry, can only be understood and validated, partly or wholly or not at all, insofar as these same trends represent a specifically utopian moment in language. Charles Bernstein's essay on "The Dollar Value of Poetry" [immediately preceding] reminds us of this. "Social force," Bernstein says citing Simone Weil, "is bound to be accompanied by lies." Poetry then can refuse to be in the service of capitalism by being "untranslatable," "unparaphrasable." In a commodity society, we might say, poetry can refuse an exchange-value to make itself available as use-value, or to use another term, text (-uality). Recent trends in poetry can be described as the attempt to deny this commodity aspect of language.

How far should we go in this project? The question is not simple. It implies that the project is historically conditioned, and developmental, and that at a certain point it will have to be thought through again when objective conditions change. In the last analysis the reciprocity between what writing *is* and what it *ought to be* becomes a question of what writing actually does, that is, politics. To judge from a plurality of practices like that of this magazine, the imperative to formulate writing questions politically is recognized more and more widely—and what is more important, by poets themselves. To place ourselves in this discussion then in the last analysis seems to be to ask how writing can relate to revolution, that is, class and liberation struggles. But not in any simplistic way. What is at stake here is the ability to give full play to the two poles of instrumentality and self-referentiality. Until the present, though, it has been generally assumed that it is the second of these poles, the self-referential aspect of language, that ought to give writing its self-nature and legitimacy for others.

But it is hard to imagine how this question, phrased in just such a way, can avoid having an eternal, once-and-for-all aspect to it. Posing the question in this way one doesn't so easily arrive at history. If indeed a utopian content were the only criterion of what a useful and acceptable writing has been or continues to be, finding writing that didn't embody that criterion would become a difficulty interesting only to the most incurable of scholastics. Yet this is how the question does continue to be raised, at least since Sartre. French Althusserianism dominates the horizon. In the view of Althusser, Baliber and Machery even classical literature turns out to have redemptive value. Not just moderism it seems but any writing, as it is assumed that Marx once showed with regard to Balzac, has its determinate moment in the inability to realize its ideological aspirations. Writing, if really writing—so runs the claim—must inherently oppose its own intents with what are called difficulties, blocks, insuperable silences. But what place in such an argument is there for history? These are the problems that anti-instrumentalist theories of writing—like Althusserianism—face.

But perhaps we can sharpen this question by rephrasing it. Is it possible to imagine a modernism that doesn't assimilate itself into the project of symptomatic reading? That is to say, into a humanism. But what about struggle then? Taking sides? Being parti pris? Or are these concerns out of date in our formalist era? Of course one assumes they are not. But if they are not, it's hard to see how they wouldn't be instrumental concerns. If all literature expresses and embodies a yearning for a non-alienated future, it isn't clear in the balance how aspirations for participatory writerliness—a readerly praxis—do not end as subjective improvements that may become indispensable to reaction itself. This possibility poses a useful limit case. For it once more foregrounds the political.

Literary history is in a sense the enumeration of past consensuses of this problem that are no longer seen as viable. Romanticism and the cult of the artist. Symbolism and alienated utopia. Modernism and the fetishization of language as product. Described in this way, however, the trajectory is one that grows increasingly melancholy. In each of these stages literature has more and more radically narrowed its rights to the public participation in the ongoing construction of society by itself—inseparable from power. A profound disjunction, that has proved favorable neither to power nor to literature. Yet both continue to influence each other, fascinate each other, and their uneasy attractiveness seems to register the uneven development of revolution itself. This specific inability to think writing and power at one and the same time then comes to have a name. It is false consciousness.

2. So perhaps we can start again and understand writing, poetry, as developed in our time as a *critique of power*. Such a critique—a denigration or disavowal—can now be usefully described and evaluated from a political-historical perspective. The refusal of the moment of power in the transition stage to socialism becomes objectively regressive or even reactionary as the refusal of contestation. Simultaneously, though, this refusal names the utopian content of a later period. But in the transition to this later time—communism—the critique of power takes on a positive meaning and no longer functions regressively. It becomes instead the means of expediting a passing over to the era of history proper, to the dismantling of the state and its apparatuses and to the first general realization of a human social life. The legitimacy of writing as a critique of power then stands or fails in relation to its historical timeli-

ness in utopian struggles. In periods when legitimate demands are given utopian formulations, the anti-instrumental character of this kind of writing gives it a definite progressive function. In an era of class struggle, however, when political demands take on an instrumental complexion, such a writing may come to seem less useful. At this point writing may often become propaganda. Such at least has been the classical and binary model. Yet there are strong indications from our own time that the model has been broken down and that these either-or formulations have been simply bypassed.

This is the dilemma. Modernism's alliance with terrorism and disorder has become irrelevant precisely to the extent that communistic or utopian possibilities have begun to make their presence felt in collective, durable political formulations in association with the working class. And to the degree that these new utopian forces make themselves felt politically, writing is to that extent forced to rethink its abdication from power. By a consensual removal of itself to the margins of the public sphere of commodity production—in order to privilege utopian demands for use-value—writing historically founded its notion of self-legitimacy on a reintegration in the communist future. But what if in a variety of regions and in germinal form that future has *already* begun to make its appearance in the advanced capitalist countries in the West?

3. All this of course is to speak once more of the cultural revolution, and to ask again if any legacy remains 10 years after Maoism, May of '68 in Paris, the anti-war days of the '60s and Counterculture, and the Prague Spring. We know there was a cultural revolution and we know that its effects have not been simply liquidated.

What has happened? In 10 years objectively anarcho-communist forms of political organization have sprung up and proliferated wherever one looks. Feminism and the gay movement, ecology and anti-nuclear movements—in Europe and in this country both—power issues on a municipal level, consumers' and tenants' movements, the large-scale prison movement and so on—a whole spectrum of liberation organizations has now arisen. Their impact has been to raise issues in mass political organizations, such that their solution is not possible within a program advancing a demand for socialism alone, but only on the basis of making radical demands *beyond* that—to communism, in fact.

Within this perspective one might legitimately ask if the solution of writing and writers can still remain what it has been programmatically—that is, a political absence validated by the notion of a critique of power in an autonomous writing area. Early in the 19th Century this was the concordat reached between writing and society, an agreement according to which society's writing practice was from then on to seem something other than self-expression. But if this agreement is now seen as renegotiable, we will need another conceptual model in order to do it. For writing's renunciation of instrumental values in regard to language will continue to imply the negation of an attempt at power as long as writing and power are seen in a relation of mutual exclusivity. If, in other words, writing must always be either on the side of utopia or on the side of instrumentality. And if—more radically—class and liberation struggles are to persist in regarding each other with stares of non-recognition. In this case surely writing would remain exterior to power, and power to writing. But what if the situation were to change? What if at a certain point in history, class struggle were to begin to have a doubly implicating relationship with human liberation struggle? And what if human history had begun to think socialism and communism *globally* and *at the same time?*—and here the work of Rudolf Bahro might be seen as a dramatic indicator of these very possibilities. If one were to be able to think the situation in some such way as this, one could also conceive of the possibility of some collective intellectual work existing on its own behalf. Rather than instrumentality for another, writing's relation to power would then be self-expression. This new model would have profound implications for the norms and forms of writing as now practiced. For writing's 'eternal', or unreflected, premise has been that the notion of writing for another and that of writing as a commodity are in reality one and the same thing—an understanding that has made modernism possible. But let us suppose for a moment that the situation has changed. Let us suppose that this binary description is no longer adequate to the course of events. Writing now grounds itself in an *interior* relation to power. It becomes a self-expression, and a group practice. With this supposition writing's past is simply the series of discrete moments, salvageable enclaves or testimonials to what is still to come. Its present on the other hand becomes the collective intellectual practice one is engaged in at any moment. Writing would not be separate from whatever one does as an intellectual—in the body of those who both think and act, and who stand in a certain tendential, final relation to the modern Prince. That is how this reality might be mapped in the present. And here one can already see certain points of possible focus. These are probably very ordinary or predictable areas like work in mass or sectarian organizations, critical and educational outputs, the construction of political narrations or what-have-you. In all this play would be supposed. This writing would be instrumental in a new way, certainly, but never in a sense that didn't say 'we,' that wasn't freely willed. It probably wouldn't get along with commissars.

Naturally one supposes that this writing has begun and that it is only a question of locating it—and that each can begin finding it in her life or his. It is impossible to assume that this writing has not already begun in places one visits each day. Writers, in this view, are simply people engaged in teaching, political organization, community work and liberation groups, and so on—in fact in normal activities we are already engaged in. This is the opposite of modernism and écriture. Above all, a writing like the one I am supposing accepts its relation to power. It knows it has no other choice. But in this it feels tremendously exuberant, at the thought of the possibilities opening before it. And it knows too, it is embarked.

Cris Cheek, Kirby Malone, Marshall Reese
TV TRIO present CAREER WRIST
[for the international *F*estival of *D*isappearing(s) *A*rt(s)]
[from the action-sound detention wing]

"Writing has never been capitalism's thing. Capitalism is profoundly illiterate. The death of writing is like the death of God or the death of the father: the thing was settled a long time ago, although the news of the event is slow to reach us, and there survives in us the memory of extinct signs with which we still write. The reason for this is simple: writing implies a use of language in general according to which graphism becomes aligned on the voice, but also overcodes it and induces a fictitious voice from on high that functions as a signifier. The arbitrary nature of the thing designated, the subordination of the signified, the transcendence of the despotic signifier, and finally, its consecutive decomposition into minimal elements within a field of immanence uncovered by the withdrawal of the despot—all this is evidence that writing belongs to imperial despotic representation. . . . Of course capitalism has made and continues to make use of writing; not only is writing adapted to money as the general equivalent, but the specific functions of money in capitalism went by way of writing and printing, and in some measure continue to do so. . . ."

"Fourteen dollars and twenty eight cents is more attractive than fourteen dollars because of the 28."

WHERE'S HABIT FORMING

Writing can't be limited to dealing with capitalism. Capitalism is a setback. Writing as it relates to capitalism is the limitation the framework poses. The concerns should be against oppressive structures. Writing has become referential to itself—to the making of objects. When writing informs writing & writers & writing writers the systems are securities.

SHKLOVSKY'S KUGEL

Literature, rather than visual or performance work, is the only useful residue left to us of Russian Futurism.   True ☐   False ☐
There are no differences between feudal states and capitalist states.
                                                            True ☐   False ☐
Where's the structural control.   True ☐   False ☐
Language (as understood in its use in a community) is comprised of approximately ten per cent verbal elements; the rest consists of gesture, atmosphere, billboards, environmental drift, etc.
                                                            True ☐   False ☐
Publishing is imperialism.   True ☐   False ☐
I embody all that I most must hate & fear.   True ☐   False ☐

WRITING IS A CONSERVATIVE TENDENCY

If writing is to defuse oppressive structures rather than re-fuse them its first task is not to be the mechanics of escapism. Lullabies are made of words. When words set themselves up they form double binds. Narrative constitutes a parallel life which absorbs the reader leaving his/her body depoliticized. Repressed sexualities objectify themselves through the use and design of machinery. The typewriter is not a lover. The investment of sexuality in mechanics leads writers to confuse eroticism with death, the erotic with the dead. What dies is not the author but the authenticating enunciation sustained by the immortality granted the subject. Properly speaking, "glyphs" are the signatures (cuts in the ear, brandmarks) of the owners of their cattle.

NOTES TO MYSELF

Think of it as why we had to cook my poor dad's flesh. Think of it as open before using. Think of it as vanity and sink. Think of it as our own. Think of it as fresh daily. Think of it as I will behave in line. Think of it as 60 cycle hum. Think of it as proudly we hail these. Think of it as exclusive adhesive. Think of it as most folks use. Think of it as sheer bandages. Think of it as all purpose grind. Think of it as capitalism is a setback. Think of it as machines do it for you. Think of it as June 1979. Think of it as the people's pharmacy. Think of it as a small curd. Think of it as not less than. Think of it as our mail. Think of it as new easy re-close. Think of it as drink your drink. Think of it as amusement only. Think of it as a half a dozen of another. Think of it as a wet book. Think of it as a soggy cover. Think of it as money talks. Think of it as you can laugh all you want. Think of it as that means I can do what. Think of it as do you read me. Think of it as a lot to look forward to. Think of it as the author has no authority.

GROWN ASLEEP

The ghosts of eroticism, so clear in the piston & cylinder, oblique into information storage & retrieval.
". . . It was only after the remaining two had consumed what food they had—some chocolate bars, a bag of potato chips, a granola bar and cough drops—did they decide to eat Don Johnson. 'We talked to God and we prayed, and whatever else came we knew we had to eat him and we did. I want it known that we aren't ashamed. We knew it was right. God told us it was right. We knew it was what Don would have wanted,' he explained . . ."
The endorsement of hierarchies induces specialization. Mystification is manipulative. Its power misleads in appearing to be productive energy; it is not generative, it's mediocre. An objective life is undesire. When sacrifice to the revolution begins revolution ends: here we mean subjectivity without individualism; micropolitics; simultaneous multiple corners. Hierarchies control through achievement by regulating & witholding information as to the means of achieving: honesty's broken spoon. It's hard to be totally positive. "Giordano Bruno comes to mind, whoever he is." "$14.28 is more attractive than $14, it's just that way." "Giordano Bruno, I think they burned him, he was too positive."

SOME DO & SOME DO: SHAMANISM, CYBERNETICS, & REPRESENTATION

". . . Lo! The lid is raised, curiosity stands on tip-toe, eyes sparkle with anticipation, little hands are clapped in ecstasy, almost too great to find expression in words. The hour arrives—the moment wished and feared . . ."

". . . T.A. (Transactional Analysis), T.M. (Transcendental Meditation), E.S.T. (Erhard Seminars Training, not exactly electro-shock, E.C.T.), Creative Fidelity, Creative Aggression, Provocative Therapy, Gestalt Therapy, Primal Scream, Encounter Therapy, the conducting of three-day 'Marathons', a form of deep massage, Bio-energy, Japanese Hot Tubs (you take off your clothes and enter them *en groupe* as part of liberation). Then, 'Behaviour Mod' (the new generation Skinner) on how to toilet-train your child in twenty-four hours—and then on the next shelf another book advertising a method of toilet-training your child in *less* than twenty-four hours! I've no doubt that after some of these experiences some people feel better, or begin to 'feel', or feel more 'real'—or whatever the ideals of capitalism prescribe for them. . ."

ONE LEG AT A TIME

OK. OK OK. OK OK OK. OK OK OK OK. OK OK OK OK OK. OK OK OK OK OK. OK OK OK OK OK OK OK.

BIB

ANTI-OEDIPUS: CAPITALISM AND SCHIZOPHRENIA, Gilles Deleuze & Félix Guattari (trans. Robert Hurley, Mark Seem, Helen R. Lane), Viking Press, New York, 1977.
PRIVATE PARTS, Robert Ashley, Lovely Music Ltd., New York, 1977.
ZOO or LETTERS NOT ABOUT LOVE, Viktor Shklovsky (trans. Richard Sheldon), Cornell Univ. Press, Ithaca and London, 1971.
THE PRISON-HOUSE OF LANGUAGE, Fredric Jameson, Princeton Univ. Press, Princeton, 1972.
CALIFORNIA PSYCHOLOGICAL INVENTORY, Consulting Psychologists Press, Inc., Palo Alto, 1956.
LE MACCHINE CELIBI/THE BACHELOR MACHINES (exhibition catalogue), Jean Clair & Harald Szeemann eds., Rizzoli, New York, 1975.
MIDNIGHT/GLOBE (vol. 26, no. 26), Rouses Point, 1979.
THE REVOLUTION OF EVERYDAY LIFE, Raoul Vaneigem (trans. John Fullerton & Paul Sieveking), Rising Free Collective, 1979 (total anticopyright).

BRITISH AND IRISH COOKING, Sally Morris, Galahad Books, New York, 1973.
SCHIZO-CULTURE issue of SEMIOTEXT(E) (Sylvère Lotringer ed.), "The Invention of Non-Psychiatry", David Cooper, New York, 1978.
BENJAMIN OBSCURA, Ron Silliman (excerpt published above).
NOT AVAILABLE, The Residents, Ralph Records, San Francisco, 1978.
ZOMBIE, Fela & Afrika 70, Mercury Records, Chicago, 1978.
MORE THAN MEAT JOY, Carolee Schneemann, Documentext, New Paltz, 1979.

Michael Davidson

> For, as Aristotle saith, it is not *gnosis* but *praxis* must be the fruit. And how *praxis* cannot be, without being moved to practice, it is no hard matter to consider. —Sir Phillip Sidney

Since any text, regarded as a mode of production, must be capable of analysis, why not start with the question posed by the editors of L=A=N=G=U=A=G=E. The fundamental problem with answering it lies in its blurring of distinctions between two rather different ideas: 1) that writing "has" qualities intrinsic to it and 2) that writing "could have" qualities leading to a social critique. The former implies a study of internal features. One might treat the linguistic structure of the declarative sentence as a microcosm of power relations in a capitalist society. The sentence's tidy organization of elements, its subordination of action to actor, its separation of subject from object could indicate attitudes toward human labor and the material world. Or, in terms of larger structures, one could discuss the "well made" essay and point to its implied valorization of idea to documentation, its positivist/deductivist bias, its emphasis on communication over the process of thought as extensions of bourgeois/technocratic thought.

On the other hand, what the editors seem to mean is "how can writing *be made* to critique capitalist society," whereupon the ancient dialogue between formalist and materialist surfaces again. The formalist contends that by radically altering the structure of conventional discourse, by decontextualizing, fragmenting, foregrounding the material element of language, he or she will illustrate the lesions and gaps within ruling class ideology. The materialist argues that all art is essentially ideological, and that analysis is carried out between base and superstructure in any literary work, regardless of intention. In its vulgar form, this criticism looks for strictly economic, sociological "content" within the work. Obviously the answer to the question rests somewhere in between the formalist solution and the materialist theory.

Since I don't think writing has "qualities," per se, outside of a context of use, I would have to say that a critique of capitalist society begins with an art that investigates its own modes of production. I don't mean by this to emphasize self-reflexive art as practiced by current metafictionists—an art which tends inwards toward a narcissistic literature of exhausted possibilities. I'm thinking here of an art which is conscious of its own vulnerability in a world of attractive, institutionalized solutions: an art which regards itself as a form of knowledge rather than a strategy in its pursuit; an art that in asserting its objectivity and integrity does so without forgetting the realm of human concern. (I am purposely avoiding naming what this art might be since to levy various critical criteria would only serve the interests of an already imperializing criticism; obviously, every new problem demands a new solution.) The lure of an objectified, ossified art, working in the service of "materiality" does little more than fetishize the realm of language and reinforce the dualism of subject and object all the more.

But this dualism can be useful, at least in one respect, in that it contains the boundary terms within which an interrogative (authentic) writing may occur—a writing that works in the interstices between expressivist and objectivist modes. Such a writing would incorporate the moments in which language loses its purely instrumental character and becomes a mode of "humanizing practice." As Marx Wartofsky says, ". . . (the artwork) is a representation of a mode of action which is distinctively human . . . ; in short, that art represents its own process of coming into being and insofar, exemplifies and objectifies the distinctively human capacity of creation." Art, considered thus broadly, should still be able to appeal to an actual (as opposed to a theoretical) reader and might even provide some of the *energia* which Puttenham declared " . . . giveth a glorious lustre and light."

Alan Davies

$$\frac{politics}{art} = politics$$

$$\frac{art}{politics} = art$$

Larry Eigner

Much more than enough boggles, drowns the mind and empties it
– also, the more a man takes for granted, or over and above he needs to
(forego, ignore, shut his eyes), the more he goes after to fill the head. ?
Well, every day is new, at least in the morning. Take each. Here, what-
ever wakes you up says, have another. Some eternal present. It has to
be a miscellany. No time for incoming shadows, sundown, or not too
much, that is. Let's realize what there is. The variety. No regrets, or
grievance.

Rapid transit? Somebody is/was lonely? Civilian? The life of a nude
in one equatorial jungle or another? Bird? Elephant? Lion? Squirrel?
Why do birds sing. There's interest.

Books, mag..s, eventually newspapers, as well as maps, legend-
ary, make the best packages. World// Packed// All// Ways The more
books the fewer of each, as wrote the author of *Future Shock*, the
quicker the turnover they have. Is this adequate? Are there big enough
islands? Too big? X is company and Y is a crowd. So maybe capital-
ism, constellation of miracles or not, let alone quantity (/quality), is
mysterious.

O .. – mark something like sword overhead

Brian Fawcett
AGENT OF LANGUAGE

I don't want to write. I don't want to go to Eatons. I don't want to
write here because I will provide in the activity of writing a rhetoric
useful to the maintenance of the status quo. I don't like the words *status
quo*, its neutrality, taken (stolen) from a dead conservative language.
Rhetoric . . . is useful only to the ruling class. The *ruling class* upsets
me. I don't want to use left rhetoric either. They (the ruling class) are
byproducts of a universally employed process of exploiting phenomena
for specific ends without having ultimate purposes, good or evil. In lan-
guage the same process dilates complexity for its own sake, making it
opaque, thus taking the power of coherent action out of the hands of

Excerpted from an article and letter in *Periodics* #2 (Vancouver, 1977).

any single social or political unit. We (human beings) are left with an arid corruption. To write about the *ruling class* without focusing on the source of power that organizes its activity & which allows it to ignore the ultimate questions of mass justice & truth while allowing individuals the air & illusion of those qualities . . . on the third floor buying a pair of shoes made in Europe, a black wool coat with real mink grown on a farm . . . they would know what it is to be poor if there were words but words aren't here, and it's a long way to the basement where the poor buy synthetic wool checkered jackets with fake fur collars. I don't want to be in Eatons. . . .

But I do want to buy something. No, sorry, that's an error. *I want to obtain something of value*, which is a struggle altho I have the money. I'm on the main floor between the basement & the third floor. I'm a bourgeois artist struggling to find value inside a language in which Beauty can't be spoken of in the same sentence as political or economic justice. Wrong floor. Go to the eighth floor, go to accounting. There are no words, they are, like the articles proffered from the store racks, inappropriate, they don't fit, they are not of the materials of reality. I can't invent a new language, a device like the escalator to elevate me to the next level of meaning because the parataxis is broken, busted, the magic of Psyche's house is gone, is immaterial, no stairs, entrances, windows or exits . . . and I don't want to write anything that is not the materials of reality. . . .

Nothing else happens. I made no singular error in activity or thought that lead me there rather than anywhere else. Nothing is that personal. It isn't a question of the personalness of the personal opposed to vast forces moving like grand dinosaurs of 19th century historical necessity, it's the similarity of destination—into the taxonomic reflecting pools where . . . I don't want to write this, I don't want to be alone, reflecting by pools of sorrow or by vast lakes above turbines grinding the energy for these useless appliances stacked row upon row beneath sterile lights & lady in black w/ plug in hand, beckoning to me *here sir, is a fantastic labor-saving device to help the little lady help you in the morning. In just 35 seconds your morning coffee* . . .

Says Trotsky: *In a society split into classes, the democratic institutions, far from abolishing the class struggle, only lend the class interests a highly imperfect form of expression. The possessing classes have always at their disposal thousands of means to pervert and adulterate the will of labouring masses.*

Yeah says Cliff. *In Cuba it's not like you go to work for the government or stay on the outside, as if the government is an entity that's either beneficent or hostile. Those questions are answered. I mean, if*

*you're an artist, you get a wage, you work to make the revolution clear
& thorough. You stand outside, you're not an artist, you're just picking
your teeth. There is no separate culture like we have.* I mean, like off in
the closet, where I can talk as loudly or clearly as I want because it's
describable as protest, or some phatic corner or other into which even-
tually walks a joker wearing a tight blue suit & says, *Hey baby, you got
a career!!*

I don't want to write. In the guts of the city there is neither air nor a
heart, there is only ourselves, choking in the guts. Which hang over the
streets, wired for electricity and totally invisible. Crammed with cheap
goods & ideas. The agent of language is lost in these streets. In the
springs of the heart. Sprung, like an old mattress, or bulldozed to make
way for some further developments. I'm in Eatons looking for the agent
of language and the orders of the heart and the confirmation of justice,
without words of my own.

. . . Our bloody technique mongering has led us down into the
sump to the point where we've become convinced of the verity of lan-
guage that is pure *within* so narrow a context of human existence its
relatively harmless to the comings & goings of the real power in this life
. . . parataxis, beloved parataxis, functions only inside the realm of
personal emotion & the truth of our lives is that there is no *public* lan-
guage that can be understood, I mean freely heard without the control
of materials being withheld. (& this, I'd argue, is the real basis of con-
temporary marxism) So in the story I do something I've been taught not
to do, which is to invade the rhetoric of the left to see if I can bring
across what lies underneath its veneer. . . .

I'm deathly tired & ashamed of the absence of public language in
poetic thought—it isn't good enough to press the conviction that if
everybody could practice parataxis the structures that make our lives so
awful wld crumble. . . .

I think we have to destroy our poetics & our poetic techniques &
start to reintroduce all the *active* voices that make up *this* world's
thought & force if we want to really practice parataxis. The parataxis
we've learned is classical, applies to a world 2500 years gone. This
isn't Homeric greece. We have to introduce the abstract & rhetorical &
deterministic & the mathematical & the vernacular. Even the buzz.
Without fear or hope. As if poetry were a dead issue we might reify
with that risk.

Emotion is a dead issue—we know so much about its dynamics
that it has gone into the abstract (you can't have read Freud & treat hu-
man emotions as if they're mysterious). What hurts about this is that its
made all the verity the writers who taught us sought not worth a pinch

of coonshit. (If you want to test this have a look at any of Lawrence's more didactic & less careful novels [like *Kangaroo*, which I just finished reading]—his commotions of emotion & their extensions into landscape is/are vaguely embarrassing & dilettantish. Or watch the same process on the media, where its all done from the outside, & much more effectively. Id say the emotional is the least reliable source of information we now have, because its the most thoroughly manipulated.

Which leads back to my statement about the exploiting of phenomena/organization of synaptic activity (or 19th century capitalism/20th century). Both activities have taken from most people the power to act, & by that I mean to act *knowingly*. Most of contemporary capitalism (or just state control because it has more to do with industrial organization than anything) draws its power from destroying our abilities to understand our environment & the consequences of social/political activities, or at least to restrict it to those areas sympathetic to the retention of the present forms of control. I guess I share with Dewdney the notion that it isn't the existence of a "ruling class" that matters, but a ruling structure that exceeds the power & understanding of those it benefits.

P. Inman

Capitalist ideology hopes to dilute or deny the existence of anything other than the everyday given. By doing so current ideology stagnates thought, replaces the possibility of change with the statistic, frozen black on paper, legitimized by its very inertia. In rendering present social structures "natural" ideology underwrites their "immutability", whether in terms of some kind of metaphysic or positivist scientism. (. . . or in what is the sociological equivalent to scientism, it promotes all reality as relative, hoping to defuse all social idealism.)

If only as a language that is other, a language outside the pervasive ideolanguage of advanced capitalist society (which once having classified & defined, seeks to box in, contain) free language exists in a critical relation viz. capitalist superstructures. A language of the word instead of the worded, predigested, -fabricated; accepted fact. It's perhaps as simple as saying anything to make one think & examine. The degree to which language is self-concerned is the degree to which it remains unimplicated (?).

Having said this, there are a few important qualifications to the above. For me any critical theory must of necessity exist within revolutionary praxis . . . neither the primary component of that praxis, nor servant to "practice". Whether the establishment of a revolutionary counter-hegemony (Gramsci) is a precondition for social transformation or not, once critical theory has become detached from practice (or at least the struggle toward a program for action) it becomes merely another academic discipline. Scholasticism drained of any real social content, ready to be taught at the state u.

Gramsci's concept of the organic intellectual is helpful here. The organic intellectual was one who, unlike the traditional intellectual, was not a sub-class unto himself, separated from everyday life. "Theory" was not directing practice from above, but the self-expression of the proletariat's everyday struggle. (This shouldn't be taken as an argument for some sort of Gramscian orthodoxy. For starters, the whole concept of "working class" has become problematic forty years later.) . . . Concretely, it would seem to me that all revolutionary critique must begin (attempt to) with an extensive analysis of class relations within present-day society. Who, what or where are/is the revolutionary class(es) in the USA today? Critiques for their own sake obviously dont make much sense. Criticism becomes revolutionary at the instant it somehow manages to come to grips with this question.

Michael Lally

One "quality" that "comes to mind" is—to isolate and describe and record exact observations about "experience" and "objects" that otherwise are never shared beyond intimate relationships because they offer an alternative perspective to "reality" than the one the "capitalist" system (and maybe any "generally" applied "system") imposes through its control of the distribution of "goods," including "art" and "language" and other supposedly less "essential" "goods." *Honesty* is still, in my opinion, one of the most revolutionary "forces" or "weapons" we always have "at our disposal."

John Leo
/CAPITAL/   /WRITING/

The mere juxtaposition of the word signs creates doubts which unhinge and dismantle the familiar repressions, allowing for greater oscillations between signifiers and signifieds (whose fundamental misalignments it has been the business of Capital to conceal, wish away, or stabilize by mediating or diverting the interpretive process even in Capital's reterritorializing gestures). So: a countering that sets up bibliographies and an itinerary of possible projects and which assumes that a text's meaning production is always a collaboration/intersection/ exchange between two *a prioris* privileged by two names: Freud and Marx: hence *autoproduction* (the drive(s), desire, libidinal economies, the Subject) and *the real* (all institutional discourses, constraints, encodings, economies of the commodity, the Other). And names familiar and unfamiliar: Lacan; Deleuze and Guattari; Kristeva; Fredric Jameson; Stanley Aronowitz and John Brenkman and their new journal *Social Text*; Rosalind Coward and John Ellis, *Language and Materialism: Developments in Semiology and the Theory of the Subject*; and from Australia the "'Working Papers' Collection," revising freudo-marxism in such anthologies as *Language, Sexuality & Subversion*, ed. Paul Foss and Meaghan Morris.

To see as preeminent in writing its intertextual *loci*, or oriented spaces marked by relations and modes of material language in its spectrum of specific performances from speech to written acts; a recognition disabusing us of the notions that space is "neutral" or that "extrinsic or intrinsic" are transcendental categories governing writing analyses. To further question writing in its aspect as an archival repository which in turn grounds the archive (hence a hierarchy of writings, "evidence," "history"); Foucault's project, but pushed deep into Capital's Writing by Michel de Certeau's *L'Ecriture de l'histoire*. To grasp that the most devastating confrontations between writing and Capital today are critiques of the (patriarchal, ascendant) signifier (all bets on / signifier/ taken), e.g. Kristeva (esp. *Polylogue* and current work; some translations in *Tell-Tale Sign*, ed. Sebeok and the journal *October*), Hélène Cixous, Luce Irigaray (*Speculum de l'autre femme*; *Ce sexe qui n'en est pas un*; see *Language, Sex & Subversion*), all connected by their work positing primordial biosociopolitical *differences* in female/ male discourses (and thus *different* phenomonologies, semioanalyses, structurations . . .); and the continuing undoing of the hegemony of the signifier (and thus of capitalist representation) in Deleuze and Guattari, Jean-Francois Lyotard (e.g. *Des Dispositifs pulsionnels; Discours, figure*; some translations in *Sub-Stance, Genre, Semiotext(e)*), Pierre Klossowski (on Nietzsche and Sade), all of whom dance on the meeting-ground of intensities, redistributing flows, cathexes, the very possibilities of somatic (in)difference, "drive-devices," sophistry as the language of *affect*ation and desire, bachelor machines, the resituating of the phenomeno-semiotic exchanging as the gradating libidinization of Capital. With differing emphases, but still within the framework of the critique of representation offered by the deconstruction of (ideological) positionings of sign, signifier, signifieds and hence the position of the subject, a variety of revaluations are occurring of writings figurations, typologies, and logical categories (e.g. implicit causalities) as these achieve the power effects of representation (a "window" we see an event *through*, or a "mirror" *on* which we passively regard a sort of duplication of the real). Here the work of Louis Marin (e.g. *Etudes sémiologiques: écritures, peintures; Utopiques: Jeux d'Espaces*; and *La Critique du discours, études sur la Logique de Port-Royal . . .*, with translations in *Diacritics, Glyph, MLN*) and Guy Debord (*Society of the Spectacle*) is unique.

These projects share an urgency, a sense of unease, coming out of that process we call writing which, in its tensions and reflexivity, generates its metacritical possibility with regard to what it embodies or authorizes: power, ideology. These projects are attempts to undo, in all domains of writing, the substantialist techniques of Capital's containment (policing) or rupture (generation) of meaning production and power of extension by reification. These counter-writings put forward at the level of writing, of representation, Capital's substitutions, its concealed attempts at neutralization, its dependency on phallocratic/logocentric (are these distinguishable *in* Capital?) *organ*-izing energies, which are the dismembering mutations of the scopic/writing/reading drive into living estrangement. The critique of the signifier from *within* Capital but *against* it shows the meaning of such estrangements, which is, as Debord especially argues, the moving of direct life increasingly into representations, simulacra, and allegories—into the totality of The Spectacle, whose end is always itself and whose means is the capture of the gaze.

Chris Mason
LEARNING   READING   AS   A
SECOND   LANGUAGE

you read good but that one don't read good.
to learned to read i.e. impose the reading-trauma (scrrech when you
. . .) in the middelst of jurisdictional speech and habit traumas,
: the translation from print-scratcheme to syllable that rings a bell
    'oil' = /oy-ull/, but stuff for your car is /erl/

: the translation from sounded-out notated sentence to phrase that
    rings a bell in your meaning-experience (many readers that can
    learn the notation and come out with the correct sound but not reg-
    ister meanings, not remember anything except making sounds)
        the book prints 'They are going to their house.'; a person *says*
    /they gonna go up the house/ or /them's gone home/ or, etc.

: plus knowing left and right, plus discrepancies in vocabulary, plus
    being able to concentrate on those little dots, plus being motivated
    by a story about farmer duck

: a learner who is not a normal speaker of middle class white english
    has a lot more translations to be able to learn to read to get jobs to
    fulfill survival needs and have basic controls over what happens in
    her life

writers teachers employers employees readers talkers learners friends
might examine their roles in perpetuation of this linguistically based hi-
erarchy. what can poetry, for instance, do to disturb it or remove as
much of life from its grip?

stutterer doesn't just take extra time to say something, he's also a freak,
tongue hanging out there, self-hate; . . . sound-poet / crazy-talk, fin-
gers in his mouth, by transgressing limits of what's art, limits of what's
weird, can extend limits of what's normal (he takes long to say stuff but
it gives me time to think and I like to watch his tongue)

dyslexia is not a disease but a description of how one reads. 'minimal
brain dysfunction' should be dysfunctioned. we are all learning-
disabled: I can't do directions, have no visual memory, etc. kids who
have trouble learning to read should be given extra help learning to

read (learning how to follow a line of tiny ink-scratches across the page, how to discriminate between 4 identical but swiveled ink-scratches (b,d,p,q) etc., etc.)

: Tommy Hart: 13, non-reader, speech impediment, p.s. 220 special class, funny gregarious, beats me at checkers, benevolently experimental in arranging interactions between animals & humans, humans & humans, animals & animals. Librarian to Tommy: "Can you say it this way?" (/garter snake/ instead of /dar'er snate/)
Tommy: "I kalk hat way *otay* ewy day in peech; liwary I kalk my way")

good writing: t.v. & academic & etc. america promotes a perfectionism (not the localized perfectionism of increased attention towards a particular task, but a standardized perfectionism) that is basically adherence to the linguistic stylistic logical models of the dominant group. & make every utterer who doesn't measure up real nervous.

::: mainstream literature / t.v. propaganda / hill-billy words / kiss-words / kiss-off J.C. and the finger / american sign language / signed english / slap on the back and the high sign / mumble-tsk / yawn or science lawyer / black english / gay lingo / baby talk / silence / classical beethoven whistling / and so on / folk song riffs / dance-dancing / bilingual raza mix / unassimilated pigeons / mistakes   ; these-all

are communication information systems worlds with limitless semantic layers: art/performance/hanging-around/poetry could move between some of these in a fun/serious, open/critical/guerrilla way, not to construct (probably imperialistically) joycean universal language, but to interact with others' gesture-fields, to semantically high-life, to help break down the hierarchy and dictatorship of the presidents' / anchorman's english

Steve McCaffery
FROM THE NOTEBOOKS

The fight for language is a political fight. The fight for language is also a fight inside language.

Grammar is a huge conciliatory machine assimilating elements into a ready structure. This grammatical structure can be likened to profit in capitalism, which is reinvested to absorb more human labour for further profit. Classical narrative structure is a profit structure.

Grammar, as repressive mechanism, regulates the free circulation of meaning (the repression of polysemeity into monosemeity and guided towards a sense of meaning as accumulated, as surplus value of signification).

The importance of a language centered writing—all writing of diminished referentiality—is the writing and reading per se, as productional values (the writing as a production of production; the reading a production of the text). Both writing and reading of these texts are aspects of a language production. What publishing achieves is an extension of circulation on the basis of exchangeability. The act of publishing always runs the risk of producing an occultation of a use value by an exchange value.

Grammatically centered meaning is meaning realized through a specific mode of temporalization. It is understood as a postponed "reward" at the end (the culmination) of a series of syntagms. It is that fetish in which the sentence completes itself. Meaning is like capital in so far as it extends its law of value to new objects. Like surplus value, meaning is frequently "achieved" to be reinvested in the extending chain of significations. This is seen quite clearly in classical narrative, where meaning operates as accumulated and accumulative units in the furtherance of "plot" or "character development": those elements of representation which lead to a destination outside of the domain of the signifier.

Meaning is the unconscious political element in lineal grammaticization. Words (with their restricted and precisely determined profit margin) are invested into the sentence, which in turn is invested in further sentences. Hence, the paragraph emerges as a stage in capital accumulation within the political economy of the linguistic sign. The paragraph is the product of investment, its surplus value (meaning) being carried into some larger unit: the chapter, the book, the collected works.

Grammar is invested precisely because of the expected profit rate viz. a clarity through sequence carried into meaning.

A grammatical critique can be mobilized by presenting language as opaque and resistent to reinvestment. A language centered writing, for instance, and zero-semantic sound poetry, diminishes the profit rate and lowers investment drives just as a productive need is increased. Meaning in these cases is no longer a surplus value, but that which is to be produced without reinvestment. This need to produce (brought on by instituting an opacity in language) becomes the need to activate a relation of human energies.

Reference, like Capitalism, is "metamorphosis without an intrinsic code" (Lyotard). There is no code beyond referent reality, for referents are the destination points of codes. Reference, its placement both in and outside the triangularity of the sign, territorializes the flows of code as a constant movement into absence in destinations outside of itself. Writing can be modeled on energumen (on a semiotics of circulation and flow) and so work towards the redistribution of flow and a complication within the vectors of reference.

A language centered writing not only codes its own flow but also encodes its own codicities. It is not, however, a code of representation but a regulatory code of the intrinsic, differential and oppositive flows of words. The Capitalist rationale is : you can produce and consume everything and everywhere providing it flows and providing it's exchangeable. Reference marks a point of extreme liquidity in the Sign. It is, in fact, the line along which the Signifier liquidates itself, exchanges itself for the Other by means of the flow occurring along the surface of a grammatical meaning. Reference is indifferent to either Sign or Referent. Reference is the flow, the liquid progression of a liquidity itself already marked to be undifferentiated absence. Reference needs no code because it is the end of codicity. It is the destination of code per se and its sole teleology is the institution of flow (alterity) territorialized into a vector out of a presence (the graphic forms on the page) into an absence (= that which can never be inside of language).

Meaning finds its place in bourgeois epistemological economy as a consumed surplus value; the extract from textual signification, found wholly as a surplus value at the end of a reading (whether sentence, paragraph or entire text). Meaning in classical discourse is NOT a productive/productional use value: that which a reader herself produces from a human engagement with text.

The consumption of text occurs historically at that point where the reader herself is consumed and dehumanized by the text. Signs are consumed when readers are alienated from signification. Text, as a human issue, as the conjoint concern of reader and writer, with a destination in recycling a process rather than in a reified semantic object might eliminate meaning as that which meets one's gaze, fixed, in isolated distance.

Capitalism—a decoded equality where all is equalized into exchangeability commodity promotion, loss of self, human serialization. And the reproductive organ of Capitalism is metamorphosis.

One thing a language centered writing desires is a presentness that language primarily focussed on reference can't provide. This is not so much a presentness of language per se (whose signifying functions as representation is predicated on a certain absence (of the term stood for)) as the reader's presentness to language itself. A presentness promoted by diminished consumption. In language centered writing referential reality recedes in order that the quality of the Sign as signifier, as imprint or mark, might be experienced as a "presentness before". As language centered readers do not consume signs so much as confront them as opacities or produce them from ciphers. A language centered writing dispossesses us of language in order that we may repossess it again. A productive attitude to text takes the form of a writerly stance on the reader's part and is the first step towards a humanization of the Sign.

Michael Palmer

THE FLOWER OF CAPITAL

(sermon faux - vraie histoire)

> . . . and the old dogmatism will no longer be able to end it.—
> Adolfo Sánchez Vázquez

The flower of capital is small and white large and grey-green in a storm its petals sing. (This refers to capital with the capital L.) Yesterday I borrowed Picabia's Lagonda for a drive through the Bois. A heavy mist enveloped the park so that we could barely discern the outline of a few silent figures making their way among the sycamores and elms. Emerging at Porte de Neuilly the air grew suddenly clear and ahead to my right I noticed M pushing a perambulator before her with a distracted mien. Her hair fell disheveled about her face, her clothes were thread-bare, and every few steps she would pause briefly and look about as if uncertain where she was. I tried repeatedly to draw her attention with the horn, even slowing down at one point and crying her name out the car window, all to no apparent effect. Passing I saw once more (and as it developed, for the last time) the lenticular mark on her forehead and explained its curious origin to my companion, the Princess von K, who in return favored me with her wan smile. We drove on directly to the Château de Verre where the Princess lived with her younger sister and a few aged servants. The château itself was encircled by the vestiges of a moat now indicated only by a slight depression in the grass at the base of the walls. Or: we drove for hours through the small towns surround-ing Paris, unable to decide among various possible courses of action. Or: they have unearthed another child's body bringing the current total to twenty-eight. Or: nine days from now will occur the vernal equinox. Yesterday in the artificial light of a large hall Ron spoke to me of char-acter hovering unacceptably at several removes above the page. The image of the Princess and of M who were of course one and the same returned to mind as I congratulated him on the accuracy of his observa-tion. L knitted this shirt I told him, and carved the sign on my brow, and only yesterday they removed the tree that for so long had interfered with the ordered flow of language down our street. Capital is a fever at play and in the world (silent *l*) each thing is real or must pretend to be. Her tongue swells until it fills my mouth. I have lived here for a day or part of a day, eyes closed, arms hanging casually at my sides. Can such a book be read by you or me? Now he lowers the bamboo shade to alter the angle of the light, and now she breaks a fingernail against the railing of the bridge. Can such a text invent its own beginning, as for example one—two—three? And can it curve into closure from there to here?*

* * *

A FOLLOWING NOTE

The problem is that poetry, at least my poetry and much that interests me, tends to concentrate on primary functions and qualities of lan-guage such as naming and the arbitrary structuring of a code—its fra-

---

*Reprinted in Palmer's *Notes for Echo Lake* (1981: North Point Press, Berkeley).

gility—the ease with which it empties (nullifies?) itself or contradicts what might simplistically qualify as intention. (And I might add conversely, its tyranny—how it resists amendment.)

Poetry seems to inform politically (this being a poetry that does transmit material of some immediate as well as enduring freshness) beyond its aspect as opinion or stance. Thus a Baudelaire, Pound, Eliot et al may render a societal picture of transcendent accuracy. Note of course the political "intelligence" of Shakespeare's Tudor apologies, of Racine's hierarchical poetics, of Dante's vision. It is clear that political "rectitude" is not necessarily equivalent to political "use" in a larger sense, though we can also find instances where there is a coinciding of poetic and immediate historical impulse, where in fact a poetry transmits its energy from a specifically political moment. Paradoxically I am thinking of a politics that *inheres*, such as Vallejo's, in contrast let's say with the more practical motives of much of Neruda's work.

Politics seems a realm of power and persuasion that would like to subsume poetry (and science, and fashion, and . . .) under its mantle, for whatever noble or base motives. Yet if poetry is to function—politically—with integrity, it must resist such appeals as certainly as it resists others.

The call to language in a poem does not begin or end with its discursive flow and does not give way to qualified priorities. Not to make of poetry a "purer" occasion, simply to give credit to its terms and the range of possibilities it attends. Poetry seems a *making* within discrete temporal conditions, and I would happily dispense with the word "creative". Poetry is profoundly mediational and relative and exists as a form of address singularly difficult to prescribe or define.

A poet's political responsibility is human, like that of a cabinetmaker or machinist, and his or her activity is subject to similar examination. Synchronically the results are predictably various. We treasure and perhaps survive by those moments when the poetic and political intelligence derive from an identical urgency and insight. Recently I came across Terry Eagleton's quotation from an article by Marx in the Rheinische Zeitung, "form is of no value unless it is the form of its content." "Simple," as Zukofsky used to say. And is it if it is?

James Sherry
A,B,$.

The Ground: Looking closely at words increases their materiality—
Curves of letters, repetitions of shapes and phrases and sounds. That
and the materiality of discourse, definitions that turn back on them-
selves ("contagious hospital" is the famous example) begin to generate
new meanings. Yet since the 18th century, the tendency toward stan-
dardization of spelling, capitalization and punctuation as well as revo-
lutionary content (Romanticism), more and more, has forced language
into the service of the subject and the idea. Common usage usually al-
lows one to see through the words to the meaning, intention or subject:
"Pass the butter, please.", but why should literature, writing that is in
the first instance writing, be instrumental, in the service of . . . ? Value
is not inherent in language any more than it is in commodities. All
value is attached as exchange value or use value. Why should lan-
guage have only exchange value? Yes, exchange language for butter, if
that is the goal, but if writing is the goal, a more specialized use value
must be at least a possibility. Is language always a commodity? Clearly
not in the case when blank paper costs money and a poem put on it
cannot be given away. So, consider the possibility of meaning that is
not seen *through* language, but meaning that is embedded, as it is put
on the page, *in* language. But the main concern is not instrumentality,
but to question what use we expect from writing. Whatever we develop
is going to be misused.

Language Models—*Industrial Conglomerates and Fetishism of Struc-
ture*: Suppliers take control over demand and manufacturers, with the
aid of transparent language (A lot to live, Ajax cleans), control demand
merely by producing and selling. But traditional divisions of industrial
production by product disappear, and, although we still say razor
blades please, the company that makes the blades is a tobacco com-
pany, and what controls that company is not a person who is expert in
either tobacco or razor blades, but rather a manager who creates
groupings of industries and contrives to disrupt the flow of other com-
panys' profits or supply so he can step in at the last moment and ap-
pend a real estate firm to his empire. What is the underlying organiza-
tion that makes the company more resilient to the vagaries of the
economy, nature and other's predatory instincts? Japan might be a
model and a warning to those who do not need to be convinced. Al-

though conglomerates are not organized around the commodities they produce, they still exist for two purposes—for profit and to maintain those in power in power. The literature often referred to on these pages does not exist for the purpose of critique, but because it elucidates our concerns: it has to be written because there is no other literature that can be so-called now.

Change Models—*Humanism?*: So language, the chief and continuous communal endeavor of the species, must be an agent of its change. If I am dissatisfied, I look to language to soothe my wounds and change my attitudes. I tell myself . . . Not only language, but language used fittedly. (Polemics are another transparency. Sometimes more is needed.) *Fittedness* used: Attitudes are revealed in the way one says change takes place. To say "the order must be changed" has a different implicit attitude than "the order is changing" or fatalistically that "order will change." Attitudes are revealed in the tense as much as in generalized language "views". A new idea is an agent of change, but only incidentally revolutionary. Language glorifies, gratifies, indulges, elucidates. The choices we make on that level reveal attitudes *and* expose the structures of the system. Shall we take a polemical stance or try to un-cover more? Because "Commodities . . . are functions of the human organism," even materialized language use or structured language use or sincere language use will be commoditized. Even non-instrumentality is an unreachable goal if writing is to be comprehensible. (Non-instrumentality is an asymptote.)

Avant-garde as Commodity: Standard patterns of syntax refer to the way things used to be. New patterns reveal the present. Any other per-ception of the relationship between style and change is alienated. Old ideas show that not everything is changing at the same rate. The most avant-garde barely keeps up with everyday life. "In the future we will be freer, because the most advanced writing is more free of the referent than past writing" or "We are freer, not than we were, but because how our newest work indicates what freedom is." The former is a com-moditized and alienated view of "language" writing. The contrary of it is equally alienated, but the second statement might be some help. (While we do it, we get . . .) The point is not only *how* the elements of the social structure are revealed in language, but the attitude we our-selves take toward that social-economic structure as writers. We do not need to strike poses or attitudinize. Our *works* are our *attitudes* and *expectations*. What are those three.

Another Example: Wittgenstein says, "When we speak of a thing, but there is no object that we can point to, there we may say is the spirit." If I reply that "language" writing is more spiritual and instrumental ("subjective") writing is mechanical and technical, I missed the point of this article. The philosopher's words reveal a way to speak to the spiritual. This goes for poets and their critics.

Ron Silliman

IF BY "WRITING" WE MEAN LITERATURE (if by "literature" we mean poetry *(if . . .)*). . . .

Any writing, regardless of genre, referentiality, whatever, has the capacity to make such a contribution. However, very little does. Why?

Language is simultaneously a product of human activity & a critical mediator between the individual & all else. Any privilege it may possess as a sign system rests with its social role as the code thru wch most, if not all, meaning becomes *manifest, explicit, conscious.*

Language is one strategic part of the total social fact. So is art (including lit). Beyond, if not before, art's long-recognized function of the transmission of ideology is its role as the tuning mechanism thru wch the individual is trained, often unconsciously, to organize her responses to the medium at hand. Thus painting (partially) organizes the code of sight.

Most art forms encode media that are not, otherwise, the subject of formal learning processes, consciously reproduced at the institutional level (save as instruction in the arts per se). Not so language. The position of writing, both as sign system & art, within the structure of the total social fact is therefore exceptionally complex. Its code is that of *manifest* perception, comprehension: you know that I know what you mean, because I can tell you in "my own" words.

But the words are never our own. Rather, they are our own usages of a determinate coding passed down to us like all other products of civilization, organized into a single, capitalist, world economy. Questions of national language & those of genre parallel one another in that they primarily reflect *positionality* within the total, historical, social fact. It is important here to keep in mind that new forms occur only at the site of already digested contents, just as, conversely, new contents occur only at the site of already digested forms.

Thus black American poetry, in general, is not language writing because of what so-called language writing is—the grouping together of several, not always compatible, tendencies within "high bourgeois" literature. The characteristic features of this position within literature have been known for decades: the educational level of its audience, their sense of the historicity of writing itself, the class origin of its practitioners (how many, reading this, will be the children of lawyers, doctors, ministers, professors?), &, significantly, the functional declassing of most persons who choose such writing as a lifework.

Any class struggle for consciousness must occur at different levels in the different sectors of the social whole, precisely according to the question of positionality. Bourgeois literature can either reinforce or undermine the historic confidence of the bourgeoisie, that its role, if not "inevitable," is at least "for the best." Or not.

Characteristic of this position in society (& writing) is a high degree of sensitivity to the constituent elements wch enter into the overall struggle. That the formalism of modernism (including language writing) both examines such elements in a quasi-scientific fashion, while often appearing to cleave them from their material base is no accident, as all movements in art (however small or explicitly "anti-establishment") tend to present both progressive & regressive sides: symbolism brought polysemic overdetermination into consciousness within an individualized, romantic ideology.

All meaning is a construct, built from the determinate code of language. New meanings exist only to the extent that they have been previously repressed, not permitted to reach consciousness. But it is necessary to seek the social base of any meaning not in the self-reflexivity of the text, as such, but in its relation to *the social positionality of its audience & author.*

Unlike most programs, wch are self-limiting, that of writing in the framework of capitalism carries within itself the admonition, typical of an economy predicated on technical innovation & the concentration of capital, to "make it new." The function of a truly political writing is to, first, comprehend its position (most explicitly, that of its audience) & to bring forth these "new" meanings according to a deliberately political program. Let us undermine the bourgeoisie.

Lorenzo Thomas
IS IT XEROX OR MEMOREX?

Neon, though not the opiate of the people (and though it provided a title for an interesting poetry journal edited by Gil Sorrentino in the late 1950s), is harsh and instantly nostalgic. It will also, all you dear dear "Retro" fans, become even more funky when the "energy crisis" gets a fool head of steam. The advertising/propoganda/mass "communication" industry is about to be revolutionized by calculated want . . . then it'll be back to banners hanging over Main Street and travelling medicine shows.

The weather person is talking about winds and rain. "There are," she says, "46,000 people in the San Antonio area without power tonight." She explains that this is due to natural causes reported and predicted (all but the tragedy of the powerlessness) by the National Weather Service according to her maps and radar graphics.

Johnny Carson is talking about the disaster at Three Mile Island (the US government/utility industrial complex's sequel to Jonestown) and looks properly grave. "I have good news and bad news," he mumbles. "The bad news is that radiation is still escaping from the plant; the good news, it'll be twenty years before we know who got sick."

No one applauds.

Moving right along, lets get to the rest of the best news that's come along in a long time. . . . Soon, both nuclear energy and ecology will join the nostalgic annals that now boast phrenology and other half-assed campaigns. All failed scenarios.

We have been fooling ourselves. Our science says that hypothesis is meant to fail or there is no production of progress. We all believe that; worse, such principles also believe in us and act accordingly.

The Christians say that "faith" is all . . . that this is a dying world. They sing about that on their television shows.

I'm at a literary meeting. One writer says, "I just don't feel qualified to judge these foreign language writers." He's talking about people like poet Ricardo Sanchez, Alurista, Rolando Hinojosa. I look at this idiot in all amazement and wonder, Since when is *espanol* a foreign language on this continent?

Most of the people in prison in this country are functional illiterates. It's possible to function without being able to read or write . . . but it is not possible to live like a human being up to snuff. Expectations that the media breeds are beyond the reach of them what cannot reads. Teach them to read and they can work. Perhaps they will not mug you.

With millions of Americans who steal and take the falls because they cannot read the instructions, who has time to contemplate the morals of our grammar? Magnetism is undeveloped still . . . even as neon is going out. All all all all over this land.

"Capitalism" is a snobbish term for poverty and exploitation. A fiction. If there were a "capitalist system," would there be more subordination of clauses than in some language born and borne by another form of political economy? Would "socialism" eliminate the personal possessive pronoun from any language?

Do you know anyone who can read? This? The *semiotistes* have nothing to say to those of us who function as illiterates. That? Anything? Don't ask.

Barrett Watten
WRITING AND CAPITALISM

Form is identical to content.
When first I opened my eyes, I saw. Before that, I had structure.
Words work.
Yes, writing is social. I am immortal because middle class.
The petit-bourgeois has no class interest of his own.
Editing is act.

Hannah Weiner

CAPITALISTIC USELESS PHRASES AFTER ENDLESS

TITLES ARE USELESS
THAS A HINT
what about the houses
this is a house and it is next to ours & ETC period I DONST CAPITALS
I just dont like quaint phrases anymore adds s THAS SQUINT

I just dont like Pilgrims anymore ampersand their heads off
I just dont like signs ampersand money that this is the way
our quaint phrases
I just dont like I dont speak it language I JUST COME IN
SPEAK LIKE OUR INDIANS
CHARLES CHEATS next line offends
cheating is OK if yo TOUGH GIRL ure in the boring way of it
HANNAH THAS A HINT
CUT ITS SHORT
THAT MEANS MEANS
I meant our houses are stolen from us OF COURSE IT IS
that means I have no home and I live with somebody else always
thats not clearly understood
MEANS IS OUR LEADER
AND HE DOESNT CHEAT ON IT
and they knows it in his jail
WHAS A JAIL
SENTENCE ENDED
USELESS PHRASES ARE STUPID THROW IT OUT
WHAS A PHRASE
too many words waste paper separate line
Hannahs you cant worry about capitalistic phrases you cheated long
sentence on them Bernadette anyway add s
nos code poems published wasted energy someone helps
just add up the money
BANKS
WHO OWNS IT
SOME ADJECTIVES LIKE DESCRIBE
long adjectives hurt and you know it
MENTION THE HOUSES AGAIN
WHO IS COMMITTED
END OF PHRASE STOP THIS SENTENCE
STOP WRITING THIS OMIT NAMES AND CHEATS ends sentence
mention Charles names stupid sentence omitted
its our society stupid upside down and the flag waves again that hurts
us we are indians and we live in trucks
SOME PEOPLE THAS ENOUGH
we just dont like quaint phrases
save Charles
I JUST QUIT
helps other people stupid and stop next line
complaining

BRUCE I SAID NO NAMES LIKES IT ENDS LIKE THIS BORING STUPID
ENDS SENTENCE thas a structure
I JUST GIVE HINTS THAT I GIVE UP HINTING
thas a capitalistic phrase
I DONT SIGN MY PAPERS EITHER NO SIGN AFTER WHO SIGNS IT ADDS HANNAH
                                                        NO SIGNS IT

Steve Benson
FROM A LETTER TO AN EDITOR

I think the problem of being in bad faith, if you will, vis a vis one's political position so-called, is one that everyone who claims any position at all (really everyone, since the claim to no position, political agnosticism, is one as well, and as open to question as any) must deal with forever, whether vigilantly or intermittently. I am absolutely suspicious of those who claim a political righteousness at the expense of others. I am deeply encouraged by those who do politically propagandistic work of whatever kind that manages to encourage others effectively to consider or freshly interpret their own political roles in their social culture without fronting some kind of obligation. The 'social contract' is not some kind of binding obligation, *obviously*. I am basically puzzled at the need anyone feels to point at their role as politically correct or to colleagues' as politically incorrect, since it seems that political change comes not from the recognition of categories but from a revelation of the nature of the functions of social experience as they effect one's life inextricably from effect in others'—a revelation that takes place through social relations, usually I guess through work. For the likes of us, this *may* be accessible largely through something that happens in literary work, BECAUSE we take our role as literary workers seriously. That role of ours is not likely to be taken seriously by those who aren't writers. Of course there weren't many in Dickens' time who took the role of factory-worker seriously either, outside the factories themselves, and it seems that his writings did make some little differences, both in easing a few burdens and shifting forces around so that the bourgeoisie might sit itself more comfortably on the cushions without the springs poking through. Whether the revelation of the political dilemma of fine artists is of interest to other than other fine artists today or not, certainly it is necessary that artists take note of, respond to, however ambivalently, what that is. State it, *throughout*.

Ron Silliman
RE WRITING: MARX

The poetry of societies in which the capitalist mode of production prevails appears as an "immense collection of books"; the individual book appears as its elementary form. Our investigation begins with the analysis of the book.

The book is, first of all, an external object, a thing which through its qualities satisfies human needs of a literary kind.

Objects of reading become books only because they are the products of the writing of private individuals who work independently of each other. The sum total of the writing of all these private individuals forms the aggregate writing of society. *Since the writers do not come into social contact until they exchange the products of their writing,* the specific social characteristics of their private writings appear only within this exchange. In other words, the writing of the private individual manifests itself as an element of the total writing of society *only through the relations* which the act of exchange establishes between the texts, and, through their mediation, between the writers. To the writers, therefore, the social relations between their private writing appear as what they are, *i.e.*, they do not appear as direct social relations between persons in their work, but rather as material relations between persons and social relations between texts.

However, a text can be useful, and a product of human writing, without being a book. She who satisfies her own need with the text of her own writing admittedly creates reading-values, but not books. In order to produce the latter, she must not only produce reading-values, *but reading-values for others*, social reading-values. (And not merely for others. In order to become a book, the text must be transferred to the other person, for whom it serves as a reading-value, *through the medium of exchange.*)

Steve McCaffery
BLOOD. RUST. CAPITAL.
BLOODSTREAM.

ADOLPHUS, J.L.: LETTERS TO RICHARD HEBER. ESQ. (Containing Critical Remarks on the Series of Novels Beginning with "Waverly" and an Attempt to Ascertain their Author) 8vo., Boston 1822. The theoretic interest in rust emerged from investigations into the bridge between metallurgical and physiological identities BAILLIE, Joanna: Miscellaneous Plays, London 1804, 1st Edition 8vo., pp. 1-xix + 1-438 (extra leaf advertises Wordsworth's Lyrical Ballads). Rust throughout is treated as the mineralized transform of blood and thus the oxydizational connective with the human breath and bloodstream. "BROWNE, Sir Thomas: WORKS, London 1686, fol. 1st. ed. with engraved portrait in facsimile" (Wing B 5150 Keynes 201). Rust also relates to critique and the need to negate ANY GIVEN FORM whilst as a metallic growth and pathology it relates to carcinoma and the encompassing ideology of the parasite. BURNEY, Fanny: CECILIA or Memoirs of an Heiress, London 1784 5 vols. 4th. ed. 12mo. full contemp. tree calf milled edging in linguistic form. The Parasite finds most powerful manifestation within quotation and allusion i.e. in the precise manner (the site of the cite) that creates in any text a biological device for drawing off signification by means of echo, index, association, interruption and supplementarity (pp. i-xii + 13-164 Glasgow 1751 printed by Robert Urie 8vo.) Rust tends to occur as an activity within a pre-existent wound and as such is to be classified as a post-incisional practice. It is what writing writes of itself within the aura of its own excess (contains 1st printing of SEMELE) "trimmed" London 1710 3 vols. in 2 incl. The Old Bachelor, Double Dealer and Love for Love Vol. III = pp. A1-a4 + 1-492 and as a mineralogical agency enters the bloodstream as capital to carry the microformations of a labour force throughout the human organism. DAVISDON (Joseph) . . . nto English Prose, ondon 767. 3rd ed. (i-v). It might be described as the corpuscular theory of the proletariat. cf. THE ECONOMY OF HUMAN LIFE by Robert Dodsley (London 8 vo. 32 woodcuts by Austin & Hole 1808) a work often attributed to Chesterfield. Whereas cancer (after nosological elimination) is reattributable to a biopolitical-linguistic scheme and functions closest to a surplus value which is reinvested into the cellular structure of the body as pure profit. GELLIUS, Aulus: NOCTES ATTICAE, Venice 1489 (one of my rarest

books) 132 leaves, 42 line + head 6th ed. (3rd Venice) Bernardinus de
Choris de Cremona & Simon de Luere. Goff (213) lists only ten copies
in America. What is drawn off ("virologically?") from the societal cor-
pus is art, intellect and sex. In the purest analysis of the libidinal econ-
omy (to which virus is central) sex is a pure discharge, an absolute sig-
nifier detached from its signified and demonstrates best the principles
of an unrestricted GENERAL ECONOMY (Bataille) within the structural
and epistemological restraints of the restricted economy (Windsor 1788
2nd ed. with verso last leaf containing errata. Authors: George Can-
ning, John Smith, John Frere and Robt. Smith) accordingly: any poem
which adopts "book" as its vehicular form must admit its complicity
within a restricted economy. Sex then is a pure discharge and exceeds
all value to constitute an energetic subversion of the human capital ma-
chine. As a discharge sex is fraternal & sororal to all other vectors of
spontaneous dissemination: intuition, improvisation, madness, desire
and schizophrenic proproductive drives (LACTANTIUS: Works, Venice
1478 . . . "lactantii firmiani de diuinis instituioibus aduersus gentes"
. . . which together constitute a postcognitive antidote to rust con-
ceived as a surplus value and an entropy. Negentropic strategy is
founded on the full practice of a general economy, in informational
"waste", semantic excess produced by parasitical attachments and in-
terruptions to a host syntagm 12mo circa 1729, L'ESTRANGE, Sir Robt.,
Kt., London (but why London "in the Strand" pp. i-xxx active within.
The circulation of biological capitalism are numerous virus agents
(MacPherson, Sibbs, malus coronaria, Harrison Blake at Worcester,
Johnson on the life of Father Paul Sarpi, Cholmondeley's letter to Tho-
reau in 1857, bourgeois consciousness in general, Dr. Johnson's ref. to
mustard in a young child's mouth, the Rev. Thomas Newton on The
Prophecies, David Hume, Zeus, Patroclus, Chichen Itza, the word of
the Lord, virus "positioned" "as a dormant potential" "within structure
within" "this structure" Loudon's remarks on pyrus malus and the
badge of the clan of Lamont. It is homologous to the political implica-
tions of the poetical phrase MITCHELL, John: The Female ondo 793 2nd
e 125 × P grim grav frontispiece by (defectiv) . . . / WORDS being
what poems are then SENTENCES being what POLITICS is . . (suste-
nance) (quadruped) (the Duma) (Lenin during Blossom Week) . . . .
VIRUS . . . . . and at this . . . . . . po . . . int . . . . . . lexically inter
changeab . . le with the SENTENCE: "POTENTIAL" so that when acti-
vated it becomes THIS FRAMING AGENT YOU ARE reading now
(Theophrastus included the apple among the more "civilized" plants
URBANIORES rather than WILD/SYLVESTRES) fixating epistemological
boundaries which sex cannot be in such a way as to derive maximum

sustenance for itself and to prevent the operation of general economy. LETTERS OF THE RT. HONBLE. WRITTEN DURING HER TRAVELS IN EUROPE ASIA & AFRICA n.d. 6vo. VERBALLY SPEAKING an activated virus of this kind "assumes the form of either page (consecutively bound as book) or else as SENTENCE "Probably 1767 ed.") as container of the grammatical line which is itself both the victim and the vengence of a persistent ideology of perspective.) ACTIVE VIRAL PENETRATION IN ART (buds we must remember were counted every winter's eve for seventeen years) GIVES RISE TO THE INTERRELATED HEGEMONIES OF COMMODITY, CONSUMPTION AND PRODUCTION. Poems on Several Subjects, don 1769, John OGILVIE incls. Essay on the Lyric Poetry of the Ancients 8vo modern calf binding + "the fruit of the crab in the forests of France". IF IT WERE POSSIBLE AT THIS POINT (Rowe, Elizabeth: Friendship in Death in a Series etc. . . . . portrait by J. Bennett) WE WOULD SWITCH THIS DISCOURSE INTO THE MOUTH OF HER WHO IS PRESENT IN THAT CLASSROOM WHERE A SMALL CHILD SITS INTENSELY POROUS AND VULNERABLE AND EAGER TO (to) RECEIVE (receive) THAT (that) WHICH (which) WE "we" CALL (call) "SCIENTIFIC" scientific KNOWLEDGE (knowledge) THAT (that) WHICH (which) ONE "one" DICTIONARY "dictionary" AT (at) "LEAST" (least) IS is ABLE able (TO) "to" DESCRIBE (describe) AS as OPPOSITE "opposite" to TO ART (ART):

Eric Mottram
OFFICIAL POETRY & CONFORMIST ENTERTAINMENT

The current Establishment conception of poetry — indeed, of all the arts — is classicist. Horace's *Ars Poetica* is the fit monument to the living-death practices of the Movement, the Conquest conquistadors, the Arts Council's literary commissar, Radio Three's 'Poetry Now', the Dulwich Group, Oxford's professor of poetry, and the rest. There would be no point in lambasting their dullness and Grub Street jostlings for power except that their tastes and publicist talents dominate the Press and the educational system. The belief is that poetry is decoration, the accompaniment of conspicuous consumption. In fact a conjugation of Horace with Thorstein Veblen's *The Theory of The Leisure Class* (1899) can show the Romanised decadence of the predatory literary bosses, and their patrons. *Ars Poetica* lays down advice and duties for the would-be 'successful' poet — decorum and good taste through genres placed in a hierarchy of acceptable types, adaptations of accepted models, obedience to fixed criteria which criticism is believed to contain. The young are advised to imitate the older, to please patrons, to reject cathartic or any other disturbing experience in art. The poet is the servant of patronage. Poetry is a pastime. Greek originals are reduced from complexity to consumer simplicities. The artist is a conformist entertainer. . . . Form must follow social utility. The predatory class dictates the limits of creativity, and would place a boundary on extasy and the outward figure of inventiveness. Poetry is part of leisure along with comedians and cigarettes, 'my car' and 'the box'. In Veblen's terms, 'the criteria of past performance of leisure therefore commonly takes the form of 'immaterial' goods': 'shrewd mimicry and a systematic drill have been turned to account in the deliberate production of a cultured class'. If a poem cannot be owned, as part of property and possessions, or be a hymn to an established cause or cult, it should not exist. To be possessed by a poem or a performance, however briefly the catharsis may be, strikes terror to the leisure class because, like the presence of the new, it lies outside the expenditure of energy on money, property, comfort and disciplinarian hierarchy. 'The predatory culture' wishes to annex the arts, to consume poetry as a luxury or to ignore it

Excerpted from *Towards Design in Poetry* (1977: Writers Forum, London).

altogether or be comforted by its platitudes reinforcing the status quo. To ensure the correct kind of luxury art, charity is doled out in an inflationary economy, or a totalitarian one, through patronage. . . . 'But in order to be respectable [poetry] must be wasteful'. . . . In Veblen's terms, the neo-classical performer is governed by a 'process of selective adaptation of designs to the end of conspicuous waste': 'A limited edition is in effect a guarantee — somewhat crude, it is true — that this book is scarce and it therefore is costly and lends pecuniary distinction to its consumer'.

Within the criteria of the leisure class lies the assumption that design expresses a prior formed thought or feeling, clearly obvious to any untrained glance. . . . To the classicist, shapes are finite. . . . Composition is a set of decisions within choices, but improvisation can be simply repetition, as most poetry and jazz in established modes is: that is, it has become commercialized design, or it has become the fearful recapitulation of minor artists. The degree of alert creativity within intelligence and sensitivity reaches its vanishing point and is supported by patronage. . . . The artist [can] choose against patronage and critics. As Picasso is the last artist to sustain the role of Master Artist . . . so it may be that the role of Master Poet is no longer a viable position — or has to be reinvented. [One alternative to this tradition is the use of systematic procedures as in what's sometimes called systems-art and systems-poetry.] It is certainly the implication arising within Ron Padgett and David Shapiro's anthology of New York Poets (1970). A group may use systems which group them. Projective verse poets use recognizable procedures which group them as much as poets using heroic couplets in Queen Anne's reign or petrarchan sonnets in Tudor decades. . . . [Yet] poetry-form addiction may, quite as much as criticism addiction, result from a man's or a group's need for security, for a bounded sense of availability, a defense against revolutionary art, against the artist who subverts, disrupts, destroys 'too far'. . . . The function of official poetry and criticism is to historicize art, place it in linear succession so that it becomes part of something called 'tradition'. . . . The totalitarian nature of official criticism's inclusiveness is as vampiric as the state system it imitates. The New Critics of Nashville in the thirties may be compared with the State Capitalist commissars of taste in the period of Soviet socialist realism, as ideologically coercive predators. The one defined freedom as bourgeois western individualism within the encompassments of Church and State hierarchy. The other defined a line of revolutionary ideology — the editorial in Mayakofsky's *Lef* magazine stating that art must be 'the supreme formal engineering of the whole of life'. . . . The dominant critics of the era of twentieth-century criticism — a curious phenomena lasting from 1920 to 1950 — have been the servants of a rigidly conservative state and church stasis, or a return to a maturity defined as the craft freedom of a wheelright in his village shop. . . .

Susan B. Laufer & Charles Bernstein
STYLE

It is said that one can tell during a conversation that lasts no longer than a summer shower whether or not a person is cultivated. Often it does not take even so long, for a raucous tone of voice and grossly ungrammatical or vulgar expressions brand a person at once as beyond the pale of polite society. As one goes forth one is weighed in the balance and if found wanting he is quietly dropped by refined and cultured people, and nearly always he is left wondering why with his diamonds and his motors and his money he yet cannot find entree into the inner circles. An honest heart may beat beneath the ragged coat, a brilliant intellect may rise above the bright checkered suit and yellow tie, the man in the shabby suit may be a famous writer, the woman in the untidy blouse may be an artist of great promise, but as a general rule the chances are against it and such people are dull, flat, stale and unprofitable both to themselves and to other people. In the end, coherence is always a quality of thought rather than a manner of expression. The confused mind cannot produce coherent prose. A well-proportioned letter is the product of a well-balanced mind. The utterance of the single word "Charles!" may signify: "Hello, Charles! are you here? I am surprised to see you." Language, however, is not confined to the utterance of single words. To express our thoughts we must put words together in accordance with certain fixed rules. Otherwise we should fail to express ourselves clearly and acceptably, and we may even succeed in saying the opposite of what we mean. Since language is the expression of thought, the rules of grammar agree, in the main, with the laws of thought. Even in matters of divided usage, it is seldom difficult to determine which of two forms is preferred by careful writers. Everything is taken care of in the most orderly fashion: terms are defined, possible ambiguities eliminated, implications and assumptions explained, proofs adduced, and examples provided. On the whole it is safe for the writer to leave semantic theory unexplored. We favor the standards of the more precise stylists if only because we cannot be more permissive without risking their disapproval, whereas those who

Sources include Follett's *Modern American Usage*, Kittridge's *Advanced English Grammar*, Stein's *How to Write*, Modern Language Association's *In-House Style Sheet*, Hagar's *The English of Business*, Martin and Ohmann's *Logic and Rhetoric of Exposition*, Raleigh's *Style*, and Eichler's *Book of Etiquette*.

do not object to less exacting usage are not likely to be offended by the correct usage. A good expository sentence does not call attention to itself, although Strunk comments that an occasional loose sentence has its virtues. No one who speaks and writes can expect his audience to respond to connotations that arise from his own purely personal experience. Some people associate colors with numbers, but orange is not a connotation of "four". The trouble with Humpty Dumpty's stipulative definitions, if they can be dignified by such a word, is that they are entirely capricious and absurd. For sentences must measure up to standards: it is always fair to ask of a sentence, "How good is it?" Among the qualities that contribute to an effective impression, the five most essential are clearness, correctness, conciseness, courtesy, and character. For style is ingratiation; negative ideas, as a rule, should not be developed at length. And constructions to be shunned include those that are vague, abstract, equivocal, slanted, misleading, exaggerated, understated, loose, abbreviated, oversimplified, obvious, irrelevant, oblique, figurative, redundant, empty, impossible, or obscure. It would be a curious state of affairs if only those who seldom think about the words they use, who read little and who "cannot be bothered" with distinctions should be the only ones with full powers over vocabulary and syntax. Even on the grounds of free democratic choice the hands-off attitude about language receives no support. These assumptions further suggest that the desire for correctness, the very idea of better or worse in speech, is a hangover from aristocratic and oppressive times. . . . The young foreigner who apologizes for the fact that the chocolates he has bought as a gift are *molten* is told with a smile that that is not English: the right word is *melted*. —We talk to our fellows in the phrases we learn from them, which seem to mean less and less as they grow worn with use. The quiet cynicism of our everyday demeanor is open and shameless, we callously anticipate objections founded on the well-known vacuity of our seeming emotions, and assure our friends that we are "truly" grieved or "sincerely" rejoiced at their hap—as if joy or grief that really exists were some rare and precious brand of joy or grief. A sentence says you know what I mean, dear do I well I guess I do. Grammar does not mean that they are to limit themselves. More and more grammar is not a thing. Grammar does not make me hesitate about prepositions. I am a grammarian I do not hesitate I rearrange prepositions.

Lawrence Weiner
REGARDING
THE (A) USE OF LANGUAGE WITHIN THE
CONTEXT OF ART

IT (LANGUAGE) SEEMS TO BE THE LEAST IMPOSITIONAL MEANS OF TRANSFER-
RING INFORMATION CONCERNING THE RELATIONSHIPS OF HUMAN BEINGS
WITH MATERIALS FROM ONE TO ANOTHER (SOURCE)

BEING ITSELF (LANGUAGE) A MATERIAL ONE IS THEN ABLE TO WORK GENER-
ALLY WITH RATHER SPECIFIC MATERIALS

DARWIN IN *THE VOYAGE OF THE BEAGLE* INQUIRED OF A PATAGONIAN INDIAN
WHY THEY (THE INDIANS) DID NOT EAT THEIR DOGS IN TIME OF FAMINE IN-
STEAD OF EATING THEIR (THE INDIANS) OLD WOMEN
" Dogs kill otters, old women don't "
THEY REPLIED

Peter Schjeldahl
POETRY: A JOB DESCRIPTION

From the standpoint of being a poet, what is interesting about poetry today is that it is the occupation most completely without professional status in our society. "Poet" is a term without social resonance for us, aside from a few very old ones that, fading and fading, still impart a certain aroma. For the individual it can sanely mean only "poem-writer": ". . . his writings make him a poet, not his acting of the role," Frank O'Hara wrote — not that there's any role to act anymore, so the choice isn't so noble. The only true choice I see (after rejecting out of hand the ways of the academy) is in how to think about it — whether to see oneself as a member of a little tribe of atavists or band of subversives, on the one hand, or really completely alone and slipping through the interstices of the world, on the other. I aspire to think the latter way, which has the advantage of opening on the most nearly total freedom. Admittedly, it is also close to thinking nothing at all.

It is, with all due modern irony, the course of the Sublime. The economic and, outside its craft-ghettos, the social insubstantiality of poetry may be fecund if, looking them in the eye, one continues to take poetry seriously. There is a certain light-heartedness in this, as in contemplating the present world — for instance, that it is inhabited now by 4 *billion* or so of us humans — and in treating one's individual life, a thing of no consequence, seriously nonetheless. Now, the Sublime is a thought you can make nothing *of*, which is the point. It's an escape from the toils of any other thought, any minor seriousness — and that would include all attempts to justify the vocation of poetry. It is precisely in being unjustifiable in present "real" terms — meaningless in relation to the minor seriousness of a given social order — that poetry may have something — some deep, funny, surprising consolations — to offer.

This is why poet clannishness distresses me: people just throwing away their one and only significant advantage in rites of terminal pettiness and boredom. That advantage is a detachment, and a stamina, for the highest existential fun — licensed irresponsibility of thought. What could be better? Why doesn't anyone seem to want it?

Charles Bernstein
THE CONSPIRACY OF "US"

I don't believe in group formation, I don't like group formation, but I am constantly finding myself contending with it, living within it, seeing through it. "Okay, break it up boys." First, there is the isolation of the atom, looking for some place to feel housed by, a part of, & every which way the people passing seem to have that—"see it over there"— "look". But every group as well has the same possibility for insularity as each individual: this new "we" having the same possibility for vacancy or satisfaction, a group potentially as atomized in its separation from other groups as a person from other persons. This is the problem of family life. Property, territory, domain. But, "for us now", group (family, aesthetic, social, national) is merely another part of our commoditized lives—for we consume these formations, along with most other things, as commodities, & are ourselves consumed in the process. ((Putting aside here the extent to which political groupings and parties would be different from groups of 'artists'; also the place of groupings based on class oppression on the one hand and minority oppression—women, gays, mental patients—on the other.)) So we use groups as badges—shields—as much screening us off from the intrusion of outside, others, as sheltering us from the sheer invasiveness of it, them (& so allowing us a place to occupy, inhabit). I don't so much think that such shelter is a fraud, unnecessary, as much as "let's look at it, call the strictures into question, understand that we *can* reshape": a call against paralysis from a sense of boundaries fixed without, or before, our having had a chance to participate in their making. "The danger is that our demands on each other will trample what we really feel." The danger is that we will hide ourselves amidst the shuffle to proclaim who we are.

We're afraid to say poetry, afraid of the *task*—that's why simply having the goods—"Oh he's gifted as hell"—is never enough. I want to see more than fine sentiments beautifully expressed "in the manner of . . ." "He's really picked up on me" but sadly, not on *us*. One might as well go back to fruit picking. It's hard to talk about content these days, everyone pointing to the trace of their ideas as if *that* was "it" but we don't want mere conceptualizations. "*But*, I mean, that person is really saying something," which is the wrong way of making the point. But: enough of empty vessels for sure. It's necessity which makes the form, which then inheres; not just any "constructs" but the ones we live by, the ones we live in & so the ones we *come upon*—

"Getting it." "Using it." "Pretending." "Imagining." "On the inside track." "In contention." "An authority that genuinely speaks from its heart, letting us know that here . . ." "Great hips." "Thyroid problems." "Oh how come you done that." "Ain't that *Christian* of you." "Grace." "Grave." "Maria of the *fleurs*." "An open cavity, about three to six inches from the back of tongue, who . . ." "Naturally." "Over-intellectual." "With too much *effort* . . ." "Over-emotional." "Grecian." " . . . which at times one only wishes would give way to some greater sense of necessity, like why bother to write it in the first place." "From up here, the low-lying clouds obscuring the view . . ."

Language-centered writing and other art-historical epithets. For instance, you're right that the need for recognition, given that the work is important, does demand that action be taken. Cuts are made but not without enormous confusion on all sides—what's in common within & different from without both get exaggerated. A kind of blinder's vision begins as we look at the world in terms of the configurations being made. "At a given time we responded to each other's work, were there for each other." "To the permanent removal of everyone else after, simultaneous?" No. These things arise in practice, have a practical value. ((Imagine a world in which people allied along lines of hair color. Or what unified a group of artists was their use of a given shade of blue, or that they live (or grew up in, or went to school in) the same place—the impress of a common environment a constant to facilitate art-historical apprehension. How does Richard Diebenkorn get seen by those who think of non-figuration as the key issue of his generation of painters? & *wasn't* it the key issue?)) But the "final" cuts have not—will not be—made. Only cuts for "here" & "there" —

The identification of "younger" poets "coming up" by a group or community can imply the beginning for these people of inclusion within a paternalistic hierarchy—an initiation into it. —Simply, the walls must be stripped down & new ones constantly built as (re)placements—or rather this is always happening whether we attend to it or not. We see through these structures which we have made ourselves & cannot do even for a moment without them, yet they are not fixed but provisional. (. . . that poetry gets shaped—informed and transformed—by the social relations of publication, readership, correspondence, readings, etc

(or, historically seen, the 'tradition') and, indeed, that the poetry com-
munity(ies) are not a secondary phenomenon to writing but a pri-
mary one. So it won't do to just "think about the work". But it still
needs to be explored what the relation between "normal" and "extraor-
dinary" poetry is—& why both need to be more valued in some re-
spects and devalued in others (snobbery, elitism, cliquishness, histori-
cal over-self-consciousness, self-aggrandizement, &c)—especially at a
time in which there is an increase in the number of people and the
number of people engaging in art activities—not just a few "men" "out
there" doing the "heroic" work. —That poetry, with written language
as its medium, is, in fact, the exploration and realization of the human
common ground, of "us", in which we are—"that holds our sights
within its views".)

Or what we have is a series of banana republics with internecine (ie
inner) conflict as to whose to "be the" THE of the court, all that fading
with jocular regularity as we paddle our gondolas down the canals of
time and look back at the many remnants of period mannerism. You
want to name names? I feel very bloated at last & want to take this op-
portunity to thank everyone. I wish I had a quill pen. I'll take a dime for
every time they . . . "I mean some of this stuff really knocks you out."
A great place to take you date, &c, I mean it really impresses boys.
"You wanna know something—I'm glad what they done to you. . . ."
The foundations of a linguistic empire on the coinage of a distinctive
and recognizable style—"& that means don't hone in on my territory"
"& that means *you*" is about as crucial as the opera of Luca Della Rob-
bia. But not to stop there. "We" ain't about no new social groupings—
nobody gotta move over—*this is the deconstruction of team.* This is
looking at language, which *is* "us", & not creating the latest fashion
splash of the "up & coming".

What happens, which is what it is when something happens & you say
"oh, look at that —————"—already having arrived in your mind as
a —————. But not just to plug in—"oh I got it let me dig some out
for you—" The skips on the record which our pounding feet accentu-
ate, making the needle dance out of synch to the rhythm our bodies
seem to want to keep . . .—keep us honest. "Honest"? But not to
"groove into", it's to make the words that come out *that* way more
aware of themselves & so we more responsible to them, not that we
"say" them with whatever capacity our "gifts" allow us but that we
mean them with a twice told intention that puts "mere facility for im-

ages & transitions" in its place & puts "poetry"—a guild without mem-
bers, only occasionally one or another of us finds ourselves there,
or not "ourselves" but rather "those syllables so ordered . . ." & we
mere spectators, out in the public field, watching *that*, now already be-
hind us. . . .

Steve McCaffery
INTRAVIEW

Marx's notion of commodity fetishism, which is to say the occultation of the human relations embedded in the labour process has been central to my own considerations of reference in language - of, in fact, a referentially based language, in general - and to certain "fetishistic" notions within the relationship of audience and performer. Reference in language is a strategy of promise and postponement; it's the thing that language never is, never can be, but to which language is always moving. This linguistic promise that the signified gives of something beyond language i've come to feel as being central to capitalism (the fetish of the commodity) and derived from an earlier theologicolinguistic confidence trick of "the other life". It's this sense of absence as a postponed presence which seems to be the core of narrative (the paradigm art form of the capitalist system) and basic to the word as we use the word in any representational context. To demystify this fetish and reveal the human relationships involved within the labour process of language will involve the humanization of the linguistic Sign by means of a centering of language within itself; a structural reappraisal of the functional roles of author and reader, performer and performance; the general diminishment of reference in communication and the promotion of forms based upon object-presence: the pleasure of the graphic or phonic imprint, for instance, their value as sheer linguistic stimuli. Kicking out reference from the word (and from performance) is to kick its most treasured and defended contradiction: the logic of passage.

Excerpted from *Centerfold* (1978: Calgary, Alberta).

Bernard Noël
THE OUTRAGE AGAINST WORDS

Screams. They begin yet again. I hear them, yet hear nothing. I'd like to know what they are saying. I knew. Now I seek what censors them within me.

Revolt acts; indignation seeks to speak. From the start of my childhood, only reasons for becoming indignant: the war, the deportation, the Indochinese war, the Korean war, the Algerian war . . . and so many massacres, from Indonesia to Chile via Black September. There's no language to describe that. There's no language because we live in a bourgeois world, where the vocabulary of indignation is exclusively moral — well, it's those morals which massacre and make war. How can one turn their language against them when one finds oneself censored by one's own language?

For a long time, I've not known how to formulate that question, and now I can't find words to answer it. Not that it requires other words than ours, but that they arrange themselves spontaneously according to structures which correspond to the moral order of society.

Language, like the State, has always served the same people. We ought to distrust all of which the bourgeois say: With this system, at least, we can speak. This system is already a traitor even if it has not betrayed. In the context of order, in dialogue with it, one can only serve it.

The police are even in our mouths.

In one's own solitude, one only holds a dialogue with oneself to stylize oneself.

One does not write in order to say something, but to define a place where no one will be able to declare what hasn't taken place.

Censorship gags. It reduces to silence. But it doesn't do violence to language. Only the abuse of language can violate it, by distorting it. Bourgeois power bases its liberalism on the absence of censorship, but it has constant recourse to the abuse of language. Its tolerance is the mask of an otherwise oppressive and effective violence. The abuse of language has a double effect: it saves appearances, and even reinforces its appearance, and it shifts the place of censorship so cleverly that one no longer notices it. Or to put it another way, through the abuse of lan-

Excerpted from Glenda George's translation of the postscript to a reprint of Noël's *Le Château de Cène* in *Curtains* (1978: Maidstone, Kent, England).

guage, bourgeois power is made to pass for what it is not: a non-constraining power, a "human" power, and its official policy which standardizes the value of words, in fact empties them of meaning — whence a verbal inflation, ruining communications within the community, and in the same way censoring it. Perhaps, in order to express the second effect, it's necessary to create the word SENSURESHIP, which by referring to the other would indicate the deprivation of sense, not of speech. Deprivation of sense is the most subtle form of brainwashing, for it operates without the victim's knowledge. And the information cult refines that deprivation even more by seeming to stuff us with knowledge.

Freedom of expression is evidently dependant on the state of language. Apparently, I can say what I like, but in reality I can only do so within the limits of this state — a state that current usage of language conceals from us. The words, it seems, are there, always available, always equal to themselves. We use them so spontaneously, and they're at our disposal so naturally, that we cannot suspect them. They're a currency which seems unable to be false, at least at the specie level. How therefore are we to perceive the sensureship? It's true that words are words and that sensureship only insinuates itself in the game of their signifieds, but the words we have abused, abuse in their turn. Whence, at this point, the appearance of a new ambiguity: sensureship which acts on us through words (while censorship acts through us against words) acts in other respects on words with a sensureship effect: it obliterates their significance, that's to say, their matter, their body. Thus we discover that the moral order aims at erasing its materiality in every being, in every thing.

Shit: up to what age did I dare not say that word? And how many other coarse words thus forbidden? All the words of the body. Good taste is one of the morality police. It serves it. It squeezes it round our throats and over our eyes. Good taste is a way of adapting the death of others into the forgetting. And even here, I experience my impotence to chase out my own. How can I treat my sentence so that it refuses the articulation of power? It would necessitate a language which, in itself, was an insult to oppression. And more than an insult, a NO. How to find a language unusable by the oppressor? A syntax that would send back the spiked words and tear apart the language of all the Pinochets? I write. I have cries in return. There is no liberal power: there's only a smarter way of fucking us. For every televised fireside conversation, each of us should have replied with a parcel of shit posted to the great shit at the Elysée. Who would salvage that language?

Writing, trying to write, the primordial question becomes: how to get rid of this? Bury syntax, comrades, it stinks! Okay, but we make sentences even so. Go on and speak without taking on a subject, a verb, etc. We seek dodges. We change our seduction. We even ask the reader to lend a hand instead of always letting it be. The great thing is that we are among the bourgeoisie and that, under such a regime, there are only the morals which can serve the collective bond. Only, in order for the morals to function, the sentence must also function, and the words truly say what they say. Well — that functioning is rotten — rotten since our fathers massacred the workers, the colonized and even their brothers, all the while continuing to play the good father. Your civilization has big teeth, o fathers, so big that it ended by gobbling itself. Now, we must pick over the pile of shit and each seek his piece of tongue/language (langue). No history, everything's putrified!

I write whilst saying to myself: I don't want to be possessed — and yet they trample on my back. I write against meaning, and I write to produce a meaning. Always the same overload, and the body is exhausted — yes, the body of words burst beneath the weight. I'd like now to work on the level of the sound of language. Or perhaps to *miswrite* (mécrire) as Denis Roche says, crying so rudely: "Leave your tongues, little fathers (my tongue, my tongue, shit), eat your tongues, old dogs, while there's still time!" But there's no more time. And that squawks, squawks in our throats, while what would like to rise, tumbles and falls in the hole.

3.

Readings

READING STEIN

(We asked a number of writers to respond to the three short selections from Gertrude Stein's Tender Buttons *(1914) quoted below — to give their sense of the ways of reading this text — what it means, how it means, & in what ways it might seem relevant to their own concerns in writing. What follows are the Stein selections and the replies.)*

from TENDER BUTTONS

A CARAFE, THAT IS A BLIND GLASS

A kind in glass and a cousin, a spectacle and nothing strange a single hurt color and an arrangement in a system to pointing. All this and not ordinary, not unordered in not resembling. The difference is spreading.

GLAZED GLITTER

Nickel, what is nickel, it is originally rid of a cover.

The change in that is that red weakens an hour. The change has come. There is no search. But there is, there is that hope and that interpretation and sometime, surely any is unwelcome, sometime there is breath and there will be a sinecure and charming very charming is that clean and cleansing. Certainly glittering is handsome and convincing.

There is no gratitude in mercy and in medicine. There can be breakages in Japanese. That is no programme. That is no color chosen. It was chosen yesterday, that showed spitting and perhaps washing and polishing. It certainly showed no obligation and perhaps if borrowing is not natural there is some use in giving.

ROASTBEEF

In the inside there is sleeping, in the outside there is reddening, in the morning there is meaning, in the evening there is feeling. In the evening there is feeling. In feeling anything is resting, in feeling anything is mounting, in feeling there is resignation, in feeling there is recognition, in feeling there is recurrence and entirely mistaken there is pinching. All the standards have streamers and all the curtains have bed linen and all the yellow has discrimination and all the circle has circling. This makes sand.

Very well. Certainly the length is thinner and the rest, the round rest has a longer summer. To shine, why not shine, to shine, to station, to enlarge, to hurry the measure all this means nothing if there is singing, if there is singing then there is the resumption.

The change the dirt, not to change dirt means that there is no beefsteak and not to have that is no obstruction, it is so easy to exchange meaning, it is so easy to see the difference. The difference is that a plain resource is not entangled with thickness and it does not mean that thickness shows such cutting, it does mean that a meadow is useful and a cow absurd. It does not mean that there are tears, it does not mean that exudation is cumbersome, it means no more than a memory, a choice and a reestablishment, it means more than any escape from a surrounding extra. All the time that there is use there is use and any time there is a surface there is a surface, and every time there is an exception there is an exception and every time there is a division there is a dividing. Any time there is a surface there is a surface and every time there is a suggestion there is a suggestion and every time there is silence there is silence and every time that is languid there is that there then and not oftener, not always, not particular, tender and changing and external and central and surrounded and singular and simple and the same and the surface and the circle and the shine and the succor and the white and the same and the better and the red and the same and the centre and the yellow and the tender and the better, and altogether. . . .

Gertrude Stein

ON READING STEIN

Stein has been haunted by two antithetical criticisms. One proposes that her writing is all play, that it derives strictly out of her early researches with William James and motor automism and was later invigorated by Cubist formalism. The other proposes that Stein is a kind of hermetic Symbolist who encodes sexual and biographical information in complex verbal machines which contextualize their own environments. Both views operate on either side of a referential paradigm; one wants her to mean nothing and the other wants her to mean intrinsically. But what makes *Tender Buttons* so vital is not the strategies by which meaning is avoided or encoded but how each piece points at possibilities for meaning. Unlike the Symbolist who creates beautiful detachable artifacts, Stein's prose is firmly tied to the world—but it is a world constantly under construction, a world in which the equation of word and thing can no longer be taken for granted. "The difference is spreading" not only foreshadows deconstructive thought; it recognizes that between one term (a carafe) and a possible substitute (a blind glass) exists a barrier, not an equal sign, and it is this difference which supports all signification. Stein interrogates this barrier in order to break open the imperial Sign and leave "a system to pointing," a language that no longer needs to contain the world in order to live in it.

What's the good of all this? Obviously we know what a carafe is or nickel or roast beef, but Stein doesn't much care whether these things are self-evident. She *does* care that we've come to regard writing as the discovery of concrete counters for feelings, objects and places, that human memory is valorized over human mind in the act of creation. "A name is adequate or it is not. If it is adequate then why go on calling it . . ." she writes, inveighing against the noun's authoritarian stasis. What she wants is movement, a shifting of words among other words—not to erase their ability to refer but to make that act as polymorphous and perverse as any sexual play. *Tender Buttons* as a title suggests words binding the fabric of language together but also the sexual (clitoral) excitation potential in all linguistic play.

Each of the pieces in *Tender Buttons* seems, at some level, to refer to Stein's decontextualizing strategies. "A Carafe, That is a Blind Glass," is "about" the difference between a term and its multifarious substitutes ("a blind glass," a "kind in glass," a "spectacle") or its attendant qualities ("a single hurt color," a "difference . . . spreading"). The unitary object is dispersed among words in "an arrangement in a system." The objects themselves are commonplace—as common as the carafes, bowls and guitars of Cubist still lifes—but Stein's disjunctive prose removes them from their commonality and accentuates the gap between object and description. "[It] is so easy to exchange meaning," she says under the heading "Roast Beef," "it is so easy to see the difference." What links roastbeef to such remarks is the idea of transformation and change present in foods and language alike. Roastbeef exists as the sum of many processes, some of which involve cooking, preparing, eating and digesting; it is the least permanent of things, and yet for the creator of literary still lifes, it is expected to stand in an eternal brown glaze on the verge of being carved. Stein's carving exposes the fallacy in a whimsical rhetoric of permanence: "in the inside there is sleeping, in the outside there is reddening, in the morning there is meaning, in the evening there is feeling." Without knowing what is "outside" or how meaning relates to "morning" or "evening" to "feeling," we are at sea, but by creating a larger grid of specious comparisons and fake equations, Stein undercuts all logical continuity. The logic is entirely her own, and the shifts of predication and assertion (the very stuff of reasonable discourse) serve to expose the mutability which lies at the heart of consumption, whether of food or of language.

What this implies for the act of reading is that there are no longer any privileged semantic centers by which we can reach through the language to a self-sufficient, permanent world of objects, foodstuffs or rooms. We must learn to read *writing*, not read *meanings*; we must learn to interrogate the spaces around words as much as the words themselves; we must discover language as an active "exchange" of meaning rather than a static paradigm of rules and features. The question is not "what" she means but "how." If such activity is difficult it is only because our habits of reading have been based on a passive acceptance of the criterion of adequacy; Stein undermines the model with the simplest of language only so that we may read for the first time—again.

Michael Davidson

A CARAFE . . . GLAZED GLITTER   ROASTBEEF
(through a glass darkly)

Ok murky in after all end, unpredictable day, with rain shine any degree night, the sun kin warm and hot. Enough stone or other jugs lineup of whatever is In Through Out That's light as much as known Differences evanesce Like, where and/or what on the equator might be french or spanish Longitude and latitude, yep yep sure Americana

But could someone mobile with us sleep downstairs, in case of some needs? The amount of variety, seen small, or a knockout maybe in fact. Going deep and strong suddenly three times, though not any more in a while. Mystery on occasion frightens, hurts what you don't know. Sleep came and nothing in square feet changed and later morning is too again there.

And however long the new days all. Every new second minute at least. But the more there is the less you have in common, knowledge of pieces, experience taken in. Bit by bit or in what or how many dimensions. Is there any further inch to a holograph of a spread? Lightning's fast in bed or anyplace. Monuments mixed in haystacks lost.

Nothing is too dull.

Larry Eigner

Writing is intentional denotation (you *choose words*) and reading mirrors that, is read as denotation and intention (mix of the words/what the author is 'trying to say', technique composition context). Of course, strict denotation is a myth: ambiguities/extracurricular meanings can attach to any word(s) read. But it's a myth reinvented at every word ("If not, why use words" — Zukofsky): "breakages" mean breakages, "Japanese," ditto.

The (A) point of *Tender Buttons* is the play between what the pieces are said to mean (the objects, the titles, Stein's theories, Paris Impressionist through Cubist still life) and how the words exist and interact in saying what they do say.

She insists on an (intuitive) identity between her portraits & the objects, arising from avoidance of memory, breaking through crust of habit to actual perception, seeing something continually for the first time. And it's done with *words*: "I became more and more excited about how words which were the words *that made whatever I looked at look like itself* were not the words that had in them any quality of description." (Portraits and Repetition; my italics)

She's proving that she's seeing it by a continual athleticism, leaping free of the gravity of the familiar. Yet "words that make what I looked at look like itself were always words that to me very exactly related themselves to that thing . . . ." (P's & R's)

So, related (a kind, a cousin), but at a necessary distance (not resembling), breathing room for the object to *exist* (the difference).

Anomaly needed to keep us awake (a kind *in* glass, not of; a system *to* pointing). In A Carafe I see her saying she sees and seeing to it that she says so.

But this sounds like systems of more or less stretched metaphor. Occasionally, yes, "the round rest has a longer summer" (round, resting on a platter, roast, summer, opulence, flavor) — I can hook up my intuition with what I guess was hers. But often there's no 'very exact [outward] relation' I can see. First 2 phrases of Roastbeef, yes, rest of paragraph, no. Rocking along on the sound, patterning, slides into lecture against memory: mounting, *resignation, recognition, recurrence,* mistake, pinch, wake up.

In places I wonder if she hears/sees/thinks the word just before or as she writes — or only after. Does she 'mean it', or is it just *prattle* (singsong, babyish joy in denotation [standards, streamers, curtains, bed linen], grammar becoming a 'weak force').

But "it is so easy to exchange meaning, it is so easy to see the difference" and on through the rest of the excerpt is definitely not babytalk, is exemplary in its variety of use, surface, suggestion.

Can't pin down what puts her on the interesting side of language's openness. At best her words displace all others. From Cups: "The best slam is utter."

Bob Perelman

TRANSLATIONAL RESPONSE TO A STEIN SINGLE

a carafe that is a blind glass

she types clarity
relations to a scene
a seen in
zero

queer ones in the pain
of pattern
wheeled directions to
a fullness

that negated more to
more what chaos enters in

no one same article
unlike a wide.

Steve McCaffery

WHOLE HALVES

Bisection, leaving one half hanging over, the drapes are clean. You look as if you need the third from the bottom, the keyhole, nicely in a row. That brings up heat, McCartney's words are blue. It's sort of molded into a mountain. South socks all metal by air sideways, the trim set back from the teeth, the white trim, beginning to stand there. What's back is clear, gently crumpled without creases. White line leads to ferrous flair to private stuff side by side and side by side side by side invitation to an address. Lines rise. Pillow's overtime. Questions: round blue orange white yellow thin and horny. Once top on another without looking very far up. If they stay up, moving in up, and the board leads line a tongue right this way. And then the tongue two three four. Stripes are everywhere, some hanging down or looking up face down or up and left open ready to be lit: answer. The face got a new invention. Buttons no longer don't make any noise. Because what's switched also's identified. And instead of going straight on a round surface straight means the French word for alright. Right at the middle you get wet. Then people save you. Green spots connection. New buttons never have to curl over one another. The old rigidity, the old holes the fading tension aware of its collaboration, the new tension, uncovers the covers. What's a head no longer needs what's ahead because more and more buttons are right to be pressed, propulsion hovers on exhibit. It's stacked, easier to lose the thought of finding, insulatable craft against the checks. The rivers that run to the sea oh boy, use the floor as a step out the door. What's discolored indicates the presence of routine, suddenly the hard weight of the sun becomes mold, mold molding the frame, frame framing the water, water drying up. And ancient actress sees at once. To occupy, having an erection nothing is the same nothing is the name nothing is the frame. Pursuit is as temporal as openings and closings buttons relieved pacify. No one seems to know the right hand way to go, going down, which leaves the middle and the left facing the trees and the hills and the local stuff and the cagey touch flame away from glass. To be here now means how can no one respond to buttons. They all have to be accounted for. When you work in countries the next step is staying home, using buttons, could be in the air like the old Chinese pool hall. Nobody's outside without a shirt not moving lips without saying speed. Before there was even a black hole a table right beside it. A chair. A pair of reroutings means inside. Outside's very tangible, actual, substantive, understood, outside's very material, always there to be reached trying to be touched. Adhesives as well as collections and bone as well as plastic and current as well as fastening and sewing, the next step's stamping. The next step's diffuse. Solid. Volume descends to Richard's only throne. Division of the aspect into verb as seeing progressive form point-action verbs indicate is waking up is working out. Think of it as a as: my whole life has change. In between the round ups everything happens. Billy the Kid counts peas. Rock forms. PVC does not burn. But as we entered the harbor some kind stuck, made stucking sounds. Three bars equals ten dollars. Three buttons means one is missing. That means make it tighter and only maybe somebody'll have to wait. One more thing, light. Looking closer or closely looking used to mean less light. To be precise include everything. Listening used to mean use your head. Then Picasso said even here means a lot of work. Even here being hear, you mean there Alice said. Here here refers to there, permission prohibition, love marriage, button unbutton, press release release press. To be precise precision excludes almost everything, what's left, under the light, clean dirty, includes everything. In the north in the potato country roads are there when you're there or when you're here. Here roads are here wherever you are.

Peter Seaton

READING A SELECTION FROM
TENDER BUTTONS

I start reading "A CARAFE, THAT IS A BLIND GLASS." I go from word to word, seeing the shapes of the printed words, hearing the sounds inwardly, noting rhymes, assonances, alliterations. Where an image is suggested, I see it inwardly. I hear the alliteration "kind," "cousin," "color," with the near-alliteration "glass." The rhyme in "strange" & "arrangement." The alliteration of s's: "spectacle," "strange," "single," "system," "spreading." The assonance of short i's that binds the three sentences ("system," "this," "difference") as does the ending of each sentence with an "ing" (which is reinforced by the short e's in "resembling" & "spreading"). There are also the 2nd sentence's rhymes ("ordinary," "unordered") & the alliterative sequence "spectacle," "pointing," "spreading." The three sentences are a bound system of sounds.

But can I specify anything beyond the sounds? To use a phrase I first heard from Spencer Holst, it gives "the sensation of meaning," but can I connect the meanings of the words as readily as I find their sounds connected?

Beyond the obvious fact that the carafe is made of glass, I can see only certain connections of meanings: "a blind glass," "a kind in glass" (I didn't notice consciously the "blind"-"kind" rhyme before), & then "a spectacle" (something seen or to be seen, but also "spectacles" are "glasses"). Then "nothing strange," "not ordinary," "not unordered," "not resembling," & "difference" form a meaning sequence. Another sequence of meanings: "blind," "spectacle" (with the intervening "glass"'s causing the ambiguity of "spectacle" which might not have been as apparent without them), & "color," that seems to carry over to "arrangement," "pointing," "not unordered," "not resembling," & even to "spreading." The sequence "kind" (with its two meanings), "cousin," "nothing strange" seems opposed to "not ordinary," "not resembling," & "The difference is spreading.": a meaning movement from near-sameness to greater & greater difference.

"A single hurt color" is the most emotional phrase, altho "blind glass" with its implied oxymoron (glass is usually transparent—at least we first think of transparency when we hear the word "glass"— & when it is made into spectacle lenses, it helps people to see better) is perhaps even more so. Maybe the "single hurt color" is the blackness of blindness. The whole poem suddenly seems to be about seeing!

But what of the "carafe" that starts it all? Why is it "a *blind* glass"? Ordinarily a carafe is one of the least "blind"—that is, the most transparent—of glass containers. It usually contains plain water. The OED defines it as "a glass water-bottle for the table, bedroom, etc." Its Romance forms (F. *carafe,* It. *caraffa,* Neapol. *carrafa* (a measure of liquids), Sp. & Pg. *garrafa,* Sicil. *carabba*) are related by some authorities to the Pers. *garābah,* a large flagon, & the Arabic *gharafa,* to draw or lift water.

Why, then, is *this* carafe a *blind* glass?

Is the whole poem then a "pointing" from the ordinary transparent carafe ("nothing strange") to one "not ordinary"—one that is "blind"—an orderly ("not unordered") movement "spreading" from transparency & clarity thru the "single hurt color" to the implied darkness & opacity of blindness, a movement condensed & made explicit in the title?

Jackson Mac Low

TENDER BUTTONS

Undergoing *sight* (& by 'sight' thinking feeling looking remembering even inventing imagining certainly tasting surely listening hearing talking) meaning potentially all human process, as almost academic ('art-school') exercise undertaken for the species' joy in it, less talking & listening than looking to know that words can do it, making nomenclature consort of nature (1911, in Spain) in the perfect understanding that *that seen* makes a name, this time (accommodating strangeness of verbiage in process of gaining exact usage), only because (mutton flies into the sundown upwind upstream already) all time/everything is. Artist never fell.

Sad story, now, apparently. Real im Traum, 'before the War.' Today, a hearkening back, as longing, not the reality of the word, not the faith that makes composition of the world, riding on that everything, permission given. She could say anything.

Now some further difficulty of access, as the nature of human experience slips away from the ad-men as makers of language unconvinced, in the last resort, of any *necessity*.

Before I die.
Before I die.
Before I die.
Before I die.
(Robt. Creeley, *Pieces*)

—resolve echoes. Names repeat.

But it's the same imperative, that one might undertake now in the absence of conviction, that anything was, that a word might mean anything, that she addressed with certainty: ". . . looking at anything until something that was not the (conventional) name of that thing but was in a way that actual thing would come to be written." ("Poetry And Grammar")

•

"TENDER" says entire activity of the artist's portraiture (subtitle: "portraits of objects, food, rooms")—not 'studies' of objects etc. nor 'still lives,' but (*portray:* 'to draw forth, reveal'; from root, 'to drag, move') dramatic engagements with things-given-the-sort-of-attention-that-humans-get often in motion, 'alive,' as well—so you get a verbal-formal offering, that stretches out to move through circles of light (attention) in which "beginning again and again" transforms into a "continuous present" in which words one-one-one actively engage as single-frame sequence (". . . this our period was undoubtedly the period of the cinema and series production") something all right, tendered, right in front of you. "BUTTONS" just means everyday domestic objects (which are??) nudged—'on the button.'

Ok, 'tender' because new-born—& all right, word-buds, tenderly regarded.

•

What poetry *does* (see "Poetry And Grammar"): realization of new nominatives—(not neologism but) whole text, in process, "replaces" worn-out, now-merely-conventional name offered up (in title, commonly) to be melted down in crucible of language process attention forging other access to the ongoing of what's what.

T.B., as *early* 'phenomenological investigation,' is interpretative/as it is revelatory—the whole storm of passion, discernment, definition, feeling//carried by language//brought to the 'budding' of the thing—three together, through time, make the name.

•

It's not 'snapshorts' (moves; don't copy nature), & it's not 'the pathetic fallacy' (though it includes much of the artist's process). And it ain't 'abstract.'

(In this context, for L=A=N=G=U=A=G=E, I want to say I think it's
at best a 'creative misreading' of Stein to take her work as a whole as a
primary instance of 'language-oriented writing.' Not only her some-
what less arduous later work (*Autobiography of A.B.T.*, *Brewsie And
Willie*), but *The Making of Americans* (a history of her family & com-
pendium of sketches of every possible kind of human being), *Lucy
Church Amiably* (an 'engraving' or romantic portrait of life in the
French countryside) & her long poem "Stanzas in Meditation" (written
shortly before the *Autobiography of A.B.T.* &, if anything, a prototype
of confessional poetry) all are intent to make new ways to say some-
thing—show her thinking language not as object-in-itself, but as com-
position functioning in the composition of the world. With the excep-
tion of some verbal experiment, with Williams & Pound, Stein's basic
concern as a writer was to confront the imperative MAKE IT NEW how-
ever possible—'IT' being, equally/simultaneously, sentience, world &
language as relation between these. *T.B.*, specifically, exists *as* such
confrontation—& to take it as a variously interesting arrangement of
words, alone, is to perpetuate the initial journalist-parody response to
the work as 'nonsense.')

•

But can it be done, as a *task*. *Was* 1911, or. . . . *Even now.* . . . "It's a
mild, mild day, Starbuck" etc. . . *So* quiet, in America. . . . 1977
rhymes with 1911 (*is* it, already, 1978. . . .) Seemingly timeless lull on
the brink, this time, of the extinction of something other than the Pe-
quod as American westward-expanding enterprise (or craters in the
Whiteheads' lawns). . . Beautiful fall day, clear even to the horizon
. . . though the reign of conventional names, reiteration of terminology
as fixed interpretation of that not happening, appears to cover the globe
several times over, 'ruling' air & land & waves. . . . What a moment,
nonetheless. . . . *Yet again*, that chance to (two by two, alpha & beta,
assess & elephants) call the roll, look to words to show & tell the pres-
ent orders of. . . .

•

". . . Think of all that early poetry, think of Homer, think of Chaucer,
think of the Bible and you will see what I mean you will really realize
that they were drunk with nouns, to name to know how to name earth
sea and sky and all that was in them was enough to make them live and
love in names, and that is what poetry is it is a state of knowing and

feeling a name. I know that now but I have only come to that knowledge by long writing." ("P. & G.," 1934) . . .

Robert Grenier

ZYXT

Michael Andre, editor, *The Poets' Encyclopedia* (1979: UNMUZZLED OX, N.Y.)

[Last entry reads:]

The last word (here, in English, in the OED): an obsolete Kentish form, the second person indicative present of the verb *see*. Language even ends in the eye. In a book, if we are enjoying ourselves, we often reduce our reading pace measurably in its final pages, luxuriating slowly in the joy of words & syntax (unlike that of ideas & referents, where the onset of the conclusion only accelerates the reading), anticipating an inevitable sadness wch follows the end of the (always erotic) body of the text. The book closed sets loose an emotion tinged with jealousy & grief: its presence (wch includes our own reflected in the text) is something we can never again possess. Rereading is not the same: words harden, aura crystallizing to define a wall no quantity of inspection can penetrate. In this after*word* we sense ever so briefly the immense relief we felt in having been delivered awhile from the weight of directing our own psyches. This is the restorative value of any text (reading is a kind of sleep, a return to the senses). Now we can only wait until this wave of sorrow subsides before seeking the seduction of another book. There is no alternative. You zyxt.

Ron Silliman

ARAKAWA & MADELINE H. GINS, *The Mechanism of Meaning*

(1979: Harry Abrams, N.Y.)

"Ambiguous zones exist with each statement or representation across the conceptual distance which separates them." Arakawa and Gins, in 15 sections, investigate the processes of meaning in terms of degrees, scale (expansion and reduction), splitting of meaning, reassembly, reversibility, texture, feeling of meaning, logic and so on. The basic unit of presentation is the map—color painting/grid used as often archly funny method of optical/verbal investigation of meaning as perceptual field. Object of meaning viewed, rearranged. Puzzling technical/scientific-looking diagrams confront and remove and replace assumptions about labels, identification, differentiation, measure, spatial depth. Brain is visually astonished, jolting confines of memory, geometric expectations of axial relations. Recurrent use of juxtaposed pictures and words, each saying (pointing to) something at an angle to the other; words question picture, picture casts shadow over accuracy of accompanying words. "Shape is used to plot sense color to relate quality of nonsense." Color as senses (coloring meaning). Color as feeling. "The distance out of which, who, repeatedly hypostatized, speaks. (That angle of tone at which is arrived a concensus of modulations through/along the blending scales of apperception and perception)."

Charles Bernstein

RAE ARMANTROUT, *Extremities*

(1978: The Figures, Berkeley)

> Going to the desert
> is the old term
>
> 'landscape of zeros'

> the glitter of edges
> again catches the eye
>
> to approach these swords!
>
> lines across which
> beings vanish/flare
>
> the charmed verges of presence

EXTREMITIES. Paths lost found forgotten. Border margin beginning. Birth/Death. Inside/Outside. She/He. Moving/Staying. Finding/Losing. The unity of opposites, Epicene, Androgyne. According to Boehme, in the beginning Adam was the primal Androgyne. After the Fall, God separated female from male and the primal harmony was lost. Armantrout in these poems wants to begin again. Like H.D., her search is for that lost prelapsarian state which may have existed only in the mind — back in the pre-history of childhood. It is a search for harmony in a bewildering time. GENERATION

> We know the story
>
> She turns
> back to find her trail
>
> devoured by birds.
>
> The years; the
> undergrowth

Gretel lost in the forest of generation, the undergrowth of years. Not a word that doesn't belong. We all know the story — but we still don't understand the undergrowth. " 'Just wait Gretel, till the moon rises, and then we will see the crumbs of bread which I have strewn about, they will show us our way home again.' When the moon came they set out, but they found no crumbs, for the many thousands of birds which fly about in the woods and fields had picked them all up." Imagine the Moon then!

Not the city lights. We want
— the moon —

The Moon
none of our own doing!

Like riddles the poems in *Extremities* are terse, precise, subtle. A riddle
is a puzzle. A mis-leading. The novelty of a riddle is that by depriving
something of its name, we render it unrecognizable. A dislocation of
perspective similar to the fear expressed in XENOPHOBIA (fear that
one is dreaming). In a riddle every word counts, is a sign. A signifier.
Words both hide and reveal. Fear of riddles with no solution.

this same riddle:
IS IT ALRIGHT?

qualm that persists
on the bus ride

"Tonight there's
the movie"
a woman soothes her son

A female Knight off on her quest, Armantrout has armed herself with
enigmas, paradoxes, wit, and cunning. The intensity is religious, pure
in the best sense. And it is a quest undertaken with the awareness that
in the search there is no sanctuary. In SAVED reading Lao-Tze she
makes speech a raft, and in TRAVELS thinks for a moment

I had recovered silence

The power to be
irretrievably lost

Oliver Cromwell to the French Ambassador — "A man never mounts so
high as when he does not know where he is going."

GRACE

I am walking

covey in silent flight

PROCESSIONAL

The smallest

distance

inexhaustible

In XENOPHOBIA she isolates each fear by placing it in parenthesis as if a printed wall could contain the idea (fear of sights not turned to words). Again, it was the primordial Adam to whom God gave the power of naming. Imagine a world without names! SPECIAL THEORY OF RELATIVITY

> You know those ladies
> in old photographs? Well,
> say one stares into your room
> as if into the void
> beyond her death in 1913.

In the brave new world of Death there are no names.

LXXXVI. When born they wish to live and to have dooms — or rather to rest, and they leave children after them to become dooms. (Heraclitus On the Universe). The sort of paradox these poems are made of. I love *Extremities* for its intelligence and curiosity. From the first poem, the title one, the first extremity — Armantrout stands poised at Lacan's ecstatic limit of "Thou art that" the point where any real journey begins. "to approach these swords!"

the sentence
flies

In medieval times the idea of earthly knighthood and angelic knighthood were intertwined (militia). They pre-supposed economy and discipline. The medieval Latin for a knight is miles.

Susan Howe

SOME NOTES ON THOMAS A. CLARK

Sincere. *Sine cere.* Without wax. No filler. Object. *Ob jaceo.* To throw against. A destination. Aimed at. Focus. Thomas A. Clark speaking: "Years working in a short space . . . the trouble was, how to distance it from one's own mind. The language became more and more self-referent and 'obscure' in the worst sense. So I've been making poems using texts which were 'outside my own head', and treating them in different ways: permutational, fragmentary, etc. I set about experiments like cutting columns in half, or placing frames over a piece of prose. I think that knowing to look at all and knowing what to look for is rather a lot."

And so it is. *The Secrecy of the Totally* (1969) collage and chance generated works.

> ragged party of docile
> and romantic sunsets

Emphatic Forms (1971) with epigram from Wittgenstein: "We make to ourselves pictures of facts." Pieces gathered from assorted language primers. The act of isolation being the poet's only intervention.

> to speak distinctly
> to speak loudly
> to speak softly
> to walk straight on
> to stare fixedly
> to see clearly

To see clearly! Eye poems. The Stein directive: write not what you see but what you know is there.

> why have you not eaten this piece?

In *The North Bohemian Coalfields* (1970) the language and approach is slightly more oblique, dramatic and speech-oriented in tone with punctuating slash marks further suggesting abrupt shifts:

Work cited: *The Secrecy of the Totally* (1969: South Street Publications, Sherbourne, Dorset); *The North Bohemian Coalfields* (1970: Bettiscombe Press, Bettiscombe, Dorset); *Emphatic Forms* (1971: Bettiscombe Press); *Some Particulars* (1971: The Jargon Society, Highlands, N.C.); *Pointing Still* (1974: Arc Publications, Gillingham, Kent); *A Still Life* (1977: Jargon).

/ there falls here also the /
/ image of the bridge /

/ through the moment when
there is nothing /

the broad daylight /

Light and function a persistent concern in all these works. Illuminated stillness. The poem's workings. A Basho-like sensibility. Completeness ever deferred. Not particulars but *Some Particulars* (1971). Selection. Choice. Burton's *Anatomy of Melancholy* cited on the title page: ". . . I have laboriously collected this Cento out of divers writers. . ." The cento itself a literary patchwork. In the fifth century the Empress Eudoxia composed a life of Christ in verse with every line drawn from Homer.

Clark's sources: the 18th century British naturalist Gilbert White, the Life and Letters of Samuel Palmer, Walton's *The Compleat Angler*—all anatomists in their own right further anatomized by Clark. A strong tho distilled taste harkening back to the original. Illumination. What would normally be overlooked in the perusal casual or otherwise is brought into the light. At times almost miraculously. The last piece in *Some Particulars* ironically titled "Note"

on the 11th
of April 1971
across the centre
of page 117
of Burton's
"Anatomy of Melancholy"
there was a rainbow

".....and bees amongst the rest
though they be flying away, when
they hear any tingling sound,
will tarry behind."

These are spectral works. Beautifully deadpan.

Pointing Still (1974) records (and only that) six incidents of watches lost. Time frozen but rediscovered and re-articulated in the virtue of its factness. Pointing here or there. Still as in at rest or yet. Suspended.

A Still Life (1977). Picture in a frame. Or a quiet life. Both resonate here. Present as in the earlier works is an affection for and a studied observation of nature. The presentation of images self-informed and complete though transient and accidental. Poise. Balance. Discernment. The first piece in the book sets the tone and isolates the manner of the music to unfold:

> Place words end to end as dry stones.
> Using only local materials, arrange them
> sparsely to admit plenty of ventilation.
> They will stand among the fiercest winds
> and keep the sheep out.

A wall extends horizontally as well as vertically. Light bends to make a spectrum. Light's torque.

> "Rainbow"

> At the end of each arc of speech
> the treasure of rest.

Ray DiPalma

CLARK COOLIDGE, WEATHERS

What he takes from Olson is not the Hey-you-guys-set-out-to-sea-in-the-leaky-yawl-I-have-provided but the I-want-to-get-Gravelly-Hill-into-a poem/diorite-stoney/the-secret-I-can't-speak-is-dark-in-here Olson. The geology of Weathers (the poem thus far) is there to be read as metaphor of language in its dense histories, its screed presence, but not really. It's there because CC is fascinated by rocks. This is Black Mtn projection, the individual writ big, Specter-of-the-Brocken writing, Kerouac he much admires : CC wants to write *his* life. Any attempt to go by earlier models for how to do that would never *be* "my" life, which, as all might know, since it's fact, is composition of thwarted desire with misdirected intention come right. So he puts pebbles in his mouth, thus to shape his utterance to figures having that in common with his life : not personal poesy à la I-take-the-hose-into-my-mouth-&-switch-on-the-ignition, this speaks through a medium & knows it. The medium has to be huge, as the person it gathers to contain, conceal, present, prevent, explain.

The same afternoon CC "answers" "questions" re his writing at 80 Langton St, SF, the publishers of *Jack's Book* are at least 20 blocks off at the Old Spaghetti Factory throwing a wake for the anniversary of that resource's death, there on the North Beach which nostalgia wants to say anyone who was anyone was present at the "flowering" of : witness (same day) Sunday Supplement idiocies re poets disparate as Kyger, Weiss, Kandel ("I went to Big Sur with Jack & Lew"), Ferlinghetti (Mrs.), Kaufman (Mrs.), McClure (Mrs.). "It was the greatest love scene between a poet & a lady since Robert Browning & Elizabeth Barrett" — Eileen Kaufman. How that yearning to cry, "I lived!" banalizes all thus touched, denied sufficient form, is surely known to CC, who presents the book instead : which is why we are here & not there. But Beckett & Kafka (CC alludes to as heroes), minatory of, however protracted-grace-of-an-art, ultimate frustration, need this sentence to be here.

It proves extremely difficult to secure an actual answer to a real question, e.g., How did you know to let the misdirected intention ("canyon") come right ("crayon") : for Coolidge writes his fascination, which is at some remove from the questioner's procedure, which can be characterized as if-I-were-to-write-the-poem-tradition-dictates-here-it-would-go-exactly-like-this-interruption-instead. Or say I concern myself with how this sounds/means to others; CC, writing, is lost/found in his child's play, rearranging his magic objects until a pattern (on the instant become *the* pattern) creates (note : creating subject vanishes, alleviated as by magic) a sufficiency : "Stonehenge" is *not* the analogy, that was communal, not private, magic; Clark is crayoning rocks in his coloring book & will not be diverted by "Dinner's ready!"

Therefore it is the persistence of the child, fascination's ability to resist interruption, we read in Weathers, rocklike; apart, & the incommunicable portion any severed individual needs to be aware he/she includes; the contents it offers as its evidence could be, theoretically, anything — although in practice can't be but what CC happens, projective, upon. This will be missed when the academies take up this man's work. The patterns *in* the work will become ground of *that* debate. But the various gestures he brings to the writing from previous models & that suggest thematic recurrence, narrative continuity, etc., are only here to say "Hi."

Wordsworth's "Anecdote for Fathers" can show us the futility of such questions Weathers might raise :

A boy five years old. His father : "had you rather be
on Kilve's smooth shore, or here at Liswyn farm?"
"At Kilve." "My little Edward, tell me why."
"I can't tell, I don't know." The father persists.
Edward raises his head — and glittering bright, there,
he sees a broad & gilded vane. "At Kilve there was no
weathercock; & that's the reason why."

I think Romantic art apotheosizes once again in Weathers with, as ever,
that sense of having-come-to-some-terminus-beyond-which-impos-
sible-to-push these instances invariably suggest : BUT it will permit so
many misreadings, so many creative mistakings, that it strikes me as
useful to say that this is highly traditional art of the West & not in any
radical sense deconstructive, demystifying or prophetic; & as grace-
ful/grateful to remark that, incurring the complexities of its genius, it
alters our world beyond its intentions, which I think may be great.

David Bromige

CLARK COOLIDGE, *Own Face*

(1978: Angel Hair Books, N.Y.)

Clark Coolidge is restructuring language to inhabit his personal
chromatic scale.

In the early seventies, using only prepositions, pronouns, conjunc-
tions, articles & nouns in visually spaced-out arrangements (that in-
ferred subjects, verbs, phrases etc. around them), he succeeded in con-
structing technically induced texts. (*Air*, Clark Coolidge, 1972). Using
these elements as a sort of semantic glue he *realized* the 'induced' text
in subsequent work. This process, almost methodological, is in itself
quite significant, it resulted in the achievement of "A page that is
nothing but words written by itself." (*This 8*, Clark Coolidge, 1977).

It is in the light of these very regular emissions, (from the vantage
of a decade) amounting to wave-texts whose frequency is determined
by crests & troughs of semantic referentiality, that *Own Face* stands out.
Own Face is a very personal work originating in Clark Coolidge's or-
pheatic obsession with the *real* underworld (note Floyd Collins' eyes

on the cover). Syntactically, the book is congruent with the over-riding flow of Coolidge's methodology. Thematically, the spelunker/cave biography of *Own Face* is reduced to collocation, which, although nominal, is nonetheless efficient. And it is at this level that *Own Face* arrives, in a trough of semantic referentiality, bearing a very revealed Coolidge.

The text is an anti-quantum morphemics where each successive unit of meaning re-defines the manifold.

Christopher Dewdney

*

From *Own Face*: "A Note"

I think then I live in a world of silence.
The language has become lodged in itself a background,
wall of rock, black and resistant as basalt, then sometimes
as viscous as heavy grease, poetry must be reached into
and rested from in a cry. Meaning is now a mixture, it
recedes to itself a solid fix of knowledge. The words
of poems, once rested from the mass, cry shrilly and singly,
then spring back to that magnetic ore body of silence.
The longest poem has become a brief crack into light and sound.
The candle flame through the sliver hums but must be tricked,
wrested out for a mere tick in the radium dark.
The rest is all a walk in stillness, on the parade of
the tombs of meaning. Or is this all still the highest ledge?

Clark Coolidge

31 ASSERTIONS, SLOWLY

Christopher Dewdney, *Spring Trances in the Control Emerald Night* (1978: The Figures, Berkeley)

Here language goes back to the spring we see it come out from.

The air is geology.

Eye is born in its sac.

Each integer vibrates the space between its neighbors, domains in line.

A star a dream of light from which a universe awakens.

Persons are volumes of live matter raised in meeting to 451° fahrenheit or cool in water.

Each version is solid eschatology.

In every passage a great whale blocks the sight from the sight but not from the whale.

Towns are beaches onto which wash.

Through these visions runs a tiny naked and frothing vision.

From the chosen vantage, fireflys are acres of light.

Large balls of silence roll past and through each other, on a border of nerves and delight.

Sense data fills cylinders with its saturated solution.

Each fossil a photograph of a comet, then, and also.

The literature phosphoresces in slow biologic warp, seeing desire untied of desire.

Dreams coat the inside of beings, the underside of sight.

Going out in air, the lungs envelop stone history.

A statement nearly restates another, it must be stating itself, must itself be stated.

Metaphor is one word for two: family resemblance.

History bumps itself off.

Preordination fosters statues.

Organisms are preferred which voice without breaking open their layers, rather case in them.

Far away objects are simple on protractor limits.

A body part is a testicle of motion.

The aliens are contentedly at home.

360° dreams 0°.

Inside brain a knot surfaces, to be solid text.

One mosquito syphons blood from the fucking body.

The future holds, sustains, each present in sounds.

Preference is an asterisk.

The author escapes from a paragraph, eloping along slightly bottomless discourse.

Alan Davies

THE ALPHABET OF STRIDE (on Ray DiPalma)

> The world is a text with several meanings & we pass from one to another by a process of work. It must be work in which the body constantly bears a part, as, for example, when we learn the alphabet of a foreign language. This alphabet has to enter into our hand by dint of forming the letters. If this condition is not fulfilled every change in our way of thinking is illusory.
> —Simone Weil, *Gravity & Grace*

A unity suffering its inception.—DiPalma

Everything makes a move, is fixed, moves on—. *Between the Shapes*: an early 'collection'—what is the sense of writing that inspires a person

Works cited: *Between the Shapes* (1970: Zeitgeist, East Lansing, Mich.); *Works in a Drawer* (1972: Blue Chair Press, Bowling Green, Ohio); *Planh* (1979: Casement to craft these poems?—& yet already the (a) twist ("early in the turkey/ the ground had a pedigree") and a (the) sense of *words stacking*, breaking down the syntax of pictorial representation into strata of words, *things* ("Above the tracks/ a slight embank/ ment. Limestone./ Mud. Weeds. A/ concrete wall . . . "). *Night*: & immediately (from a more sprawling . . .) to a crystallization of form, only what is necessary ("the condition was relative to a measure"), stillness (fix of words); here the syntax opening up by ellipses—one pinpointed detail next to another, concentric ripples not touching; items, words as objects existing side-by-side; yet the movement of one unit to the next—a progression of sightings . . . which gets very rapidly (*Works in a Drawer* &c) to a subtle detail, refinement, that gives weight to each syllable ("sooner or later the sun cracks rebecca") & it's apparent that there is a constant attention to order & balance (in the sense that a coordination of elements is always at play, as is the recognition, though not necessarily the recreation, of a specifically geometric arrangement). We take this into the visual placement of words in the more than 100 pages of *Sgraffiti*, name derived from a graphics technique in which the surface layer is scratched into to reveal a different colored ground. A complex play of cut-out, design, procedure—always delineated, articulated—intelligence dancing through the words & rearranging them. Or *The Birthday Notations*: in which it's not the syntax that gets broken up to bring out the plasticity, ping & pong, of word against word—but a syntax— "After lunch I slept almost all the rest of the day; another man would have made it his duty to go and see the waterfalls"—that gets looked at with a gaze that makes it plastic, so we see it *as* its mode of language at the same time as enjoying its 'content'. Time having moved us away from these syntaxes—the work composed entirely of citations from 17th to early 20th Century diaries, journals and letters—but that distance also allowing us to see them with an angle of gaze that reveals their meaning with renewed intensity. Genre writing: well each way of proceeding establishes its own kind of rhetoric but never assumes it, so the language work is always active: " 'You must talk with two tongues, if you do not wish to cause confusion.' " More recently: the rubber-stamp books, which create a pictographic grammar, where repetition, blurring, juxtaposition and serial ordering page to page (of a fixed 'vocabulary' of stamp images) give rise to a movement of meanings realized solely by this specially made coding ("plane *falls on* horse, sheep *falls on* tractor, soap *falls on* boat, chair *falls on* bear, cow *falls on*

Books, N.Y.). Author's mss: *Night* (1968); *Sgraffiti* (1971–73); *The Birthday Notations* (1974–77).

car, . . .")—but codes not for sake of conveying some message by use of symbolic elements, but for the sheer joy of the cipher: their internal movements & their transformations. — & next, what new gaze ("Planh"), clumped with "rolling vision/ from staring eyes". —A sequence of illuminations, clouded, pulsed. "When in the dark move faster, make your own light." — Hats on.

Charles Bernstein

TIM DLUGOS, *Je Suis Ein Americano*

(1979: Little Caesar Press, Los Angeles)

How can you care about your neighbor if you can't understand what he says? I thought I was going to fall down backwards, and began to laugh with delight. Twelve stories up you can feel the damp of subway excavations, see the damp good looks of the workers. No revolution without them please. We are ready to meet anybody here, little brother. Do what you want. You walk into the empty parlor, sit down, and play the only song you know by heart. You draw your own breath, then I draw mine. Part of it is staying in the earth. Another part is moving in the wind. The birds fly away, they shed their reputations like their history. I'm the space explorer. We take off to the museum and watch the individual colors as they surface in the late works of Matisse. I don't want to go home. I am afraid of the country, too. But everyone, no matter how far the physical distance is only a phone call away. In the breeze, the river reeks a little less than usual. I feel the sun in my face. I see the light through my eyelids. It's bright, intelligent, free of all cares. My life on other planets has been pleasant, but now I must return to my own people. Some of the words are meaningless. All that you have to give is in your eyes.

Steve Hamilton

LYNNE DREYER

The writing changed my life. I was thinking how my affections would be thrown out, my feelings would be cast aside or just internalized. I know for some writers it makes them keep thinking, but I'm interested in the rhythm of words, and how combined we receive their story. Like when someone asks if "ya get the picture" and you do. I'm not a very intellectual writer, yet I feel I learned to think when I started to write. I need to emphasize my feelings and thoughts — make them clear to others. The way words grow out of words and phrases, light on other words — an icey voice. This happens when I start to write and when I forget myself. This is what is most important to me. I think the thoughts form themselves when I lose myself in the writing. I'm learning, making it clearer I like to get carried away by the words — but I need to be understood not hide by abstractions, vagueness or drama. I need to know it's real.

Lynne Dreyer

LYNNE DREYER, "Letters"

(1978: in *Tottel's* #17, San Francisco)

Letters to friends about: "Every possible motive of action" & "The freedom to use it", awareness of what we say, "unknown qualities" taken for granted. The extremities of norm: darkside. Manners learned off tv "slightly off course". But the issues are embedded in the woman, not doctored out. Lynne gets hectic with restraint. "He would lie down and be interesting." Could? Inneresting? (Voyeur. Observateur. i.e., "a new kind of tune replaces the new." "In the persona of modern-day woman-child, Ms. Dreyer considers a day she 'didn't T.V.' simultaneously a victory over her own ennui and high praise for the author who so stimulated her that she didn't need tv; contrary to Plath's solution, one we can live with.") Meaning comes out of the language uncommented on. I know what she's talking about, because it could only be talked about that way. "Embarrassed" and "logical": I don't know what to say, because I don't need to. The metaphor is humanism.

James Sherry

JOHANNA DRUCKER, *From A to Z: Our An (Collective Specifics) an im partial bibliography, Incidents in a Non-relationship or: how I came to not know who is*

(1977: Chased Press, Philadelphia)

A typography that reflects a thrownness into text—a big way of saying it—"wise she so willing to approach the insidiously inadequate signifier, with TOLERATION & ON." Which means we are faced with a WHOLE HEAP of letters—here, nothing can be seen more physically than the literal lettrist composition—& yet this is a work not of reflective imposition of a form but of a form emerging from the energy of the making. "It's the vision that matters, the real & worked out clarity of vision." So, like Hannah Weiner, what appears as an interruptive quality of variant type faces & sizes (in the make-up of single words & whole pages), which is continuous throughout this book, doesn't so much have its roots in cut-up or program (the 'imposed' form) but comes out of the writing "ON". "The energy runs through eVerything when it's going. I go with it, making the moVes according to the opportunities." So what we have is "constructivism" that comes out of "trust (in) the intuitiVe aspect of the organism: to function through the totality of the being". I.e.,: the construction collapses back onto its own necessity, a short circuit which refuses to allow for anything but an integrated thing. But, & note, Drucker's "primitiVe driVe" isn't just a *self*-defined *writing* exercise (viz: Mayer)—this book poses as its 'external' condition to set all the type in the printshop & make a book ('internally') come *out of* "that". "I have a serious interest in the synthetic integration of thought." &: "For the actual purpOse of deliberate cOmstrucTiVe thOughT." Which doesn't even get to the humor of the 'narrative' here: "I mean, I figured you're just not that bright, right? Nobody ever said you had a great head. But you're still a pretty man, & if you turned out to be a nice guy, then that would be okay, I couldn't expect you to have everything, after all." Here, she's going for both.

Charles Bernstein

LARRY EIGNER NOTES

                              "Who wants to see himself"

I see . . .

   the noun states accent in air

   so much that an "on" or "hard" takes on
   solidity of noun at line-end

   the prepositional phrases: a thought he's
   using only one unit, over & over again
                        (Cezanne?)

   every line hit to a conclusion; the prepositional phrase
   pushed up against its noun-wall; the single noun,
   preposition, whichever, its own wall; each wall
   a cut in space
                 "a wall was thick

                 air was a wall"

   a nounal/prepositional universe. verb slides . . .

   an invisible & steadying "is" behind everything

      "my own hands are distractions"

   all particles in the pile soon to reach
   nounal state

                 "Names are the colored barrels
                 we trip over inside."
                              —C. Olson

     "or arrows

         slopes   room for all

             particles
                     outlines"

each line a new mind (focus)
rather than divisions determined by breaks
of sound, syntax, etc.

air, his medium, air, the medium of voice (waves) and
image (light) immediately inward/outward, as one.

the word "air" & its immediate prepositioning

the sub-vocally/sub-optically heard/seen

    "there is everything to speak of
      but the words are words"

these "scenes" don't exist, never have.
these words comb them through mind.
The poem is built.

pages, hammers, boards, trees, garage, cars,
horse, bowels
             : his tonality

  "or peas

you shift

  practice"

          making a landscape by motion
                              (*Another Time* 45)*

a hard movement of the words
allows equal solidity to the spaces between.
otherwise such seemingly "fragmented" structure
fall to the bottom.

Eigner is an *on-going* register. His movement.
and from poem to poem must be spaced, noted.
 (why, for example, *Another Time* so much the better

* *Another Time in Fragments* (1967: Fulcrum Press, London)—eds.

to be read than *Selected Poems* with its imposed
and titled interruptions)

Air, his medium. every thing, hangs up & out.
a window, all ways.
and the word "air", his serial point of closure.

each line
equals
its own completion

and every next line
its consequence

wholes are only made by motion

"Sight is the only sense in which continuity is sustained
   by the addition of tiny but integral units: space can be
   constructed only from *completed* variations."
                                          —Roland Barthes

   "Part & particle is a noun."
                        —G. Stein, *Portrait of Man Ray*

A network of blind people, inventing
new methods of telephoning.

"what you like
  is a plain object"
                . . . enters the whole air of his poems

space of singled-out words increasing speed
toward attaining a whole line, sentence, stop.

scarcity of enjambment (a word of meaning
far from its sounding), so its occurrence
has weight of event.

Sound creates silence. Images produce the blanks.
                         "material
                            gapping"

Each poem sights into a distance of all the
others following.
                    "the whole is divided as you look"

The Imagination.

to Williams a very present physics of the senses.
a synthesis of presence.

word-activation of the imagination in the act of seeing.

                    "the bird
                    of wire like a nest

                    is all through the air"

start made at a word
everything to follow
the word its word
again the following

I do not think of Eigner.

                                        Clark Coolidge

LARRY EIGNER, *Lined Up Bulk Senses*

(1979: Burning Deck, Providence)

air mostly. 7 pages. enormous resonances. word, line, vowel/conso-
nant function alternatively and then– relatedly. Eigner scales his focus
moving designedly forward, even as he re/covers ground– line is the
life is a birth– syntax joining the words in an eddying motion *this/is a
calendar/the wind/past it and the wall* wch might be read bkwards *past
it and the wall/the wind/is a calendar/this* vowels/consonants sound-
ing across lines. 4 ends *sky/variety/it/fields* multiple sounds/visual
slimness adhering in the vowel *i*. & 7– *a certain newness in/ few trees*.

words resourcing their varietal meanings– *the clock being of hands*.
Light running type moving down each page successive page (as in the
capital cover). A tribute of days. to life. thanx at birth *the future more
direct line*. Out. sound from the chair window wall *out of the fences
now* & in. brought in. past=wered=writing. this writing synonymous
wt. breath 1. projected extent extant heaven. to be taken 2. acknowl-
edged ingathering *the past taped* (obscure threat). Writing this writing
looks back– layered *lined up bulk senses*. each succession a listening
to turn the line, to build dense verticals that move. on. Place reverts
into space and returns to page– *line* at the bottom. I think of Eigner's
earlier *diversions/distractions merge/if no dead line* and the fullness
of air from my eye to the ground– granular sleight of sight, in what is
NOT empty air– *Silence lost* in the creation of a sequence of molecular
particles powering in $^{on}_{as}$ wind. it is a flood, high, as one dreams it

add + here Eigner's reading, Grand Piano fall 78– optical potential re-
covered in time, in language-reading as opposed to speech, the play of
music or film (yet these might be rewound). There– Eigner's voice a
stratum of half understood sounds/ the type opaque-projector projected
crawling round and up the page/public finding necessary mouth inter-
mediary mouthing– *it was there/which had to be taken/what you
made*. here– in print/meant to be read/the page measures, is time, line
achieves polyphony, the mind an instrument

Abigail Child

BARBARA EINZIG, *Disappearing Work*
a recounting

(1979: The Figures, Berkeley)

Recording witness to a life through the mind, a narrative of "what re-
mains" (Merleau-Ponty), is Einzig's coming to a language of memory
with the case for poetry met in a unique diction of brevity: the evolving
post-negative function in signifying being the route taken through the
mind towards the succinct. This refining sets-down a hermeneutic, a
"recounting" that is in every sense of the word parataxic and ends-up

on the page in the positivism of the head's organizing swiftness, and, more, caught-up *voce*. Any decision to think "like this" is elaborately binding in the choice to at once notice and define a specific design in thought, and carry it through into the key gesture of "figuring" (historicity). The insisting motion is from mind to page and, though evenly exegetic, is random in its phenomenology. Simultaneity and approximation root the material persistence of "story" in a phasing that oscillates between corporeity and absence. Rare in any book, *Disappearing Work* countermines the full reach of a substantial centering thesis.

Andrew Kelly

I would be this cool, this deliberate, with my jumpiness — address my impatience to the sky. "She brought orange juice into the sauna. Shocking cold in her mouth and throat and then all the way inside her as she drank it there palpable," — *that's* what I felt, guzzling something wet down till stuck in the craw. Enough, — the thing one gradually comes to find out is that one has no identity that is when one is in the act of doing anything. The joker there being, that one "gradually comes to find out". Various ways to draw mountains. SF Review of Books reviewer scolds *Disappearing Work* for not being a novel . . . wants fists brandished against an indifferent sky. Event in *DW* includes the sky, skies — not "cosmic", but aware how we would like to eradicate what we can't summate. The crisis is over, I sit & write on an exceptionally smooth & even surface. Words of many lives, in random order yet carefully kept. First you notice how different the words are from hitting the nail with your hammer. But then, how useful compared to hitting it with your hand. What has happened will cause sense to pass through us on our dash toward meaning. Letting the book fall open anywhere, I find myself drawn on. No, this is myself, being drawn on. Shadow & object form one being, reading life, including those who'd tell us how to.

David Bromige

ALLEN FISHER, *Stane* [Place, Book III]

(1977: Aloes Books, London)

A dozen years ago I was hailing the birth of a Poetry of Information—it would grow from lore and data no less than from sensory experience, precisely because data are sensorily experienced. My Olsonian hope has borne less fruit than I portended, but one utter triumph of such a poetics is the ongoing work of Allen Fisher, of which book III appears as *STANE*. This English poet, with a clear musical sense and breadth of what constitutes *interesse*, has a work going on that continues to challenge close reading. It *is* close reading, and what it reads it carries forward, addressing the deepest epistemological problems of literature: the shifting primality of reading before writing. Fisher is not mounting a Poundian suasion, but experiencing a lively compulsion to which he is subject and subjects in turn what he reads — a compulsion to be lyric, just like that traditionally reserved for flowers and fucking. These are not 'found poems' — far from that. Fisher has lost his texts into a discourse in which he feels at last free to speak. Poetry is making one's own. His work excites me by his exacting feel for method.

Robert Kelly

REMARKS ON NARRATIVE: THE EXAMPLE OF ROBERT GLÜCK'S POETRY

Robert Glück, *Family Poems* (1979: Black Star Series, San Francisco)

"There is a story being told about you. . ."
—Marx, cited by J.P. Faye

. . . The stories and poems collected here seem to present themselves to us as a series of developments of narrative possibilities in poetry itself . . . [as a] critique of many recent formalistic tendencies in poetry, par-

Excerpted from Boone's introduction.

ticularly the new trends toward conceptualization, linguistic abstraction and process poetry. . . . What isn't said here might be called a kind of absent present existing only offstage — the metatext that is spoken from the present — while onstage appear conventional anecdotes, such as these narratives of someone's past, of ethnicity and family life. . . . At the end of the "Mangle Story," for instance, we find that through some sleight of hand it is we ourselves who have become the narrator of the story, and through a linguistic ruse the subject of these stories has become only a conveniently transferrable function. And the narrator has become the object of a new narration being told — this time — by ourselves. What the narrator seems to be claiming then is that it is the act of narrating itself that causes the narrative function to slip across the invisible bar of separation — from him to us. . . . [Such] devices constitute a transfer of the subject from a local determination in the speaking narrator to a more profound and generalized function. . . . In a larger sense what the stories of this collection narrate is society itself, and the exchange system of this society as it continues to narrate only death . . . as it tells us the story that continues to constitute it. . . . The poems may in this respect appear as bringing out a strongly judgmental or juridical aspect of this narrative function in a tradition which up to now has not adequately or politically appreciated it.

Bruce Boone

TED GREENWALD, *Native Land*

(1977: Titanic Books, Washington, D.C.)

What is here is here in relation. There too, and then. Continually, then. You want to pay attention to as much as possible. At once. States of affairs give way. This dissolution of relations, in favor of new sets of relations, might later be called the instant. Its measure would be the line. Schematically, the space between the lines is the continuum. Could association ever really be free? There is logic, permitting inclusion of as wide or narrow a range of possibility as you like. Its rules are the unfolding of its form when it's developed. They punch out logic. Their logic makes itself comfortable at speeds up to and including the next guy. You talk I listen. Then we switch. There's light in room, supper on the way. We want to hear what's said, and so we do, again in the head, in relation to what's going down there as to what's next, which we would include also, even insist on, so to get on with the fun of it fresh in mind. Some of the time, not all of the time. That's when something's happening. Between those times you test the limits, weather, unconsciousness, provide for meal times, times together. Desire inevitably opens a hole in the static. There's no telling when you're in the turn how things will turn out, hence no time sense, all presence. There's a generosity in this way of taking things in, leaving them open to change. An assumption of common ground between talk and thought. There's access, out, person to person, by virtue of the open endedness in dealing with voice and a tough minded refusal to consider sequence as circumscribed by any prior formality, or line as pinned down to final value. It's an up.

Kit Robinson

PIECE TOGETHER BROKEN SWEAT/ MILD CONCERN

Ted Greenwald, *Use No Hooks* (1980: Asylum's Press, N.Y.)

There is a relationship between reading and writing that seems unsunderable. To the extent that there is a set of repeating signatures, one learns to recognize as appertaining to something that could be called a Greenwald poem, it has always seemed as likely as not to have developed as a part of an emergent *style*, or voice, or writerly persona, more or less connected to an *actual* person, in New York, with a certain Queens accent, who was to be seen, or not, at certain places around town. Admittedly such recognitions (this, here, is a Greenwald . . . e.g.) arose not only out of some more selfed armature of presentation to the exclusion of familiarities in other aspects of the writing. A somewhat *socialized urbanized 'relaxed'* mode of discourse could have been held up, as epitomizing, as an hypothetical model, and matched with a similar more formal contextual focus: continuities of relationships, friendships, lovers, bars, parties, evenings at home. This sort of identification came with the accrued presence of the writer and his work on the horizon so that, eventually, there seemed to be something that in being called a *Greenwald*, for example, as style, appeared as a realized thing which could conceivably span, comfortably, almost any exigency of *subject* and still reside, undeniably, as a work by this author.

In part the not inconsiderable effect of reading a book like *Use No Hooks* seems due to the way one's expectations of a writer midpoint in his career are destroyed — through, and *as*, the structure of the poems themselves are torn and ripped and pressed and pushed to the edge of organized utterance recognizable as the writer's parameters, — and beyond. The *envelope* is thoroughly reconstituted. Edges are sheared off or repeat like a monitor's rollover. Often the face of the prosody is stripped past the stratum of *consensual artifice*, deeper than the *bones* of the sentence, to a ledge of basal utterance. World is accounted as something that may enter the *field*: a pipe, phone's ring, a hat. What was thought of as what *made for* a Greenwald poem turns out to be both more and less than it seemed. Any convivial perhaps casually expansive mode that seemed to be what could be called the *style* was, after all, it now appears, only a collection of *temporal* approximations tailored for what it seems the work, generally, *then*, had as an *aboutness*. This was not how he had to write, that was what he chose. The force of this book's form, the way it epitomizes, lines up, with the pain and loss, anger, reaction, and hope, the terrible dissolves that it springs from, that it takes up the colors of, impels the reader to a new assessment. Anyone who can so across the board, after twenty years of writing engineer, or, rather, render, such sweeping changes in his writing has to be thought of *differently*. What we thought of as a *Greenwald style* was all wrong, it was something tailored. What remains, what *resides*, a hard edged, tight, unrelenting *way of looking* that emanates from this book, and now, in a sense, more clearly, from the older work, that is the uniqueness.

There are certain things one isn't supposed to say. Even the most exhibitionistic of the late unlamented confessionalists, apart from other more formally debilitating adherences, can now be seen, if anyone cares, to have hewn to certain mores of decorum. The most *searingly bared* revelations in the first person were still clothed in the inclusiveness of the monolithic lyric *I*; by the middle of the century the presentation of literary self was sufficiently bogged down in a morass of convention that it no longer constituted any great sally to say that this *I* was capable, or engaged in, the *most terrible* affliction or infliction. If it wasn't completely worn out as a mode of discourse it was encrusted with as much study as any of the older readily compatible fitting prospects on objects (landscapes, etc.).

The residual tags of disguise, enfeebled necromancy of narration and taste in lyric *thus constituted*, stand out most starkly in the rote fictionalizing reference this kind of writing called up when the sense of a *personal place* could no longer be avoided. There were still certain things one did not say. You didn't name names, at least not the real names. Did Sylvia ever write the word Ted? Even now, in the kind of writing where that subject survives, when one half of a couple mentions the other it is in the context of washing the dishes or babysitting. Some of the constraints on this kind of particularity are self-evident, seeming to have more to do with social binding, decorum in that sense. Similarly, certain accusations or lacerations too clearly labelled are out of bounds. Another major influence in the context is the familiar charying desire to set the writing apart, to push it up to another *realm* by the deletion of various proper nouns and the odd mundane reference.

At this point in time to make the decision to include these sorts of hyperpersonal reference is to imply a critique and realignment of the literary presentation of the self that injects a healthy note into an increasingly tendentious argument. It is an affirmation that that which places writing in a place or *signature* which is some way a *beyond* has little to do with discretion or *attach*able entrances into the basis or source of the work. In twenty years no one will care anyway.

The formal component of this openness seems rooted in an attitude, a non-exclusion taken to its logical conclusion or development, which, as it realizes more and more as *pertaining* to that which is *connected, evidentiary, important, illuminating,* is impelled to present, to *include,* that much more.

Michael Gottlieb

ROBERT GRENIER, *Sentences*

(1978: Whale Cloth Press, Cambridge, Mass.)

The work is unavoidably an object. A production number—five hundred index cards, boxed, one poem per card. Intended to be read in any order (ideally all at once), it denies book format, in which binding would give only one of all possible readings page-by-page. Any sequence is a chance ordering, any poem could come next. The words rise off the page as the mind would like—well-lit, pure, detached—"in eternity." The heavy white paper (field) sets off the IBM Selectric type (thing) as utter contrast in order to dismantle the apparatus of conveyance and release the word and its effect. Yet the work is physically awkward, a mechanical problem, and calls attention to itself as visual format. So the object (box) is a complex pun, a narrative grotesque fixing time in ironic termination of desire, as much of the actual writing puns. The blue Chinese cloth box with ivory clasps might hold the murder weapon or a biological anomaly, while the heavy white paper exists in opposition to physicality itself. The box is both fetish and transparency, and is identical to the work inside.

Sentences is a distillation of six years' close attention to "everything going on all the time." Out of voices heard, bird calls, shape of landscape, bolt from the blue, Kerouac's "void bowl slant," some perceptible shift makes a denotative signal, as bird pistols brain with peculiar stop to all sound. One kind of perception in the taxonomy of this work then shows parallels of language to the world outside. "walking down Washington Avenue" shifts syntactic center in the way that one walking is not in any one place but *in walking*. If "walking" were enough to say this, why "down" to complete it—much less "Washington Avenue," which changes scale entirely (arrives). In many cases, though, the shift is in the panorama implied by the words, rather than in the words meeting panorama head-on and equalling it. "being downstairs / / like being awake" is a moment of truth, but not in the different uses of "being." Each line constructs a diminished narrative set, through memory (outlines hardening). The shift of direct perception losing power to mind specifies its synaesthetic moment in language. Landscape leads from perception through memory to words (nature as creator), but it is not landscape which follows (nature as

Some quotes in this essay from Louis Zukofsky, *Prepositions*, "The Effacement of Philosophy" and "Modern Times."

created not the same). The composite world picture is at the mercy of the word. Revelation is a stylistic conceit. Furthermore, the mind knows this.

Voice invested with power to make real (symbolism) is finally undermined. Any person's voice noted shows desire bending to an unyielding other. Cued by dissonance under scrutiny of arbitrary white, the sum total of the cards exposes the point in the mind where structure collapses into words. Not the work objectified (as a "point of rest"), but language brought to light through the failure of object (a "point of unrest"). The loop is a paradigm for this effect. In

SNOW

snow covers the slopes covers the slopes
snow covers the slopes covers the slopes
snow covers the slopes covers the slopes
snow covers the slopes covers the slopes

the fact of landscape appears and disappears through a kind of phase variation. The 1−2−3−4 pattern becomes a grid to distribute the split phrase. Both parallel to the perception and a voice humming to itself, the poem is first of all the property of mind discovered in seeing the poem on the page.

TWO

around twelve
at 12

"twelve" and "12" are heard differently because perceived differently, not because they are different notations of the same thing. The fact of the poem, then, is the difference in notation and its basis in language apparatus. Originally heard in exterior "materials" (crudely), the interruption of phenomena by the act of writing forces words into actual units of recognition. The question is not assumed in Grenier's work. "saids" might be one word or many. "close close" is an equivalent in language to Wittgenstein's cube. "it's you" extends the moment of the poem into any dialogue. "transference isolates" indicates a romantic landscape, greater than any one man. "searchlight distributes sky light it administers" might be movement or tautology, depending on the resolution inherent in the phrase. A vocabulary of possible experience builds from simple counting, as these "units" enumerate any notation.

The risk is that the absolute intention (number) is confused with the dramatic irony of everyday life (mass). In an instant nature closes in on the work. But *Sentences* does not collapse, because its language is outside of time.

Is that enough? There are no sentences in *Sentences*, like a glass ball nearly impossible to find. The work refuses closure (capital letter, period meaning a "completed thought") in being completely self-contained. It might be the only constitution possible for the republic in which one would want to live. Yet "it changes nothing" to note this. "You could put them (the cards) together, but not now." The story is built from denial of story, of holding back. "But even the nervous tension . . . sensitive to moral weight . . . cannot replace . . . events . . ." The box. "The rapidity with which they move as of themselves . . . compels sequence . . . concentrates action many times . . ." Charlie Chaplin made full-length features out of discrete bits. "A proportion or style . . . mixed with story and with heart-beat . . ." Accessibility doubles (exactly) the problem. "He who . . . is fated to style had at best make as much story of it as he can to be free . . ." The system is fully integrated, organic. *Sentences* locates literary style in the fact of language in American writing. There is certainly much more to be done, starting with—writing in sentences.

Barrett Watten

CARLA HARRYMAN, *Under The Bridge*

(1980: This, Oakland)

Harryman resists stasis, attacks any form of the given. "Creation not reality," she writes in the "Forward" to *Under The Bridge*. Her focus is on will; her own, of course, as the creator of this prose, "I think I made up the future in order to go away, to move elegantly." and the perceived will of others. Her very syntax points to the agency behind effects. For instance, in "Cult Music" she writes, "Fed period music in a boxcar." Another writer might have begun that statement with the words "period music," stressing the nouns. Harryman begins with the verb "fed." So someone is doing this to us. Her "Forward" ends, "The hand walked down the road."

Her emphatic verbs bridge the gap between one seemingly uncon-
nectable noun clause and the next across sometimes incredibly long
sentences as if she found nowhere she cared to pause.

> A self pleasure supermarket puny bridges defy willfully demeans
> articulation but had all the confidence not to be interested in music
> at home or locked out by a big mouth talking in swamps that hinge
> between doting or like propaganda spread two dogs changed posi-
> tion fretful crooked road sauntering up the tangled figure proceed-
> ing naturally in a remote space loaded up with characteristics, a too
> cumbersome visage opens the scroll in mud and lifts up head tum-
> bling into a frame like eels circling the heavens to make themselves
> feel better.—from "Various Devices"

Her sentences seem to proceed, "exhibiting ruthless fancy." They
"could go anywhere, but might not."
Superficially, Harryman and other writers of new prose sometimes
resemble surrealists. But sentences like: "The black tub motors by." or
"Frightening packages of detail surround the house. . . ." or "Smell of
dust in this geometry." sound odd not because they describe impossible
happenings or dream states, but simply because they are unusual for-
mulations. In each of these sentences at least one term feels out of
sync. The nouns "geometry", "detail" and even "tub" are more general
than one would expect. Sporadically, she raises abstraction to a higher
power. It is a defamiliarization technique. "Is this why I'm strange to
you as we practice being home?"
Consciousness suddenly stands back from a thought, regards it
from outside. "I am not an innocent: I was only pretending to be con-
temptuous of the mountains." Sentence turns against previous or even,
in the case above, hypothetical sentence. 'Characters' appear briefly to
make statements contradicted by the 'narrator.' Mom is "wrong" in "In
Front" and "One can't say, 'But they don't live in water,' without being
an ass." So one must be wary. You can't believe everything you read.
Harryman's writing presents both the will to act and the possibility of
error. Reading Under The Bridge one feels provoked and energized. "I
could have been in a more simple schoolyard."

Rae Armantrout

SELF WRITING / *I (lucky thought)*

> Private life asserts itself unduly, hectically, vampire-like, trying compulsively, because it really no longer exists, to prove it is alive.— Theodor Adorno, *Minima Moralia*. In reality the ego is like the clown in the circus, who is always putting in his oar to make the audience think that whatever happens is his doing.—Freud to Jung, *The Freud/Jung Letters*. To accept subjectivity as it exists today, or better, as it does not exist today, is implicitly to accept the social order that mutilates it. The point, however, is not merely to reject subjectivity in the name of science or affirm it in the name of poetry. . . .—Russell Jacoby, *Social Amnesia*.

I, I, *I*, I I, I, *I*, I. *Suppose I* don't exist, *fuck individualism, by myself, 'I'*. I don't make up the world, I'm not *self-sufficient*, O.K., not master in my own house. *Will (the verb I activate)* — not free, not responsible, not consistent, don't blame me.

No need to expose *crabbed secrets of the psyche . . . to the well organized and systematic scrutiny of some poetic form or strategy*. They're always already exposed to language, pretty well organized & systematic, which even creates them, *always first for the context —* they're worded secrets, coded: *Before you get the chance to cut and direct and reflect and get yourself in control of the flow or at least the flowering of the important parts* — I don't act; I'm 'acted' by : *things which eat up intentions, things which are always behind the one who is labelling.* . . . My unveiling (call it the demystification function of writing) places me in a system, that code, *continuous logic of structures — institutions —* of which I'm *the faintest idea, small changes*. A structuralist view, then, as a critique. *It had been written by me. Only not by me.* It had written me.

I had an invincible desire to clutch language itself through my most recent values. But I'm a dictionary, language castrates me. Individual experience is primary?, that's a myth, especially now, administered capitalism, *forces of control over . . . the resolutions we initiated,* over the revolutions, I don't like psychology, *environmental custody*, social phenomena are there in the background, *or the words coming through, and . . . Precisely at that point: vanish.*

I just know how to work myself, or what I think's myself when it's really writing *rooting around in the gym of language*. Free play of

Italicized portions are from Michael Lally's work; this essay, in part, a part of my continuing response.

meaning in writing overshadows and disperses me, it undermines my raps' autonomy, *bio style,* just like unconscious desire undermines an ego, orphans me, disrupts a narcissistic dream of me-present-to-me, me & you *(the fusion of classified information with a body). THE APPA-RATUS OF THE OTHERNESS FAILS or UNIFICATION. How Many Times Must I Marry Myself. the book opened like a vagina.* But remember: 'I'm an effect, of language, breaking up the scene at the mirror — *(I was captivated with this vision . . . this is me I see! . . . I dissolved into it)* — differences, separation, absence, meaning, all that. *All part of the motion away from our mothers. The gesture completed when we became the bigger boys and did some of the beating.* I could really identify with all those structures they put in my head to get out of our heads what was there first. When I joined the system, *the men made me one of them* but to do that they had to make me one a single solitary one to begin with. *NOTHING TO DO BUT LIE HERE AND COME APART. I knew it wasn't really my imagination that was making this scene it was the cops,* the Law, who controls who, who even distributes the name 'who' & who 'me'? and why why? *We taught him our standards, which weren't ours.* Secondhand — *you know the rules* — . . . *I hate machines and systems . . . but I got to admit I'm enjoying the respite.*

Apprenticeship of language = alienation for me, *each piece a solemn dedication to the whole* — etc. — *speech matrix / flow. Is the way we feel normal* [& stress how we're social & how social we are; socialized, not socialists. We're LIKE A SPEECH, social life speaks right through us] *if we normally feel this way,* made normal — with fixed destination, exclusive assignments, *flattened out.* Even the atmosphere the textures we grope around in are a system now not just pinpricks of the things you notice yourself. *The music then was a radio in the night, now it's a system.*

When I hear all this talk about systems, I want to say: I don't take dictation. Conventions have limits, and there're dangers in being complacent or rhapsodic about them. *The crudeness of socialized instructions* needs to let through, between the cracks, individual experience, flower, *the confusion of heads to unfold.* How self-contained & closed-off is this 'order of language' or 'Law of Culture'? What's in it that guarantees our desire, *firsthand,* to *put together truth,* or ethics, or confidence (unless they're just supposed to be byproducts of 'if all goes well' or 'I'm like everyone else' or 'genital normalization' or 'that's taboo, decadent, counter-revolutionary, etc.', etc.), etc.

If language is primary and everything we felt was central is really prefab & de-centered, then how does individual experience fit in, how can it loosen up these structures & punch through some barriers : these are some questions : If systems are determining, then is poetry just 'showing language at work' with language now fashionably defined as a system that 'works'? *They're always about themselves / (words) driving people away* . . . Or are private worlds upfront & if you say they're 'constituted by language,' O.K., *those who come apart first fill up the words later*, but language isn't some frozen merchandise. *I'm a writer,* IT'S WRITING, I'm producing it, not just to show its obstacles *(I'm a generation of obstacles)* but to show them up, disassemble the fixed programs, not just be marched along by them. *One dude plays blues harp and makes up lyrics to go with action as the arrests continue.* . . .

And all of our selves refusing to be subordinated to the selves most widely recognized, accepted. . . . To want *a poetry that has room for me, knots & shields, my tunnels and locked doors.* More than a byproduct of 'the law of one and all,' it starts with some me, *our self importance, collisions with speech, fragmented signature,* then plugs in but only afterward, when I write, read it, me, then people can share it. Otherwise it's just the conventions of the culture apparatus make us all this way then get us to 'create' its way & feed us the need to make it, succeed. Remember when 'the system' had obvious negative overtones? Is this rage for codes & systems & structuralism in the 70's more than a tidying-up of our regret & frustrated longing for getting beyond it? *And the people who know see through the collage we constructed to show them we weren't what they said we would always be but were pieces of all the things we had loved to see others make lives from.* . . .

Self-consciousness is being programmed out of existence—*it's all so subjective, as they say*—so, we're more insistent on it? *And what other way can we see the world except as extensions of who we are or would like to be* . . . *Things meant or did not exist,* they seemed to have to mean something beforehand, firsthand, *I mean me, in my solipsistic universe,* or writing didn't make them mean — HERE I AM; but this cant mean as much in words as it did in experience. If I record my raps, *sometimes appearances,* more like a transcript of heart on sleeve, *speak louder than words.* Voice — breathless throw made, personalizing, into a verse line, or a rush, a way of lacquering associations for you with a personal speech and asides and memorabilia, *the screens of our dreams' imaginations,* not just composing with them more freely but back to putting a high note in the bar where my self is. Still, stressing ME might at least give writing a whiff of what defines 'us' struggling for autonomy (whether it's blacks, feminists, bisexuals, street queens, working class renegades, or what) and in those struggles highlighting the person may (helpfully or unreflectively) be *just sunk in the language of defense* — against what's deformed & pre-formed about what's outside (all the social, the norms). *We have our codes too, let's use them to interpret our experience in ways they'll have to stretch to understand.*

Now, some (usually white heterosexual American professional-class male) writers write about 'the death of the author' or 'the de-centered self' or how 'a system of signifying practices constitutes the subject as a precipitate of unconscious discourse inscribed in response to the basic lack produced as the determinative network of oedipal triangulation supercedes the imaginary identifications of the ego,' etc. *They weren't telling their stories.* Well maybe their chance to go beyond the self & give writing freer play is like class privilege — an elaborated code. Stressing a ME filters & squeezes what the writing does — it's a restricted code, *language that is accessible to the people I come from,* but it allows me to speak to who 'I' need to speak to, including 'me': *to decrease that chasm of semantics.*

The necessary extension. Not to be privatized in a single self because I didn't see how privatized even my attempts to make the self infinitely expansive might seem to others less hounded by *my need to be in everyone,* to publicize a private mythology in order to share it, *thinking I'm still in the movies, it's an outside telephone booth.* To make me universal *(I come out with myself & find everyone),* not symbolically as a language so much as a pretty irreducible concrete thing, body, that can be anyone everyone displaced disguised — persona — *mistaken for black, for gay, for straight, for older, for younger for bigger for better for richer for poorer for stupider for smarter for somebody else, . . . I never talked about making distinctions. He was him. I am 2 of us . . . spending much of my energy identifying with all kinds of people I wasn't. . . .*

Shifters. To shift all around a lot, but a little in a vacuum, can never fully accept that the firm ground for any pirouettes in writing is *the language proves itself.* And if LANGUAGE IS WRITING, it's writing writ large not just *this is about me now.* In fact, there are no immediate first hand things in writing — not 'remembrance of my life' & not 'my eye ball view'. Everything's mediated, that is, it's WRITTEN — *this this this.* There's a whole complicated 'transformational process' separating my 'private materials' from any publicity, since reading is social. Peril to ignore this. It's writing as the whole mediation, not *distracted by some shit or sex or need to be me and say it.* That drawback is always feeling the meaning (the sharing) has to pass directly through that filter of 'I' — an identification, an interpretation, a star system, *making the decisions for everybody, the audience was what he was fucking. Property is an extension of the self, if it's time and space that's mine forever. I must become less imperative.*

Poets primary interest is not always Language more or less collec-tively, true, but where we begin is *a simple love* & growing understand-ing *of language's hidden orders. VALUES IN THE DENIAL OF OUR-SELVES.* For even to get an exemplary grip on my selves I have to see how society & language set up a context which produces the pos-sibilities & limits the meanings I can create, and you too. I'm in eclipse. *I guess it's you.* I DON'T EXIST YET. *It was a temporary victory, but what victory isn't temporary, huh?*

Bruce Andrews

DOUG LANG, *Magic Fire Chevrolet*

(1979: Titanic Books, Washington, D.C.)

A collection in roughly two parts. The first, larger section, of "prose poetry". – Material: sentences sometimes developing into some overall structure (narrative, thematic, imaged), but more often not coalescing into any kind of resumable unit. – Lots of lists, itineraries, names. Facts in the red wheelbarrow; additive work. Lang's work here seems par-ticularly resistant to paragraphs (i.e. paragraphical history; the para-graph as teleological organization). There's no chronology implicit in "the facts". Things do accumulate (resonance), but dont line up into any kind of argument. – . . . tension is between the frequent naming (labelling) of particulars & the lack of a parcel to lug all the labels around in. (punch-line, summary.). – The strong emotional tone of much of MFC works toward one's expectation of a summation which never in fact happens . . . A second section of MFC takes a more con-crete approach to the problem of organization. Press type & typewriter script are used to form words, phonetic units & sometimes purely visual formations. The press type is often broken or crumbled to underline its texture, print is obliterated by successive layers of print typed or placed directly over it. A kind of layered type-field results, through which the alphabet achieves a physical density – (presence), (materiality of the page) – physical to the point where its letters can be broken, crumbled; splattered like paint. In a piece like "Poem for Mary" e.g., though there is nothing (except for the "so" in the lower righthand corner) pronounce-able, the large press type letters seem to demand vocalization – (child-hood association with alphabet blocks?) – These later pieces point up the problem with a term like "abstraction". For these pieces are on one level "abstract": the way the letters of the alphabet are treated as categories; the lack of reference to everyday, "concrete" language; the move toward (& I dont mean this in a pretentious way) metalanguage. But in another, & perhaps more dramatic, sense the physicality of these works argues against any abstraction "conceived apart from (the) concrete realities, specific objects, or actual instances" of the works themselves. (Random House Dictionary) . . . in short, continually interesting, non-pigeonholable work. MFC is something only Lang could have written. In fact, he did.

P. Inman

ENCYCLOPEDIA / *the world we will know*

Words first — *highly merely 'words / (cor)rect (al)ly eva(l/c)uated.* Yet, key question, how *connected with the facts for which / / properly they stand.?*

REPRESENTATION — *The story called record* — official record — *restricts by accidents of its data.* It restricts by the very logic of *the old system of production,* system of reproduction, monitoring: comes across as alienating replication which devalues the work of writing. [Repression.] To split off desire or libidinal energy or whatchamacallit from such work — scrub off words, let preconstituted world of referents shine through.

Encyclopedia: Epistemology: arrange terms in alphabetical ('arbitrary') order so that use, for units of information, leans upon an accepted outside context. This conventionally fills the gap between signifieds (mental concepts) & references — relay between 'encyclopedia & the whole world' (pretension of the former toward the latter — 'comprehensiveness', 'fullness'; just like any representational text).

POSITIVISM: this imagined closure between concept & referred-to-thing-in-the-external-world. The rules for processing & combining data into familiar patterns swamp the words' reality, as if we could maintain a purity of ideas & information against the unfortunate (or disregardable) tribulations of their material inscription. Fixed concepts; lack of

The above constitutes in part a response to Tom Mandel's impressive first book, *EncY* (1978: Tuumba Press, Berkeley) from which the italicized portions are taken.

awareness of the provisional & reflexive character of knowledge; its practices independent of the knower (no one seems to need to 'do' the understanding). Yet understanding (reading is an analogue) remains an active, material process (not naturally given, deductive, or disembodied). Knowledge is subjective intervention, not its stylish banishment.

FETISHISM occludes this fact & this gap. History lesson embedded in apparent choicelessness [fatedness, mystification, mythification] of encyclopedic choices: CAPITAL expands & weaves reality around its quantifiable needs, becomes the criteria for use — is key: *our key / expanded / our key become useful / deployed become different*, becomes the stage set for meaning (i.e., DIFFERENCE — e.g., phonemics vs. phonetics).

Words then seem to be identified with their referents, NOT with their role in a framework of human conventions & NOT in a way that acknowledges their physical manifestation — world reified / sign disappears. Individual usage or creativity in language becomes a frill of interpersonal relations & not the construction & revision of the norms themselves. Meaning would become a mere spin-off from a taken-for-granted external reality.

Yet ~ Writing can articulate, brokenly, a world requiring our full intervention to be understood — i.e., cannot SOCIALIZE us. So, a heightened stress on individual usage — to break through the fetish, the tyranny of the unmediated external itself [example: the 'optical'], where we feel effortlessly & conveniently 'in touch' without first having to bring our full humanity to bear on forming connections with the world, an 'easier' & more acquiescent ("glossed out") naturalism.

So, one alternative is a fuller insertion of INDIVIDUAL PRACTICE into the (writing) process by which these conventions are otherwise continuously reproduced through acquiescence in socialization. . . . An over-all non-representational ordering of matter — LANGUAGE / MATERIAL — as architecture of lexical associations & leaks, not 'tool'.

Do this by furnishing, in a self-conscious way, the *account not* [the] *object*. MEDIATION: *light of controversy* — Light (signification) comes through 'dialectic' / practice, not just formal patternings & not pretense of 'direct reflection'. The sign; not the fetish of reference, which would be stapled to the text's compelling absences to offer illusory compensation, alienating us further (the myth of a self-standing reality: *Every satisfaction of it is debt.*) — *the supplementary cured or dared.*

For a true fit, we require mediation, an account (to answer 'Why?' questions contextually) — *plan matters to be / appropriate*. Otherwise world just happens, w/out enough self-reflection & becomes taken-for-granted regard for use (splint them as they lay, etc.). Usage can penetrate the whole — if not it's defined as *practicability*, what fits a paradigm; comprehension — *the attempt to read opinion* by complacent reliance on system $\sim$ nuancing, ornamenting the standards derived from it.

MAIN OPPOSITION: between acceptance of rules (in this case, of composition, of positivist inquiry, of discourse) OR stress on individual choices & disruptions & deviations (flows) & perspectives to the point where signs appear recognizably conventional. Thus: *The whole standard undoubtedly has been raised not to be nuanced, but made use of.* Fetish can be partially undone, seen to be constructed, *now acts as function.* Reflexively & self-reflexively. Offer access to the procedures through which structure is articulated. . . . *throughout careful by means / adapted to readers* & to the way mediating attention intervenes as creator of meaning & not the untying of packages popping off a semantic assembly-line.

I'm interested in composition issues. *Laments of unrest . . . and not constituting disorder. . . . The convenience in arrangement* [once released, 'convenient' = 'use'] *conveys in such detail point of execution . . .* $\sim$ there need be no surface: the arrangement natural to the actual workings of an awareness, not ornamental veneer or added surface [veneer analogous to 'character structure'/psychology], but constant writing action. A disturbance IN the vista: *In the whole architecture was a / flak.* So, focus on the particular, *distinct within units.* Gather omissions or *revealed omission* — a group of gaps, rather than a series of relay points: the pages' blackhole : density→disappearance. As if the choices stretch us between the supercharged disjunct plane or Uniformity / Equivalence / Exchange — *dizzy ambitious particular, or uniform.*

So. *most with the disturbance = so many lapse of time = Preserved portions. — or marred remains larger.* Physical GESTURE regains its prominence — *salient hands up : hands into notability.* Lapse = intermittent = comes in & out of focus = comes in & out of existence [stage does not remain after actors exit —] for the intermittent spectator SPECULATES, works through, thereby FASHIONS the work, not as step-ladder but mark of, stain of, her attention. *Periodical the constructive ideal, all bookish dust dribble and sputter.* Not pre-constituted according to comprehensive, reflecting, 'outside' plan (*EncY* . . .) but to offer periodic experience of writer in role of reader/understanding faced with code or system or convention. Text gives way to broken utterance, almost stutter but disorient still more:

> Control the convention then perpetrate the tratence
> then perpede furred   to any poor hil hop for mac
> hifj outer quarters crys formference
> in Afs co ad b Eu va i   porc
> Varzo ca-pr-ici-ous

CONVENTION GETS UNRAVELLED: *decreased authority perhaps carried to extreme leng . . . too graphic, more exceptions — use.* Deviations, by breaking out, do more than charge & discharge energy, however voluptuously — scramble codes, DISORIENT language. (Constant rupture constant improvisation for readers, producing flows rather than a determinate picture of 'a whole'). They stretch the boundaries of that whole, of human use, of what can be written / felt — are praxis. *Losing or dividing is the treatment.* Also, exceptions light up system boundaries, the limits that have historically been imposed upon use. (*more exceptions . . . / as consult the glaringly outside the public / . . . settled / conventions*).

To expand use, to open up the world for us. *No question of the hasty vehicle's progress* — the unseemly rush from sign to a referent which would 'shadow' that sign, or erase it, or instrumentalize it. *no longer represent* : but only experience thrown back upon itself : *be grasped, skein be created / / and crushing units to new units / / already preferred / / a case of itself / / thought unquestioned / / forefoot & aft, aware.* Thought is questioned.

Bruce Andrews

ANATOMY OF SELF

Bernadette Mayer, *Eruditio ex Memoria* (1977: Angel Hair Books, N.Y.)

Memory, history, personal history, autobiography, metaphysical autobiography, *Eruditio ex Memoria* is all of these. Yet this book projects a memory not of the self, but of the self as defined by the knowledge which makes up the self, which perceives the world in which the self lives. And in this sense Bernadette Mayer's new work is a cosmology, an encyclopedia, an anatomy, which as a genre is related to Menippean or Varronian verse satire, from the Greek cynic Menippus and the Roman satirist Varro, both now lost. The anatomy has continued in Lucian, Petronius, Apuleius, Rabelais, Voltaire, Swift, Rousseau, Peacock, and in our own century, Aldous Huxley, Wyndham Lewis, Djuna Barnes, and most recently, in *Seeking Air* by Barbara Guest. Unlike the picaresque—which is a satire of society, of its structures—the anatomy is a satire built up through a presentation of a vision "of the world in terms of a single intellectual pattern." Northrop Frye continues (in *Anatomy of Criticism*), "The intellectual structure built up from the story makes for violent dislocations in the customary logic of narrative, though the appearance of carelessness that results reflects only the carelessness of the reader or his tendency to judge by a novel-centered conception of fiction." The shortest form of the anatomy is the dialogue, but there is a strong tendency toward a display of erudition, of encyclopedic knowledge, of complications, catalogues and lists (see Burton's *Anatomy of Melancholy*, *Tristram Shandy*, Flaubert's *Bouvard et Pecuchet*, Norman Douglas' *South Wind*, and portions of *Moby Dick*).

Does Mayer know anatomies? Perhaps not. The impulse here seems to come as much from her obsession with memory, from a compulsion towards autobiography that is related to the confession such as Saint Augustine's. But for Mayer memory is never an end in itself. It is not memory past that most interests her, but memory continuing, repeating, memory in the present made *new* through language in Pound's sense. Mayer's art is not a seeking for what *was* but what *was is*, and how what *is* was made by that past. Mayer's memory is not nostalgic— as in Proust—but is a past that makes the new, makes *for* the new: an ending that is a beginning ("Each end is a beginning"). She seeks not for old structures, not for a recreation but for a decreation: "I put these words on paper because they were once written by me, no, I too yearn for a world without meaning." As she previously wrote in her novel *Memory*, "A whole new language is a temptation."

But Mayer's world, the world she discovers, is not without meaning. The past decreated gives rise to a new created, a recreated world. As with Adam, Mayer calls into meaning by naming, by naming a past. Through memory's order "Hemispheres become loose in the country, there are new forms."

Is this different from a Surrealist allowing the subconscious to create new structures, using dream images as the basis for a new reality? Yes.

Mayer's past is not a dream, not archetypal, not mythical, but a socially lived experience. These are school notes, a pre-existent *text* rewritten (?) or almost intact, a life wrenched out of chronological context not by chance but by fact, a life perhaps not *experienced* as discontinuous but was (and because was can only be *is* in memory) *is* in fact.

No coy discontinuity is this, no clever disassociations. Actually there is an attempt in *Eruditio* at lucidness, to see through the veil of *experience* to a reality of flux, of life, of duration. And in this there is a basic recognition of the ineffectuality, of the destructiveness of the written word as opposed to spoken *language* (re Derrida). "There's no use writing down Greek words if no one is going to know what I'm saying." Mayer is always after language, then, after the reality that is language. *Eruditio* is a search for that reality not as written word but as language, which as a thought process *is* the thing itself. Saying is thinking is perceiving is knowing. In fact, although this work may often seem ineffable, there is throughout a drive for an absolute clarity of language: "Add up a column of numbers, it comes to William Carlos Williams."

All of which brings us back to the genre of anatomy, which comes from the Greek *anatomé*, a cutting up, an analysis or minute examination, to to show or examine the position, structure and relation of the parts. That is what this book is to me; it is an attempt to explain, to demonstrate, to show how Mayer has come to know whatever it is she has come to know. And in that sense, this book is a sharing, a removal of the veil, an admission, an apology, a true confession.

Moreover, in that it is itself a sign, an image, an emblem of language which stands for Mayer and the world she has *re*created, an emblem like the red letter Hester Prynne wears. *Eruditio ex Memoria* ends with such an image: "In a painting I am a Chinese woman turning away from a bowl of fruit." Is this an Eve with a second chance, this time redeeming by giving up the knowledge, by releasing it? To pin the image down that way is to miss the point, is to turn back to the fruit and eat it. It is nothing more than itself, a Chinese woman turning away from a bowl of fruit, "its own sure image."

Douglas Messerli

NICE [on David Melnick]

Words might be shields—heraldic, protective—or, reading Zukofsky, Ashbery, Duncan with a sephardic eye, the 'pure light' of reference might pass thru a 2-way mirror—word being itself is no less a concealment (seal meant), postures one holds walking 'in public'—a metaphor, then, in *Eclogs*, hustler cruising Champs-Elysées, suppresses signifieds, posits mind's life in body's locus, 'classic' because articulate, thru wch comes the *trans*fer, shock of self—writ against the grain, social fact of Berkeley, the 60s, Levertov's literalism, nearness of parents, reactionary imagination of *Occident*—a work in opposition & the closet—then silence—stasis is the most natural state—only turmoil (change in one's social order) pushes us thru the entropics—study of "modern poets' views of ole Will" takes years, yields one chapter & that on LZ, *ought*, beyond wch that life is abandoned—poetry a scene, community a mystic writing pad one opts in or out of: ink flows—new beginning begins *Pcoet*, 1972, whose words are neither speech nor writing, but each within each (what has befallen anyone in the 15 centuries since Eusebius Hieronymus first stoppd reading aloud—any increase in locomotive speed blurs landscape until *that* becomes focus)—only a kabalist traind in math (U. Chicago) cld have proceeded thus, poetry precedes the language, *makes it*, & here is that sphere of light held high, dodecahedron (how see what is there without substance? if you filmd light, as from a projector in an otherwise dark room, *Rameau's Nephew*, it wld on your print have shape, but with the peculiar luminosity of animation: photon spray), thru wch all meaning, if it is to move (*into* terms as *onto* film), must pass—beyond syntax, a city's wall preventing penetration in both directions—beyond words, wch ruse referents, posing a mock transcendentalism thru wch Capital itself has manifested natural as a sunrise (Lord's guslars did not even know what the 'word' was)—language writing language writing—Moebius amulet—again after wch the necessary silence, that norm, broken only by a few performance pieces for multiple voice on themes specific in their eroticism—for no scene's benefit nor niche in artificed hierarchy of writing, but friends (*frenz*)—for this moment (a social fact) to have *solvd* writing

Ron Silliman

thoeisu

thoiea

akcorn woi cirtus locqvump

icgja

cvmwoflux

epaosieusl

~~cirtus locquvmp~~

a nex macheisoa

(p. 1, from *Pcoet*, G.A.W.K., San Francisco)

VOICES-OFF: MENGHAM and WILKINSON

. . . I want here to contrast the projects undertaken by Mengham and Wilkinson with a continental mode which long since turned its back on the unadventurous preoccupations of our own orthodoxies. Poets such as Paul Celan and Edmond Jabés have developed a mode of writing which one might term 'dialectical lyric', a mode introduced to this country by Anthony Barnett in *Blood Flow* (1975) and *Fear and Mis-adventure* (1977). The first movement of dialectic is negation; a thesis generates its own antithesis and thus negates itself. Sartre argued that all knowledge is dialectical to the extent that the person who knows, knows that he is *not* the object of his knowledge; the subject discovers the world as his antithesis and himself as a lack (as negativity). Dialecti-

Excerpted from David Trotter's article on Rod Mengham and John Wilkinson in *Twisted Wrist* 4 (Maidstone, Kent, England).

cal lyric stages the drama of the 'advertising mind', in Shelley's phrase,
the mind turned toward a 'vastness' which reveals it to itself as a lack:
disenfranchised, internally riven. Its characteristic form might be de-
scribed as a militant slightness:

> The small verse
> breaches
> because of the enclosure,
> but, not the sense.   (Barnett, *Fear and Misadventure*, p.34)

Every word uttered by the lyric voice sets a limit, announces the in-
ability of that voice to say all there is to say; it is this limit which reso-
nates, giving full 'sense' to insufficiency. The lyric voice, dialectically
opposed to the unsayable, discovers itself as a lack. . . .

The texts of Mengham and Wilkinson, on the other hand, are not
predicated upon any such absenting movement (the generation of an-
tithesis *out of* thesis) but rather upon the multiple infliction of one the-
sis on another, *different* thesis. Indeed, the difference between theses
can no longer be regarded as an alienation, and then healed or sup-
pressed by an act of inclusion (Reason, Hegel said, is mind which
knows itself to be all reality); rather, it must be affirmed. Silences occur,
but only as they are produced by the operation of one thesis on an-
other; not as motive-forces. We have entered a Nietzschean world
where forces don't enter into relation with opposites they themselves
have generated, but with other forces. . . . In the cognitive realm,
there 'is *only* a perspective seeing, *only* a perspective "knowing"; and
the *more* affects we allow to speak about one thing, the *more* eyes,
different eyes, we can use to observe one thing, the more complete will
our "concept" of this thing, our "objectivity", be. But to eliminate the
will altogether, to suspend each and every affect, supposing we were
capable of this — what would that mean but to *castrate* the intellect?'
(*Genealogy of Morals*). The merit of Mengham and Wilkinson is that
they allow *more* affects to speak, *more* eyes to observe, and so declare
our boredom with the castrated text presented by the weaker versions
of the dialectical lyric, the text whose entire business is not to deliver.

The effacing of origins in modern literary theory and practice (in-
cluding dialectical lyric) has forbidden us to ask the Nietzschean ques-
tion Who is speaking here? Traditional lyric forms, on the other hand,
have raised the question in order to answer it without delay, to erase a
potentially troublesome uncertainty. The work of Mengham and Wil-
kinson has restored the question *as a question* : neither preempted nor
resolved. Curiosity as to who is speaking in these texts seems to me

central to the pleasure we take in them. There is for example an occasional well-spokenness in Wilkinson's writing, a sumptuous intonation, a provocative snobbism which might either be residual or the revenge taken by the demotic text on itself; which must be read as the operation of one 'will' on another. Having unsqueamishly lifted the stone of totemic Absence, both Wilkinson and Mengham seem to gaze at the life beneath with a sometimes paranoid inscrutability; but we are no longer dealing with the reserve of miniature and can hardly ignore the questions they pose.

David Trotter

I can't predict my accents. Sweeping up the short vowel, it is borrowed from his cool page. Any phrase, it dives out, you'll try to divine it in our best light. Mouthings can so thinly vibrate, and hence I know I haven't been reconstructed — just for a while all parts of speech in assent, through pull of the phantom lode.

—from *Prior to Passage*, John Wilkinson

. . . Here to stay you know that the glum depart
hurrying down the noisy path partitive. In time to
landing in order to 'cope' she ponders her broth
useless beneath the lid feature the pensive flesh as as
far the shield chattering with blows of sliding.
That says what is commonly a sponge
a vanishing interest in this dilapidation of the grammar
instead of we all uncover the infested stump. Languid hammer
head down. . . .

—from *Glossy Matter*, Rod Mengham

THE MONOLOGICAL MIRROR

The No One, *Unwritten* (1979: The Press, El Gizeh; gratis)

This book addresses the sensuous and invisible difference of mythos and logos, sustaining the motion away from symmetry and away from the spiral. A stationary motion in which the "faring-well" does not entail the whirlpool of arrival.

Symmetry and spiral are the two inherited forms of the mirror: in the first, an object is re-flected into its image; in the second, the object is de-flected into its analogon. If symmetry freezes the mirror into a similarity of objects, and if the spiral (the baroque form of symmetry) is the oscillation of the mirror between two dissimilar objects, then neither can be said to attain the condition of the monological mirror.

The activity of the monological mirror defeats the duplicity of both pleonasm and tautology as pleonasm, while setting forth, through tautology as predication, the hypostasis of transcendence (red *is* red, where the predicate red, however, *is not* red).

The metaphorical value of the etymon in the predicated noun (the red) inaugurates the difference burgeoning out of the verb of predication (is is not).

The presence of predication in tautology articulates the monological mirror which, by transcending the inclusive devices of symmetry (image) and spiral (analogon), constitutes the possible world of exclusion. While this mirror negates the double, it admits the double as negation and therefore as cruelty (Artaud). Cruelty, then, is naming performed in the absence of a name. This naming is the *going where we already are* (Heidegger), which cannot be the competential place of the name but rather the event of the absent name (baptism as an act of exclusion).

The presence of naming and the absence of name yields the notion of a book which cannot be written but only read by implication. The book-written is, in fact, the doubling-over of decrepit rhetorical figures (it refers back to the content of persuasion); the book-read-by-implication is the unearthing of the content of exclusion through the very same figures.

If rhetoric is the turning of language into the figures of language, then cruelty is the turning of its figures back into language. Aposiopesis, for instance, would cease to be the name of a willful surrender to reticence and become the arrowing source of the monologue.

Luigi Ballerini and Richard Milazzo

READING OLSON

The sense of form from which the *Maximus* grows is not rational but post-rational. The *field* of the poem includes not only the data which can be comprehended by humanistic rationalism but also all that humanistic rationalism excludes as irrational, random, or subjective. . . . Olson, with his obedience to all phenomena, recognizes a possibility for order which derives simply from the contiguity of phenomena. "One wants phenomenology in place," Olson writes, "in order that event may re-arise." The freshness of space must be allowed to assert itself so it can reveal its *own* form. . . . The poems of Pound and Eliot, as Olson understands them, are the last desperate attempts of cultivated men to insure cultural order in which creation might continue to compete successfully with action. . . . The *Cantos*, despite their epic intent, are essentially lyric. They create an order—or attempt to— by arranging the artifacts of culture, both western and eastern, according to a private vision of their transcendant coherence. . . .

For too long language has remained so utterly within the bounds of representational discourse, even for the poets themselves, that the occluded forms that rest *below* the written language have failed to emerge. Consequently, the various pure languages of poetry which have appeared are, despite the power we feel in them, essentially only counter-discourse, negations, rather than languages inside of which life can be conducted. Olson proposes to re-combine the three terms of language [space, fact, stance] in a single act of writing, commentary, and revelation.

In his concern for quantitative measure, Olson is attempting to purify the language of the abstract pollutants which have been allowed to creep into it. Before poetry can be written language must be returned to itself. In quantitative measure, the duration of a syllable is an inher-

Excerpted from *Charles Olson's Maximus* (1980: University of Illinois Press, Urbana).

ent factor. Olson objects, for example, that Milton's disregard for syl-
labic quantity results in what might be called rhythmic sentimentality.
The "humanistic" elements in Milton's verse, those which are chosen,
by an act of abstract will, rather than given, the stress patterns of syn-
tax, as opposed to syllables, are allowed weight in the determination of
verse which they can maintain only if they draw authority from some
abstract source (attaching the "emotion to the idea," whether the idea
be Christian dogma, Latinate syntax, or iambic pentameter) outside the
proper concerns of the verse itself. . . . [Similarly,] in the periodic sen-
tence, the words and syllables as loci of meanings are subordinated to
an abstract structure which reduces its burden, the nouns and their ac-
tions, to mere weightless pointers which have no inherent force; ob-
jects move not by their own force but by the abstract drama of the
sentence.

The anecdotes which occur paratactically in Maximus have their
effect on the reader who, in turn, should not expect to find a hierarchy
of subordinated actions. Rather than integrating categorically or ac-
cording to chains of cause and effect, one discovers on-going associa-
tions, subject-puns, images answering to images, one moving to the
next in terms which are purely local to them. Unlike stream of con-
sciousness, however, which is passive, parataxis is active, attempting
to bring the poem to an immediate coherence by developing concrete
associations on multiple planes. . . . Olson speaks of "a syntax of ap-
position", which can be opposed to a syntax of subordination. The or-
der that emerges is analogous to the order of a map rather than the
order of a scientific law or a periodic sentence, both of which tear ob-
jects from their contexts, rearrange them, and subordinate them to a
controlling principle or, as Olson would say, logos. . . . Olson never
intends to express any thing; he insists that the poem must enact the
reality which is its content.

Maximus is a collage of fragments, a recognition that every per-
son's life is a collage of fragments, in the process of coalescing toward
the whole, where person and world are one. It does not move linearly
along a single thread of argument but through a matrix of complex
associations, juxtapositions, dialectic contradictions, puns, melodic re-
lationships, and complementary rhythms. . . . The unity of the Maxi-
mus is perhaps best compared to the unity of a zoological species: it is
an unchanging form that perpetually reconstructs itself in useful and
unexpected ways.

Don Byrd

MICHAEL PALMER: A LANGUAGE OF LANGUAGE

Michael Palmer writes a splendid poetry of displacement, of shifts and nomadic drifts of text through zones of page. The operative semantic is copulative, a linking (purely syntagmatically) of isolated units still preserving their molecular independency. He writes a double assault: on page per se and on the vector of reference. There is no place in his work because there largely is no referent incanted. Reference is rendered intransitive and instigates the arbitrary flow of linguistic signs. Referrals without the finality of reference, ectoskeletal structures carrying deliberately interior deformations. Frequently logic is placed in contest with a syntax resulting in the gravity of utterance being withheld. Sentences register as syntagms, surface activities of syntax, no entity-terminals but simply the betweenness of a trace, word motions rather than conveyed ideations. Logical relation is violently displaced by verbal relation and spacing, so that space becomes the abyss causality falls into. And this space in Palmer is less projective (a breath withheld) than the violated function of the sign: the articulation of displacement. Space becomes the agonistic surface, the zone where words displace themselves. Palmer's consummate craft is the superb orchestration of these displacements: to activate fissures, architecturally tensified, and phrases that remain stiff in a precision of placement as all meaning slides. Viewed temporally this all amounts to a consecutivity minus a consequentiality. In Palmer's poems there is, deliberately, no purpose. This leads to local composition, an investigation of grammatological space per se, of space as deferral, of placement and occurrence as difference. Constant, consecutive invention on the plane of the signifier.

The process of reading becomes a muscular activity of the mind operating in tension through disjunctions, aborted vectors, non-purposive contexts. Everything happens on the level of the signifier: semic discharge across a surface and the surface is that discharge. Page/space an utterly non-hermetic experience. Meanings localized within the isolate sign. Contexts displace to indicate, if anything, the schizophrenic predications of language. (Language as a branch plant of schizophrenic emission?) To place us in the movements of a language of schizzes is Ipseity. Dis / place / meant. Page for Palmer is the topography of the disjunctive, supporting the integral violence of transformationality. For the steady, consecutive plod of language, line after line, is at the same time its violent transformation. Such a paradox describes the horizontal identity of Palmer's signifier: a violent stability of grapheme, being at the same time a violent instability in any molar aggregate of "thought." The thing it is. Writing. Written. Not that linearity disappears, on the contrary, Palmer strengthens line but only in order for it to confess more effectively its own duplicities. The worded line identifies the syntagm as a horizontal, moving segment in space possessed of the infinite capacity to absorb all breaks in casuality and consequentiality within its consecutive motions. And thus the transparent guilt of reading. The guilt at witnessing a graphed pattern of place support a huge displacement.

Palmer's most radical displacement is the break with transitivity itself. For language has become the subject of Language and we enter, as readers, the ambiguous zone of texts without absolute speakers. Palmer makes speech subordinate to writing; the speaking subject being the intractible voice dispaced as an echo in the fissures of the spacing. Beyond voice and presence is syntactic space and absence — the consummate Palmerian domain where the phonocentric becomes marginated and writing comes closest to a pure Writing. Inscribed throughout his work, as its syntax motion, is the locale of the subject's disappearance. Nomadic topographies beyond the symmetries of line where language inscribes a sphere around itself and instigates a self-reflexiveness, the interrogation of the text's own limits. To write a voiceless writing is to reinvent speech as an order free of voice. Palmer, I believe, is transforming speech from a form and a vehicle into a content on the way to its reinvention. What he presents is speech without the social activity of speaking. Can this be anything else but writing?

Systematic detachment from the 'I' until there is no speaking subject. A subject alone is reading this and the words are voiceless speech in non-discursive space. It is — as if — the music "(was)" the consequence plus voice and so the works entirely are without music.

Steve McCaffery

BOB PERELMAN, 7 Works

(1978: The Figures, Berkeley)

"Continuity exists in the nervous system" is the prior statement I am moved to bring to my reading of the present work, the present works, which, taken in concert, insist on a like continuity.

Composition— to include the entire repertoire of generative methods here employed— "in actual obedience to what / underlies every act". Not a masque of ironies, but an earnest investigation of 'what follows'.

"The exact person ought to remain. Certainly no one can afford to stop. A person's experience must contain several meanings, or he cannot be careful." An exaction of caring that carries through the work, leads the work, fore-casting an erotic climate in which "the body / merely one side of the question" may become "the whole body".

"Each sentence is complete". A specific largesse. "There is more thought than time, more water than vocabulary." So this writing 'on' water— this "dear grim earthly intelligibility"—casual: "You want everything at once. Read my long list of fancy goods"— and essential: "A journey of this kind is no joke."

"I am prepared to hear these numbers. . . ."

Ted Pearson

BOB PERELMAN, *a.k.a.*

(1979: Tuumba Press, Berkeley)

i.

Bob Perelman is a modern metaphysical poet. Every sentence in *a.k.a. i* is a sort of critique of reason. Each interrogates the relation between mind and things. "The dialog with objects is becoming more strained." Strained to point of breaking? With Perelman, it is always a question of "an inspected geography" — the seer must affect the seen. Thus at every point we encounter a mirror. "It almost combines to be one thing, but here I am again."

a.k.a. i is largely made of sentences, or pairs of sentences, which break in 2 parts; consciousness on one side of the punctuation, "the world" on the other. For example, "The dog could be anywhere, within reason." (It couldn't be out of his mind.) "He drove to Bakersfield, so to speak." "The ground was approaching fast. It was a side of himself he

rarely showed." Perelman nearly describes the structure of this work
when he writes, "The station pulled itself apart in 2 equal halves " But
the halves don't seem quite equal. The mind is the latter half of these
equations and has the last word.

BP seems suspicious of this preeminence of mind. In *Braille*
(Ithaca House, 1975) he said "Continuity exists in the nervous system."
In *a.k.a. i* he's afraid too much continuity exists there. "Until I see what
I thought" is the danger. Until one lives "there, under the assump-
tions." If "the pictures are in the head by prior arrangement," the dan-
ger is grave. Too much continuity exists when, "Each second the fea-
tures repeat." "Told over until unrememberable, the physical features
grow so long-winded they have to be called off." "Dead certainties
lumbering center stage." Here the past is a threat, certainty is a threat,
speech is. "Thinking about them as they appear, the forms are longer
than life." Everything threatened by ossification. Continuously.

My first response to *a.k.a. i* was that too much continuity existed
in this work, that it risked redundancy. But the more I read it the more I
appreciated its structure. BP produces fresh variations on his theme
sentence after sentence — "Trees *said* to line the whole road."

ii.

In the beginning, "The baby's voice speaks, sings, cries, breaks."
In the beginning was the word. "Hello." "Saying the first thing he saw
when the screen lit up." "Delete flesh, read body of words." *a.k.a. ii* is
a curious kind of autobiography — not that of a person, but, maybe, of
Logos itself. "Nomenclature" and "sequence" become characters,
often replacing the narrative "I."

Well, *something* is moving through time and space here. Reading
a.k.a. ii is like being on a teeter-totter: "The screen lit *up*." "effect piles
up" "The rock *sank*." "The gorge *below*." "but at full throat *up* there."
"Ideal city cranked *up* to heaven." * "There would be an up a down a
back and forth." We are moving, running, playing baseball. We are "a
group of boys" faced with "a brutal necessity to add up to one." Iden-
tity continues to splinter and refract.

Moving fast because "The future was the easy way out." The future
"was" and not the future "is" puts sadness in this. "Nostalgia precedes
the focus." "A burnt offering sadly loving its milk." As usual in Perel-
man's work, the ego is gently mocked — by the word "its" in the above
quote and elsewhere in such lines as, "The echoes bouncing back as a

---

* Italics within quotations are the reviewer's.

series of tightening categories inhabited by a big personal person." In *Braille* Perelman said, "The best myth we have is the nameless pulse." *a.k.a. ii* is this myth's story.

Expectations of linearity are also mocked. He thinks he is proceeding in an orderly way and laughs at himself for thinking so. "I woke up ten times in a row, twelve, twenty. It was a winning streak and my smile couldn't have been quicker to come and go." "I listen to the correct, calm sequence and am a ring." "Sequence wakes up in the dark upset." This is the same moral universe found in *a.k.a. i*. Personality, continuity and abstraction ("An element substituted for another via the simple authority of say so. . . .") threaten to separate us from real experience. Perelman uses writing as his antidote.

Rae Armantrout

from LOGARHYTHMS

Tom Raworth, *Logbook* (1976: Poltroon Press, Berkeley)

> And I am busily sweeping up the last few words in a country without an ear, whose artists are busy filling in the colours they've been allocated in the giant painting-by-numbers picture of themselves, because they think an interview with the man (now a physicist in Moscow) who was the boy on the Odessa Steps *makes a connection.*

The connection is that imagined between something whose claim to meaning is what it was recognized for, and the subject of an expropriation, a resistance to the fading away of a subject in which the past is regulated by future needs. For the boy on the Odessa Steps was part of a diction which no longer obtains, and the physicist in Moscow will prevent our realizing the history of that. Thus the tense in which *Logbook* is written is the post-prophetical present—it will not be depleted by 'culture.' And by that I mean what culture is *recognized* as being (culture at the cognitive level):

> "He planted that word twenty years ago so that its weight is now exactly right"—that's the message of 'culture,' the real, cold, science.

For Raworth the word is not an implantation, a seclusion of meaning away from processes of renovation (there are a great number of novels and poems officially retired) but a disclosure, in a work of *dehiscence*—the discharge of mature contents. The proper meaning of maturity as of something instant, and not a state which you finally reach and then persist in.

If we think we understand this text it is not by way of consolation for the monopoly of 'literature'; 'literature' borrows its own meanings from a global repertoire and gives them only a limited territory in which they can work. This demarcation is political, like a red line on the map ignored by the elements: "For this is the battle: between the vegetables and the rocks. And we are the disputed territory—we, and the water we come from and are." In fact we are the subjects of a repertoire such that we can exclude ourselves from parts of it or force ourselves not to: "Until finally writing becomes the only thing that is not a petroleum by-product, or a neat capsule available without prescription." Writing is the excessive production from which more meanings escape than can be contained and given a place, and if 'culture' can afford to be more and more intolerant, or restfully ignorant of its subversion by writing, that is because the massive extension of criticism has actually imposed on 'literature' a greater scope than it knew it already had, persuading us of its competence through an ability to *account for* an unprecedented number of the strange materials from which it borrows—when it omits everything which it is not in order to be systematic.

> It's the front room, and the queen's picture flickers into a limp book called Jimi Hendrix because all books are dead & we live where the edges overlap.

There are other complicities of meaning some of which rely on complete subterfuge as they must to remain so fragile they can withstand the brutal coherence of civility. That maladaptation of ourselves whom writing may effectively put back into circulation is civility in the belief we are consenting members of the constituency of the book. So then it is important to traduce the accredited image of the book, and *Logbook* seems to be the record of an expedition whose parade of 'culture' might be directly provoking, and the representative value of its language could only be instated by force:

> Around us was the countryside of *Whimsy* where, huddled around leaping orange fires, the natives let their cigarettes dangle unlit in their mouths, thinking only petrol or butane could light them.

This refers to a colonial discourse like that of *Voyage au Bout de la Nuit* where the Europeans have power through a monopoly on money *and* language. We ought to note that forty years ago the question of *agency* was still an effective anxiety, and that now the honest intervention has to be whimsical. The only way in which the natives *can* know the rules is through being guilty of a breach; this is the position which writing can refuse to occupy, and it does so if it is contrary. The adroitness is a condition necessary for the act of restitution in which disobedience to the laws of consistency is freed from its social stigma of worthlessness and restored to an expressive capacity. . . .

Intermittent form is the basis of a text which *is* the presence of history, exactly like a log-book: not wholly irregular but punctuated by a regularity which is transitory, "slightly charred by the slow still silent instant." It has an essential readiness which is measured not by coherent size but the sudden insistence of its distracted parts—"a form can be used once only." Our understanding of the text is the activation of these diverging parts, the instant in which their mutual pressure is sufficient to open the text for us.

Rod Mengham

(PROCESS) NOTE: The Connection (Or, how far is it from New York to Baltimore via California?)

Marshall Reese, *Writing* (1980: pod books, Baltimore)

Marshall Reese's book *Slugs* [published as part of *Writing*] relates through its concerns to the conversation generated around Bob Perelman's talk at the St. Mark's Poetry Project in New York in 4/79. Bob proposed the issue in the form of two terms to be defined. "Artificial" as distinguished from "natural" as applied to the concept of language.

Now Bob's basic rap, which is what leads to Marshall in this discussion, is that language, as an acquired skill, is one of those loop functions for the organism. The elements of it are borrowed property, the common currency of exchange, items on loan, as it were, from the general vocabulary pool. It passes through the culture and we make use of it in various ways according to our particular needs. Okay. In that sense, given that language is all a public commodity, just stuff getting run through the cycle, how does it get to be unique? And, secondly, still be constituted of configurations which can be distinctly classified as "artificial" and "natural"?

Marshall's work is a series of pieces composed while he was employed with a printer who had a linotype machine which produces, aside from usable lines of type, a whole mess of miscast pieces. It's these cast-off slugs, from various texts (ranging from a Civics text to a history of the Southwest with miscellaneous social notes thrown in for human interest) all locked up and printed. By pushing the acquisition process to an obvious place Marshall, using what in one sense cannot at all be considered his own language, is nonetheless using it *as* his own language. For sure this is no different than any other talking/ writing process except his units are phrasiform as opposed to word form. They evolve a context just as absolutely as syntax evolves automatically in any word sequence (the absolute fact of grammar). There just *is* a logic of relation which is a matter of personal selection no matter how 'randomly' the assemblage is constructed. Choice to do it is the determinator of the form.

The conclusion here is that the concept of artificial can be disposed of having any relation to the process of acquiring the elements of language and put instead into an investigation of the use of language, which is where the selective compositional process becomes the essential factor.

Well, then, what is artificial selection? It doesn't occur to Marshall, cause he's just doing the work. The material's there and he makes use of it, simple digestion. Likewise Perelman is ripping off, collaging, splicing texts, only maybe a little more self-consciously. But actually, therein lies the difference. The self-consciousness: what needs defining as the gap, the space between the thought and its manifestation. That gap is the distinction between, the point of differentiation, the point of isolation, insularity. That which is as opposed to that which is not. So. Simple. Once you got that one the point is to get to what exactly is. Goes flat right away, because it's so obvious — it's the whole sum of those unique particulars, the choice, the combination of choices, the mess of interactions. A settlement of terms does not waste any more the energy to conflict over issues of the process. Get in there. The slogan mentality: cliches of language and fixations at points in the whole flow. Course it never finishes, never exactly originates, only begins to be aware that it is occurring then carries through whatever growth is appropriate to the logic of its own development, no, that becomes the

logic of its own development, the way grammar becomes an absolute
fact of language: because the words are such powerful objects they
command relation—or is it more simple, even, they are the units and
any sequence of units becomes a structure though, natch, there's a
characteristic there too. That's in a sense the constant variable, of
course it's always different—what should it be otherwise? Is anything
the same as, nope, be glad about it. That's the tuck and lift aspect of the
turn, the quick leap into.

What happens in an immediate sense preserves its dynamic intact,
can be edited similarly and worked through similarly. The process by
which it happens, that rush of transformative digestion, contains the
excitement of any real process — that is, its form is determined accord-
ing to the necessities of its function, so, it's clean, essential. This isn't
an argument for improvisation *at all*, it's an argument for integration
and conscious process as opposed to self-conscious process, that's
what. Because *that's* the artificial, the contrived, the thought through
first which creates a limitation on the flexible possibility. Knocks out
options beforehand, so, becomes stale in the act of its conception by
being such a finished thought to begin with. It must be larger than itself
and not understand its own limits entirely, at first, if it is to be success-
ful, and done with engagement towards the definition of its own
intention.

The working through of any real process will contain a sequential
logic according to its own particular, essential dynamic. The character
of that dynamic, which it acquires only in that exact and self-same pro-
cess, becomes its own definition. It is what it is and what it wants to be
is what it struggles to become. The intention is not a fixed ideal form,
but a process of synthetic utilization and transformative integration.
Not in the sense of achieving anything, no, no, don't want no models
of perfection, just want the dynamic process. It's got to take you and
keep you with/in the process of becoming what it is itself. Nowhere to
get, of course, nothing ever finally resolves. Things take form and then
disintegrate to reconstruct, reassemble, rearrange in another temporary
configuration. The point is to work with that continual rearrangement,
the redefinition.

So: the definition of intention the impetus, permission the cause,
dis— and integration the process with the resolution a new form, the
beginning again. And when in this process the activity makes a change
whose origin was not predictable from, the process of which was not
contained in the form of what it originated in, then, it actually is some-
thing, it gets to another place. When it all gets working it keeps on. But,
since like a combustion engine it doesn't fully realize, call that total

resolution the clear intention while the actual process is what goes down. Always that remainder to be dealt with accumulates sufficient significance relative to some point to act upon itself.

That's my process take, how I get from this to that. The rest is all the details of engagement.

Johanna Drucker

LAURA (RIDING) JACKSON, *The Telling*

(1972: Harper & Row, N.Y.)

For what Laura (Riding) Jackson has had to tell, poetry is insufficient. "Deficient," she insists; *The Telling* her first major work after renouncing poetry in 1938 as being linguistically incapable of truth telling. For writers serious about the possibilities of poetry it has been difficult to react; that Jackson intends this difficulty is evident from her vehement refusals to allow her views to be taken as the basis of a new way—a "medicine"—for poetry.

There is an unsympathy—a quarrelsomeness at times—that runs through *The Telling*, and is accentuated in some of the book's appended material. This is not a quarrelsomeness for its own sake, but the result of the prophetic—sometimes oracular—mode Jackson has chosen to write in: "preachment". There are few styles of, to her, contemporary avoidance that escape censure—from rock music and left politics to all manner of "professional" thought. *The Telling*, indeed, echoes the critique of Rousseau's *First Discourse*—that 'art' and 'intellect' have replaced 'virtue'. Jackson decries the obsession with doctrines, the new, success in the place of "articulating the human reality with truth"; it is professional learning—e.g., the poetic craft, specialized poetic form itself—that interposes itself between us and the truth of the mutuality of our one being.

Her insistence in *The Telling* is that in speaking it is possible to tell one another of that in which we each are not another—the 'Before' that is in the 'Now', spoken as 'Subject' to all 'Subjects'. Of the many things that prevent this truth telling of ourselves is the self satisfaction of carving out a voice that is distinct, actualized by its difference. "Telling differently for the triumph of difference, and not for truth's sake." Poetry dwells on the description of the distance, whose extolling, it is imagined, is a penetration into the deepest roots of humanness. This dwelling in the less-than, on the forms of our present lives, is a diversion from the fact of our "self-sameness in Being".

Since it creates a "literary reality", poetry is limited by its craft. "The liberty of word that poetry confers is poetry's technique not truths." Jackson's mode of writing in *The Telling* is able—unlike poetry, she says—to have a place for the reader in it: a speaking ideal of "normal" diction, one speaking to another of the mutualness of both, all, in being ("a method of our speaking, each, our All.") Each section of *The Telling* is—this is my experience of it—the enunciation of a shared fact; I find myself in it not in the sense of relation of personality (foibles, longing, &c) but ontologically, by the fact of my human being. (And yet in her sternness and insistence on this 'ultimate' seeing, her rebukes of all our human failings, perhaps too much—this 'all'—is asked of us—does not her very unsympathy shut-out?—for there is connection also in the recognition and acknowledging of such failings in our fellow human beings.) Although Jackson's prophecy/pretension does not allow her to admit any predecessors in this self-actualizing of words—she says there are none, that the personal concreteness of *The Telling* is diverted by such comparisons—still, I thought of Dickinson (e.g., "The world is not conclusion"), of Kierkegaard's *Purity of Heart* and *Works of Love*, of Wittgenstein's *Philosophical Investigations* (which, like *The Telling*, is a critique/renunciation of an earlier work and method), of Oppen (not 'gesture' but the 'actual' "which is ourselves"), of Ashbery's recitals. Of *Walden*: "There are words addressed to our condition exactly, which, if we could really hear and understand, would be more salutary than the morning."

In the supplemental material to *The Telling*, Jackson cautions against confusing endings for completeness. This work, dedicated itself to self-completeness, brings to completeness the promise of Laura Riding's poetry. The turning required for this completeness is, perhaps, an unexpected one; its faithfulness to itself—to language, to "us"—is manifest. "And the tale is no more of the going: no more a poet's tale of going false-like to a seeing. The tale is of a seeing true-like to a knowing."

Charles Bernstein

DOLCH WORDS

Kit Robinson, *The Dolch Stanzas* (1976: This Press, Oakland)

Dr. Edward Dolch, dear to all reading teachers, in his classic *Manual for Remedial Reading*, came up with a list of words, 220 words, which he estimated accounted for ½ to ¾ of all school reading matter, words which by the third grade everyone is expected to recognize instantly by sight. Dr. Dolch, with his usual modesty, referred to these words as the Basic Sight Vocabulary ("which should not be used in alphabetical order because that arrangement gives the child a clue as to how the words begin. They should be printed in random order . . . ") some 50 years having since passed, the good doctor's reputation in the field is secure and his name has been memorialized, these words are now commonly known as Dolch words. They are supposed to come first, the words to skip past on the way to the unfamiliar ones: yellow, five, our, put, well, always, those, gave, for, ate, pull . . .

        together or on / right / what works there

The unexpected felicities to be met in the absence of usual contrast, in a vocabulary which is all ground, or all figure. Maybe a leveller principle at work, not that it is a question of altitude, but that the words do not need dressing, that it is not necessary to import; if, as it increasingly appears, any realm of words, technical, pyrotechnical, can be found appropriate, or appropriatable, must it not also hold that the most common, the diction's lumpenproletariat, strictly those words we know so well we hardly bother with them, usually, are as readily capable, can hold at least as much charge as the most elevated, specialized, or purportedly lyric nomenclatures.

        or why think / ask / try out new hold
        if they sleep / just as off / as always
        put it to them / like this / say
        here / this want / to be clean
        open / not done / wants to know

Separating out of words, by whatever process, enjoining them to enter the poem, any sort of arrangement lying there, if it is to produce the desired, must be radically delineated—delimited (else we wld say—prose), intentions of scrutiny bring forth, what—every length or combination across the band has its resonance, its complex of value, as many and as finely tuned degrees of concern; but it seems certain vocabularies are capable of calling up wider zones of response, they may interlock into much more that is outside of them, more hookups or sprockets, or memory bits; usually these plain words are the backdrop, the links, the machinery keeping everything running; tho' through this special acquaintance—an influence unexpectedly pervasive; also known as running words, e.g. the rivers under, the underground or under the streets, what everyone is running on, what they had in them all the time, surprisingly widespread contacts, that they may be closer to that thing pertaining to reality that we are always trying to name.

> it can move fast / she is said to have / seen it go once
> once and for all / by the white way / it left out

The regions of thought the short stanzas read into are often culled from certain areas of human activity, primary activities, working, loving, sleeping, watching, hunting, playing; is it a property of these running words to combine in concentrations of other-resonance, the "we" is how many more than the author, an increasingly inclusive simplicity; and like all like minded words they combine most easily with each other—already meant for combination, unchambering each other, short primary words lines stanzas . . . and as all colors can be mixed from red orange yellow green blue violet indigo. . . .

> then is always before / no longer / than it is round

Michael Gottlieb

PETER SEATON, *Piranesi Pointed Up*

(1978: in *Roof VIII*, The Segue Foundation, N.Y.)

"Piranesi Pointed Up" and Peter Seaton follows but not before checking out the 'prisons' below, the traditions behind, or the belief/disbelief of the facts all around him. Here, where the sentences are long, bursts lead to bursts, each moment being shoved along by the moment just past and the moment (thought) beginning now. This is seemingly a logical exploration by a writer objectively looking around himself (himself as space as well as time, experience, subjectivity, etc.) and the most objective observation is the impossible suspension or isolation of one experience from all others. The frustration is in the attempt at categorizing to understand or understanding to categorize (very self-consciously); the danger is in a truth*less* conclusion. Hence, the starting over and over, the 'breathers' of short lines which appear periodically offering relief from the dense prose along with a little quieter white space of the page (a more intense reflection). The reader is *left* or *remains* with a very contemporary feeling of anxiety; the experience is honestly ambiguous. As in photography, there is an infinite number of shots; a world made up of different points of the same. The perception of all moments is externalized, projected onto, in an attempt to reconcile each and its apparent indifference to all others: a verbal hologram. A familiar desire to order with an open approach of reciprocity: being observed and observing being observed. There is subjectivity and the consciousness of the will to subjective choice and commentary on subjectivity. All of these are acceptable to Seaton, whose result is a study in perspective, and who seems to say that the next approach is now.

Diane Ward

RON SILLIMAN, *Mohawk* and *Ketjak*

(1973: Doones Press, N.Y.) and (1978: This, San Francisco)

An article in the April issue of *Scientific American* on mathematically generated music refers to "fractal curves," which show the same fluctuating patterns over time for any duration. Ten minutes of event would have the same ratio of peaks to troughs as ten years, but "the fractals that occur in nature—coastlines, rivers, trees, star clustering, clouds and so on—are so irregular that their self-similarity (scaling) must be treated statistically." In language self-similarity (statement) is irregular and constant while words can shift scale. Kid says, "You die!"—not having the same outcome as in the movies or in war. But the words in each case point an abstract finger to exert will. Imagination, thinking build on these facts of natural language: "The so-called idea of the word . . . is the so-called *word itself—the word.*"

In *Mohawk* Ron Silliman discovers/invents a kind of fractal curve from a fixed set of words over thirty pages. The scale telescopes from word-to-word jumps to page "flicker noise" to the curve of the whole, but the irregularity and energy seen in the words is constant. The fixed vocabulary and the use of the two-dimensional page give the work a flatness and autonomy; the writer is located outside the work. Coolidge's earlier investigations into word-gap led to writing in which values are primarily intrinsic—the writing occurs along a line of thought—while Silliman is involved with extrinsic dimensions—the landscape, national boundaries, demography of the words. The distance found from the page in *Mohawk* makes it the first term in a series of works in variable scale, an entrance. This distance is close to the clearly imagist quality of the words: "wet / loom / star / wicker / silt . . . ," each word a snapshot on the page.

Ketjak is written in paragraph blocks, each twice the length of the previous. Repeated material makes an infra-skeleton, though sentences used more than once take on new values. Given this mechanism, the work was deliberately written over several months. It is a fractal curve of an experience that might be reduced to "revolving door." The work's stepwise progress makes for an evaluative mode of thinking—values of the sentences are revealed in how they interact with those around them. Some are sour notes, lost handles, not repeated. Others become familiar landscapes of daily life, the noon whistle. The imagist core of Silliman's sentences invokes higher levels of visualization by means of variation of emphasis. Frozen narratives in series add up to what could be read as a completely interior novel. This activity is "an expression of an euphoria." Meanwhile the distance from the text fleshes out all manner of gossip, theory, fact. "Then we made a map of the entire country, on exactly the same scale. It was impossible to put into use."

Only someone who had thought intensely about the fate of other peoples' lives could have written *Ketjak*. The morality is in the distance from the text and in the insistence on particular facts. Silliman allows ideology into his poem along with information not usually accepted as important. These elements demand evaluation, then there can be a change of state. One is outside, invents a position in order to insist on what he sees. Conflict produces the purest types of writing. To imagine another life without power gives value to the fact. Identity is all that literary politics can produce. *Ketjak* is a political act. Identity in Silliman's work is open-ended.

Barrett Watten

KETJAK IN SAN FRANCISCO

> This is the zone. Words, where you are, as in a trail, not forest but
> thicket, pine needle modifiers, shingles of a pine cone on which to
> focus, buy syntax, syntax was the half-light.

Ron Silliman read on Saturday September the 16th all of *Ketjak* (This
Press, 1978) on the sidewalk in sunlight at One Powell Street, where
the Powell Street cablecars turn around at Market. I came in on my way
off the BART train from my job in North Oakland, at 3, roughly, know-
ing the reading started at noon, and came up the stairs not knowing just
where in the intersection it would land me or where Ron would be. The
impression of bazaar had hardly hit before there was Ron declaiming
book in hand before the front steps of the Bank of America, book neatly
clutched in right hand, left hand grasping offwhite canvas bookbag
with "no on 6" (anti-Briggs) button at center out, pacing back & forth
facing the sun in a patch of light between shadows cast (before him) by
a tree and (to his right) by the building, on whose steps sat maybe 12
people I knew; 6 or 10 others sitting or standing between me and him.
The reading was insistent emphatic and lively with an energy intoxi-
cated by its own vigor and exactitude; it was chatty (unusual for Ron's
reading) in its thrilled, maybe sometimes even giddy playfulness with
the rhetoric of its phrases in all their possible relevancy to this heteroge-
neous, very live occasion. He was clearly reading the reading of his
poem and using this to illuminate as if from behind (and taking pleasure
in the illusion as though from within) the poem itself. The recurrences
variousness & personality of the text discoursed directly and one-on-
one, as in a most democratic and definitive garden party of the urban
streets, with the prolifery of the situation. . . . Ron's gestures quite evi-
dently spontaneous, isolated in the left hand, the voice and the pacing
(sometimes stopped). The experience was available to those passersby
who didn't expect it equally as they were available to it. A man walked
up, slowing down towards the poet, and then passed to his right, as
though uncertain only whether Ron meant to be an obstacle but con-
fident in any case that he should negotiate a passage. A woman with a
friend turned around abruptly after passing the poet when she heard
"She loves to give head"; shocked, she tried to make out whether he'd
been exposing her or somebody else; others say she smiled in recogni-
tion. A drunk tried to mimic Ron's phrases into catchy blues. Ron read
as though too busy to acknowledge all this formally but cognitive of it
in all its valences of continuity and implication (or you may say fact &
what might happen next). You could stand or sit anywhere. You were

on a major streetcorner, already crowded with long lines of tourists waiting for the chief picturesque cablecar line already besieged by hawkers gawkers shoppers hookers and religious maniacs— September being the warmest freshest month in the city. Recurring and original lines and people. By juxtaposition the names, images, terms called out by the words were clearly present as such rather than as objects for fantasy to compose over. The rapture of the occasion sprang from the access to a shared awareness of being *there*, the significance of this then ready to be begun, again at any moment. The writing evoked neither this nor any particular other consistently, & so seemed never to claim any particular responsibility for reproducing, but freely aimed at the experience about it.

Steve Benson

RON SILLIMAN, *Sitting Up, Standing, Taking Steps*

(1978: Tuumba Press, Berkeley)

nominative phrases ("Not nouns.") (sister to questions of "Sunset Debris", a nominative phrase) . . . When you accept the limits (boundaries) of a SYSTEM, Ron sd. something like, you find you have as much (more) freedom as/than acting (writing) w/o restriction,,,tho (Ambivalence, an autobiography) here: "A system, an argot" (i.e., more or less secret vocabulary & idiom peculiar to a particular group) . . . Structurally informed, as so much of modern/post writing & music, by possible film form ("A linguistic emulsion" less material difficulty): here, like expansive KETJAK, the loop. Here, a primary loop — high gray sky, high gray sky, high gray sky. There, repetition w. montaged expansion (w. slight variation: slips in the gate, the refrigerator comes on, lose count thinking of if then). Beg. w. surrounding objects then drifting to past or possible realize & returning, modelly mind of the sitter (doubtless tho culled from long times notebooks); strains (man, hippie, San Francisco, language, things, Ron) & disconnectednesses & altered recurrences (wrecks in dill weed, Afro blow-outs) & silly alliterations & "Color films of dead people" (MM on platform, strains of blond, deep, deep red; duck soup) &&&. Man (pink blouse, bruise on her thigh, mole on upper lip, the bitterness, constant knocker, cheese-like discharge, itchy balls, cumshot, rim job, butch, good buddy, bachelors together, her, Her), (the planet, foodstamp office, Phil Whalen, Kefir), (bay, fog, China, Paradise Cafe gone, fern bar, towaway zone, bay, cappucino, Alcatraz, meter maid, Patty, San Quentin, Brown, morning in North Beach, Chinatown, Rincon Annex, China, a restful orange, bridge, pompadour sheriff's yacht), "language" (pronomial anaphor, an attitude toward the verbal, more pronomial anaphors), Ron (list lover, strains of blond, calm blue eyes), hardly a trace of commie. 3 kinds of prose, 2 kinds of films. Brief tune long solo shape advanced bebop, like Eric Dolphy on "Serene" on OUT THERE, snap back at end, had forgot where you started.

Henry Hills

LAYOUT

Michael Frederick Tolson et al., Untitled book, 50 pp., white wrappers

Three traditions of putting the project of representation into brackets: the expressionist, the constructivist, the conceptual. This, the third, with tinctures of the first two. Exhibitions of linguistic material — display cases. Instructions. Lists, grids. Documentation. A bag, stapled to a page, containing *i, h, s, c, u, y, a, e, t.* Take positions. We read the detachment, and feel no rapport. The texts extend by linkings, by graphic displacements of letters, by shifts of focus, and subtraction, by accumulation. Other, more complex, modes of composition and of establishing an independent (or intrinsic) presence for language are declined. Instead, try to focus on many labeled areas simultaneously. "i hate the mentally paralyzed" "i want hypnotic yourself stimulating whose eyes" The words become mere tokens of *re*-arrangement and cleansing conspicuous disruption. Not even the pleasing ribs of overall structuring. But at least they are not used to form the primary material of transparency. That transparency is an illusion. a mental operation made more difficult here. "attach idea." Muddled. Muddied. Control is too slight. "th(v) disruption(s) int(v)ntionally (v)xagg(v)rat(v)d" Only a

few frames simultaneously. But an abolitionism of the word does not
occur. "Siuce the wisreaquig of morps iuvolves au iuversiou of the sep-
neuce or sbatiotewdoral orberiug of letters' he qesiguatep this tyqe of
error as a ,kiuetic, reversal." "Since the misrepaing of omprs involves
an invreismo of the besucuee or adsittomeoprla broreing of elttre,s he
deisganbet this tbye of reorr as a k'iteni'c everrsl.a"" "Since the mis-
reading of words involves an inversion of the sequence or spatiotem-
poral ordering of letters, he designated this type of error as a 'kinetic'
reversal."

Bruce Andrews

LETTER TO THE EDITOR

"
(f) g
....&/or t h (f)
(f)v(f)n root of a - # &/or (32 &/or 66) &/or wh(f)n &/or ....
....
2 bruc(f) andr(f)ws & t h(f) r(f)ad(f)rs of l=a=n=g=u=a=g=(f),
1st r(f)action as r(f)spons(f) 2 r(f)vi(f)w of
book unlab(f)l(f)d, unnam(f)d, 2.
t h(f) book X m(f)
t h(f) r(f)f(f)r(f)nt 4 which consists of
t h(f) non-mat(f)rializ(f)d punch-outs
from a transpar(f)nt l(f)tt(f)r/what(f)v(f)r st(f)ncil.
(65 print(f)d surfac(f)s, $3 (n(f)gotiabl(f)).
mad sci(f)ntist/dcompos(f)r/sound-think(f)r/thought-coll(f)ctor
manif(f)sting/xpr(f)ssing via writing
(occasionally).
l(f)ss tradition than r(f)occurr(f)nc(f).
car(f)fully consid(f)r(f)d manif(f)station of
awar(f)n(f)ss of
anything is anything,
tim(f)
(consid(f)r substitution),
s(f)lf, spac(f), humor, #, & r(f)ad(f)r/writ(f)r r(f)lationship,
at l(f)ast,

cr(f)at(f)s obliqu(f), subtl(f), & v(f)ry pr(f)s(f)nt structuring
(sparing &/or poking ribs).
r(f)j(f)ction of
t(f)chnical at xp(f)ns(f) of psychical,
r(f)fin(f)d at xp(f)ns(f) of raw.
qu(f)stion ur conc(f)ption of what is intrinsic in languag(f).
abolitionism of word also non-occurring in ur r(f)vi(f)w.
ur quot(f)s, paraphrasing, & articl(f) in g(f)n(f)ral
r(f)v(f)al substantial non-obs(f)rvation of
m(f)ntion(f)d structuring,
much significanc(f) & vari(f)ty,
& som(f) non-dnotational implications
((f) g non-intro grid)
(not quot(f)d 2 avoid loss du(f) 2 cont(f)xtual displac(f)m(f)nt)
but,
ur critiqu(f) of c(f)rtain abs(f)nc(f) of control,
(f)sp(f)cially of t h(f) non-r(f)f(f)r(f)ntial implications,
as accurat(f), dsirabl(f), & appr(f)ciat(f)d.
(although, consid(f)r ur, & oth(f)rs', succ(f)ss in that ar(f)a
2 b satisfactory 2 m(f)
(&, th(f)r(f)for(f), not as int(f)r(f)sting 2 xplor(f))).
(m curr(f)ntly mor(f) int(f)r(f)st(f)d in
dtaching languag(f) from physicality
(i (f) (f) g sound, writing)
in incr(f)asingly autistic
(from artist 2 autist)
way,
non-us(f) of languag(f),
& sound thinking
(as n(f)ith(f)r sound nor sil(f)nc(f)),
at l(f)ast.
n(f)v(f)rt h(f)l(f)ss, m dlight(f)d as r(f)spons(f) 2 xist(f)nc(f) of r(f)vi(f)w.
micha(f)l fr(f)d(f)rick tolson (f)t al
?
"

Michael Frederick Tolson et al.

THE HUM OF WORDS

Rosmarie Waldrop, *The Road is Everywhere or Stop This Body* (1978; Open Places, Columbia, Missouri)

> I veer toward the endless
> distractions of the foreground
> even while clamoring
> for wholeness

This book contains a sequence in 80 parts, and pages, shot through with road signs and seasonal photographs, taken in motion, radiating *a cone of attention*. Rosmarie Waldrop's largest book in half-a-dozen years. She stakes out for us, gradually, a parallel between 2 senses of traffic: *the movement (of vehicles or pedestrians) through an area or along a route* and *the information or signals transmitted over a communication system: messages*. So we find content doubled, folded back into the constructed spaces of the page — first, revealing and articulating an experience of motion (and of mind/heart/memory/body/dream in motion through everyday traffic): second, doing the same for an experience of speech/words/meanings/writing as this second perspective actively unfolds from a transcription and embodiment of the first. The writing entertains a constant retrieval from one plane to another. A bifurcation, which registers gradations in both, *translating / one measurement into another*, so that the intervals achieve solidity. We notice then that the facticity of the everyday world is incomplete. Such a double vision is one of the book's achievements.

Comprehension (a *sequence / of ready signs*) bleeds through. It is performed in a space & in intermittent shapes we can measure, as an abstraction we are *obliquely conscious* of. This abstraction is our ability to frame and reframe the flows around us, and the explosions which *fracture the present*. Body becomes its own flow: the person is a matrix of those flows & exchanges & messages. Person is a communicative system, a traffic.

The *mind floats headlights on time*, & transforms what is immobile into a secret generation of desires and presence: *words / germinate on their own obstructions*. Syllables are implacable; they secrete their own space, dislodging our breath at an angle. They congest in the unbroken slowness of the gaps they make, where mind speeds ahead of body, where perceptions become symptoms.

And don't those gaps — and the line breaks & disruptions which highlight them — begin to remind us of another, more social gap?? A gap between our desires and our experience, between the outside which encloses us and the inside which projects and endorses us. *damned-up friction / knots want into / need widens : as if the future had to be / remembered words*. This resembles Ernst Bloch's idea of the 'novum'— what "has not come to be in the past, . . . which is drifting and dreaming in the darkness, in the factual blue of objects . . . as content of the deepest hope."

This difference never happens without words — a tumescence which consumes all representation in the affections of solid paper. Precisely & secretively — particularly here as the last word of a phrase often begins a new physical line and a new grammatical unit; as if intentions and conventions are bi-valved, perforated, condensed, accelerated, paralleled: *the / double sheet of the / way back of / the outside rises up. Surface / doubles the depth* just as *talk / doubles the frequencies*. Both assert attention, weaving & unweaving, giving us the material enticements of text as well as a recollected sighting from a landscape — an outer landscape which is not separate from the languagescape of the text. The flows we see — these sightings are not retinal flashes. We find them embodied, as the journey reapproaches the surface (the site of the structure). Light is ink, a series of displacements taking shape against any object, while *words make you your own object*.

Illusion dwindles into the page's margin. Yet the atomized self cannot live without these illusions. At times, *the blue bodiless shock of the air* is too much for it. At best, writing *can't find a center for its / surfaces superimposed in constant / articulation*. At those points, all obstacles recede — both the taken-for-granted self and taken-for-granted illusionism. Otherwise (& this is the danger constantly tempted here) surface bursts and yet still slackens into familiar versifying, where disruptions seem ornamental, imagistic, comforting, rhetorical. A constant activity would be a surface without grips — what is most courageously desired, what *accompanies / the tissue of pleasure inside / pleasure*.

Bruce Andrews

DIANE WARD, *Theory of Emotion*

(1979: Segue/O Press, N.Y.)

I/you. If the mind of the woman's voice, this positive gesture in a fact of feeling *that* farce, the desiring element in the change in intending, an extruding emotion over facing tongue, lapsable. "In the heat... ...into for hours." –=– One/two/others. The ongoing elimination of *worth*less elements through the elevation of worth*whiles*, and the tonal difference between the thought and the word for the gesture of selection, and the (barely) multipliable noneliminative personae. "two hands per person... ...reproduce." –=– He/them. Or the repetition *could*, *not* stop, in an intellective movement strong over chance, the nonevasive triumph of this (this *one*) axis of arranging the pronominal motivative mind in sentencing its years, any ear this time. "He mingles... ...to them." –=– She/you. Such that no imitative gestures unfold of the imitative life, or, no, no extremitous life stubborns itself into reducible speech; that that is the weary isolation of mind (speech) surrounded by speech (mind). "She stops... ...she repeats." –=– You. With which the at last isolate pronoun performs furthered noun, the heady off-cutting of sample and concomitant tribulation; breathing nebulous specifics into exact studied air, a temperature through which to mount an alphabet. "by the window... ...and run away." –=– You/I/we/"Darling" The center of an immovable constelle of fluctuant invariable or curvaceous experience, the tendency to drive, an insurgent motion words make over lips over valves over life; over the need to repair. "Darling, visual acoustics... ...the basis of representation"

Alan Davies

DIANE WARD, *The Light American*

(1979: Jawbone, Washington, D.C.)

What's left is a bigger opening. . . . Light play brightness & dark. All grey. . . . Leaves about to feet about to luck about to company about to rationalize about to further about to catch about to feel about to direct about to past about to nude about to fall about to turn about to sharp

about to wake about to mistakes about to cushion about to match about
to soak about to answer us another big one relation lotus one postcard
size social comment the stuck immigration very big broad dark over at
ends of halls or around corners sort of in social scenes leaning a power-
ful finger for you. . . . Eye me beyond the scratch mark able to or able
to understand. Time to rub them out. Time considers what gets close &
rubs them out. . . . Gum worded up. . . . Son of restless clarity. . . .
The attractions are depth humor pain & loss of manipulation the power
to pull you from security the creator of desire. . . . Trigger two reac-
tions: silent movies. . . . Isolated movement like reaction to another
movement real outside. You're the movement & the tune 'blue moon' is
the single sound you hear. . . . Please confuse us more, keep us inter-
ested we're creative please tell us you don't and then do. . . . Be vol-
umes of *History* world of solitary . . . . I'm the confiscated tactile agent
of reductive aesthetics. . . . Out with nerves. The main brain shut
down nerve. . . . Cover over mistakes. Takes place same moment.
Voice underneath the place confines us . . . . . . art being more aca-
demic than writing in the sense of cloudy. . . . The color aura the
sound disaccord. . . . Intrinsic limits to peripheral vision & bottomless
jerked motion implications to every word. . . . The taste's the same &
what goes what goes in limited and packages are packages contents
and got involved money and unwrapping and stacked sounds of sym-
bols and unwrapping insect conversations and idioms and meat and
meat and issues and what goes in eliminated and sound obsolete a
communicator and way back first eye contact and what was called nos-
talgia and constant non-movement feet compacted into motion as if
through a garden from the ground vibrations from the rails couples.
. . . Lush dialogue & the sound of tongues licking. . . . Reflect per-
sonal historical fingers masks at night & alone music & musical lan-
guage a willingness to disarrangements annotated happiness. . . . And
the room fills with people encases by invisible flowing atmospheres
dulls movement words are one by one instantly recorded & forgotten
like all relationships there're no more relationships.

Text excerpted by Bruce Andrews

DOUBLE OR QUIT

Geoffrey Ward, *Double Exposure* (1978; Infernal Methods, London)

The afferent idiom through which the best writing now takes the measure of its own compass-work is often a Pyrrhic triumph. The reader will be quick to resign from a text which seems to be all strategy and no tactics; the cost of absolutely interminable resuscitation of active reading is a greater number of casualties than even poetry has been used to.

We're unable to estimate the outcome; meanwhile we can look to *Double Exposure* as a characteristic advance. This new order of work exposes the volume of social inscriptions which seem of a piece in sharing momentum. If there seem to be points of control over this momentum they are points where the effects of control are produced: such is a judge or an author. Superimposed on the homeostat is a group of fixatives, cultural ready-mades, media phrasing, the hyperbolic naivete of poetic sentiment, the prayer-negotiation/poem as visitation of Truth. The work is at once a filatory of jumping threads and the impasto design its after-band — a double exposure on one plate — her dress, like her language, is a galimatias of several countries.

Contrast the maieutic, parliamentary drain on poetic resource which has wide currency, the prosecution of tabloid epiphanies for which *Double Exposure* is satiric depository (" We're kept snug and amused as TV innards newsreels old workmates repeats and their catchphrases rerun on similar lines below "). The routine theology is cued, made imploringly histrionic, and is precisely contravened by catcalling, writing the oath, with its physical counterpart the excretion. References to punk rock recall this profanation of the Host (the Pistols vomiting on their audience) of which the typical exemplar must be the invert Howard Hughes with his cultivation of dead matter: hair, nails, urine. The principle of work is writing as e-limination, the expulsion of dead truths—" wipes away dirt like a dream " — wastrel action as the only freedom in art, writing as rubbish — " pertinent; essential; the most intricate presence in our entire culture" (Prynne) — burning on the city limits, pushing itself in every sense into the margin.

The greater part of what is still referred to as the avant-garde is still concerned for wheedling re-valuation, the vulgarization of Truth as a positive control, justice dispensed as a pill. (There is supposed to be an 'alternative' society, an 'alternative' truth: " Pretence that times are changing outside technology".) On the face of it, *Double Exposure* assigns itself to Nietzschean de-valuation of all values, and in fact the stages of a career in Ward have the delightful consistency of inversion; the early interest in TM leads him from the cultivated nomadics of *Tales from the Snowline* directly to the indecent politics of *Double Exposure*: a movement from passive to active nihilism, a 'Buddhism of action'.

The commonplace poetry of to-day is inefficient through mis-allegation of one or another substantiation of its presence. But new work can excise the ground of any such operation by " damage to / and peeling of / the original negatives", an ablatitious force that diminished gravitation to given meta-discourse, seen as the negative of photographic print. The contemporaneity of 'double exposure' is exact: the way *The Orators* was, the way *Behind The State Capitol* still is.

Rod Mengham

BARRETT WATTEN, *Decay*

(1977: This Press, Oakland)

Where are you going your feet along those parallel lines. One place or two. When you 'get' there will you be together one or two.

If you hold regularly to the ability to say what you do say, your legs will take turns; you can go on, saying it.

*

In this writing each word points at those nearby. Each sentence.

—the way Duchamp's snow shovel points at his urinal and the hat rack, in retrospect. And in the initial fact.

"One word used in connection with the wiring of houses is current — this." The last word points with its little finger at the one just back of it. Look! But this is an obvious example of what is the case throughout.

You gain every thing by stepping consciously from stone to stone, so they tie back and forth and around.

*

Music is muted. Not silenced, but tamed and caressed. The whole thing is erect in the face of a reader. A light spreads up around our lips.

When you walk into the light, holding to thoughts as you do, an instance is filtered by its own parameters, aesthetic weight balanced, not interfered with, registered mildly. It is a word and a word, what else.

*

It is too easy to say he could not come right out and say it. It is possible to hide back of words but you don't do that.

Language a thin skin of somewhat-changing identity, on which mind projects, locating through structure.

Some reality is not presented here, but not held back; present. You hold down the world fingers around it. —this lets no thing escape though only a few things be held to. A portrait landscape forms under that pressure; complete, and aired. Sparks of meaning set off where none is apparent.

*

"I was there. I am not here.

Time is a sensible by-product, of motion between two poles."

Why we keep setting these things down, words. Because we do not ever know a difference between every thing and no thing. A language making it seem there is a difference. We write a way repeatedly through this dilemma.

How do you think of your work as coming.

*

You write it proves every bit a dream. Not indistinct the way most forget, to be awake; attentive to each particular, waking continually from that a sense of the nailed down confusion. We can call it confusion.

*

Each writing comes from, out a voice with precision sharp edges. Concaves of burnt and cut angle that permit only a most exact delineation of detritus coming in and straying from the mind, never relaxed.

You walk over the minute stones and there they remain.

A mouth whispers small notes.

We don't choke because we let it go.

These words tie themselves into accuracies of what is there about them. It is all there, contained out where only parts are spoken. A kindness to have handles perfectly the few things and let them be.

Alan Davies

MAKING WORDS VISIBLE

Hannah Weiner, *The Clairvoyant Journal* (1978: Angel Hair
Press, N.Y. and New Wilderness Audiograph tapes, N.Y.)

We all see words: signs of a language we live inside of. & yet these
words seem exterior to us—we see them, projections of our desires,
and act, often enough, out of a sense of their demands.

Hannah Weiner, in her various poetic works, and, most especially, in
the long poem she calls The Clairvoyant Journal has taken this fact of
living a life inside of language most literally. "I *see* words", by which
Weiner insists that the letters that spell out the various words and
phrases of her work appear in various sizes and colors on other people
and objects, but also, more importantly, on her self. Her work, then,
consists of taking the dictation of these seen ciphers—she calls them
voices—and weaving them into a text.

To "see words" is to be inside language and looking out onto it. For
Weiner, this has involved an actual seeing (clairvoyance), although at
the level of the text it is present as a pervasive citationality (both in the
sense of a sighting and a quoting).

And yet, because Weiner's work is so rooted in the momentum of the
act of writing,* the diaristic energy manages to totally submerge (im-
merse) the citational shards into its flow. She has herself said that she is
interested in an electric energy that completely fills the page, trans-
forming it into an impermeable field. It is this element that manages to
fuse the eruptive fragments ("voices") into a continuity. So that the
three voice simultaneity that makes up her text reads out as a linear
syntax, while proposing an awareness of its paratactic method, its
shard-like materials. Yet, finally, these different voices set up a syntax

---

*Weiner's work stands as a remarkable extension of the diaristic tradition in litera-
ture. The sense of writing out a life, the enormous force that words have to come on
their own, is graphicly portrayed in Truffaut's *Diary of Adele H*, where the writing is
more overpowering for the writer than anything else, largely because it is never re-
flected on. This question of intention pervades the reading of all of Weiner's work,
where the unsettling fact that the words may be in control is dislocating and alarm-
ing. Bresson, in *Diary of a Country Priest*, also focusses on the keeping of a journal;
here the paper absorbs the ink of each word penned as if it were life soaking up so
much blood.

that is not linear or monologic (the continuous strip of the prose line) nor do they simply establish a discourse that is dialogic or reflective. Here, the mind is constantly interrupting—intruding upon, commenting on—its own processes with its caps THIS GIVES ME ORDERS and its italics *don't make so many generalizations stupid silly*. ("How can I describe anything when all these interruptions keep *arriving* and then tell me I didn't describe it well WELL") But, more than this, the text makes one piece of (*with*) all this activity, continuously integrating "outside"** elements into its compositional field without compromising their vertical disruption of the uniplanar surface. ("Each page a state of consciousness.")

The sections of her Journal that Weiner has chosen to publish in the Angel Hair edition are characterized, even more apparently than some previously published sections of the work, by a recurrence of the most commonplace mental static that is as much an example of obsessiveness as a method of release from it. I can't think of a book which has more insistently faced these materials—"BIG OK SIT STILL   RHYS COMES *PREGO*   INstructions this morning: BATH,   SIT FOR AN HOUR *bathrobe* A LOT OF RHYS   thinking of going to Jerry's reading   it's at 2   saw 2 OCLOCK   Still depressed, dreamt I was being married off to some fat Jewish boy   I had to wear this shower cap *be careful* tonight *don't dream.* PUT SOME CLOTHES ON   Is that Peggy, the same as GET DRESS   There's a lot of energy in this *30's* robe can see

** "The poetry . . . begins . . . when the composing factor—the dictation, the unknown, the outside—enters the work and . . . begins to construct a poetry that was not lyric but narrative. . . . It involves a reversal of language into experience . . . a polarity and experienced dialectic with something other than ourselves. . . . A *reopened language* lets the unknown, the Other, the outside in again as a voice in the language. . . . Here is the insistence of . . . outside, an other than the reasonable is said to enter the real. . . . The voice arguing the necessity of an outside may strike the reader as odd since the outside, in whatever sense one takes, is usually assumed. . . . Its placement here as a composing factor in the poem disturbs our sense of a settled relation to language. It does . . . insist that language is not simply relational, but rather a knowing. . . . It is within language that the world speaks to us with a voice that is not our own. This is, I believe a first and fundamental experience of dictation. . . . In the reversal of language into experience (visibility and invisibility) fold into one another and unfold, composing as voices in our language. . . . To understand the 'outside,' that curiously naive-sounding insistence of this work, it will not do to take off on those supernaturalisms which precondition and explain the experience. The dictation remains persistently of the world. . . . The outside as it becomes technical to our experience re-poses a tense discourse, which interrogates the humanism and anthropomorphism of what is usually thought to be the poem's expression." (From "The Practice of Outside" by Robin Blaser in *The Collected Books of Jack Spicer*, 1975: Black Sparrow Press, Santa Barbara).

parts of me light up *glowing"*—nor one that has looked out on this world with a more pervasively whimsical refusal to take oneself— & these facts of life—too seriously. That this book is largely composed of debris may account for some of the anxiety in reading it.

In her work, Weiner has explored—come upon—the language that fills, and often enough, controls our lives (every day, *common* place: she says "group mind"). That these elements are *seen* in the work, hence physicalized, palpable, gives us a view of what is given, what has been handed down: & by seeing language operate, we can start to free ourselves from a compulsive obedience to it. The darker other side of the coin is equally evident in Weiner's work. When we begin to see words we may find ourselves tyrannized by them if we cannot at the same time question their authority. —Yet explorers run a high risk of falling prey to their own discoveries. A hope is that others might yet learn from these without falling prey themselves.

The citational: shards of language, ciphers to be examined for evidence, yet which we are forever beholden to . . . which holds our sight within its views. The purpose of writing, Weiner says, is to "change consciousness". —This work is, for me, heroic because of its radical reaffirmation of a commitment to writing as a specific kind of object making, an investigation rather than an aestheticization.

Weiner's writing is a chronicle of a mind coming to terms with itself, quite literally: for the terms are, in fact, made visible. We all see words, but it is our usual practice to see *through* them. Weiner has focussed her gaze not through, not beyond, but onto.

Charles Bernstein

BERNARD WELT, *Wave*

(1977: Jawbone, Washington, D.C.)

Bernard Welt's poems tell what goes on in the head attuned and committed to paying attention to itself in all the forms customary language takes, as clearly these grow more arbitrary and various. The lines, stanzas, poems, sentences are as relentlessly and casually formal in their occupation as any. Here it seems second nature, virtually de rerum natura / the way things are —

These are voices in the mind that are no less for that in the body. Their tone and import take from all the gestures of moment that happen in the inward-looking roving mind the gist of their curb ("this pleasant, slightly confused murmuring"). BW gets a positive rush of courage out of sinking feelings, while the whole turmoil comes across in the blankest verse, direct as it is erring, voluble as it is laconic, glib as it is searching.

Wave is a long poem of some more than 13 pages, dedicated to Diane Ward, much of it virtually prose and the whole more loosely structured than other BW work I've seen. Its sections are discrete but not numbered and there is no interruption. The tone is of a voice deliberately talking on, such that no distinction need be made between figurative and literal speech. The conversation is as literary as in Conrad, and there is no joke about talk.

Part of the project of *Wave* appears to be to say something given that it is difficult. The difficulties are various, and named when possible— "You have nothing to talk about, / and no way to say it"; "The words fly off into the air, / one by one, slowly, like / thought balloons, escaping analysis / into their immediate constituent units"; "You will say the same thing over and over again, but in different ways." There is no difference between puzzling over and celebrating here. The poem has the air of a disquisition on being here, or is it relationship, or address, but leans not on prepared terms, strategies, syntaxes, known ideas, but hurdles them. It is of and in movement, with a consciously rhetorical resistance against though amid the kind of stasis bred of getting anything down — "the matter / becoming an end in itself, / the individual waves / obscuring the sea, / and then you're lost: lost because you have found one place to be safer than others, and it is, but what has happened / to the motion. Absorbed / into the lines. / You have to support / what you can't avoid, / and that becomes automatic, so that it's as much a rule for those who use it to make things easy, freeze the motion, as those who learn to ride the wave, though the latter course is fraught with obstacles, 'monsters,' even; still, there is no reason to be proud of this because you have only done what you had to."

Along with the unwillingness to assume or grant the rightness of any given topic or form runs the assertion not only that any given perception or act is adequate and inevitable but also that each is, perhaps however one happens to see it, a casual paradigm. The indirection of

the poem's investigations and the distracting imbalance of its resolu-
tions, which is egged on to generate another momentum, paradoxi-
cally challenge and confirm this almost matter-of-fact fatality — the
energy offsets romantic and classical attitudes, which are both felt
deeply and problematically. Evidently the poem was written with 2
hands. Reading it, dialectical faculties are called into debate and de-
constructed. The poem is heartfelt, with that innate music, enough that
the consequence is a sort of dance, albeit tentative and ceremonious
like two contemporary friends meeting on purpose together who don't
know each other yet — although you might say there is nothing to fear,
casualness, generosity, even a show of vulnerability seem requisite as
much to indicate one's autonomy and separateness as to elicit sympa-
thy and response. The poem is less incantatory of the image of such
discourse than of its issue in what one may take it that it needs to be, as
though the voices barraging one from inside the head might be recog-
nized as just as worthy of trust as the whisper in one's ear from an ideal
friend, as though the focused deflection of all aural experience through
the conch shell were actually the ocean's chosen form of address to
me, whether arbitrary indeed or reiterative or intended for this moment
all along. I myself find this rather upsetting. BW persistently raises the
stakes of the poem high as possible without losing them from our mu-
tual view, challenges ideals of action, perception, and utterance and
what can be said of them, however ironically, sparing no direct refer-
ence to the weaknesses noticed in coping with them.

Steve Benson

PROOF

John Wieners, *Behind the State Capitol* (1975: Good Gay
Poets, Boston)

DOES one ever develop a thought ?
How has density proven ?
C O H E R E *if* itinerant in their attention, coded, spaced out,
clipped from a book; likewise chance changed address ?
A good jostling now and again — taking mathematically into account
irrelevant connectives, or quoting ignoble demolitions ((a method-

ology of confused doubt, or the *i n v e r s e* of doubt, indexd in some contrary or erratic way for ... for doing what ? for solidifying random and heedless acts attached beyond comprehension to the everyday; since that everyday is confused too broadly even for the chronicler or the semblagist)) : does this outshine parsimony ?
If shadowy interference nonetheless shifts our place, do we need complete dislocation, or disjuncture ?

CAN someone simply *decorate* the gaps, and lacks ?
By what manner, in manners, in a manner of speaking, is decorum the sensible adjunct we want to a sumptuous surveillance ?
Do I preen fetishly in reading, with a total comprehension, smothered in decorum ?
Is this my reading ?
And who will avenge this murder by which each single event is invested with dignity ?

AND how (and where) is consternation in the realm of reason a confrontation of the unknown, and do we know it ?
Or just, "You think I'm normal, they do a lot of things to my mind" ? : a senseless indecipherable deluge, where nothing contextualizes an other thing ?
Not a frame outside, and not a kernel inside ?
Are we all collage, all dense, tensed, & unlocatable ?
The soundless permeation of madness upon sanity : would this be the quandary gotten by viewing the language as the cure for the artistry ?
As a rebuff to social order, to emotional and perceptual order ?

WELL there are within it ACCURATEd voices of other places   former silences and far events   forgotten opposition   and those gregarious references' experience — simultaneity for want of better words — having become a plural intimate response : but is this without cost ?
Disinterested (priceless?) content ?
As if   we forego prior lucidities — to gain fresh condition   perhaps or less referral to the past   an independence, a genealogical morale — & then involve ourselves needlessly in prior obscurity ((the VOICES droned on)) ?

IS that what behooves to haphazard : passion's desire to sound representable identity ?
Not to be transfixed in the plural ?
Or the, without a syncopation, self construed wishfully by absorbent

intellect, the record of one, stylized and self-conscious ?

I = declaims use, for could one expect he should have the qualities of doing almost everything else ?

Disclaims use, isn't that it, for knowing an answer : it's a womanish heart ?

HOW can we construe this ? : by caverned fall in — a vertical dimension — caring of sounds, abutting solidity apart, cramming for brevity ? Or, with mere words, rhetoric ? — so back to the believable histrionics to finally learn the diction ? (learned minutely expressed things dictated without choice, direction in discourse as a duty-found definition of alleged purpose) ?

NOT to belabor either fact or to imagine a world devoid of nabobs and fulfilled in reality, yet still in forebearance of any genuine appearance : what have we got here ?

None of *trompe-l'oeil*, so therefore language an act of sharing words ? Or both realism and make-believe, caught in that dilemma ?

Yet how to get beyond both: first, that kindled embrace of past observation (the simple glass mirror, which allows subterfuge to glow forthrightly) and second, that condition of mankind dependent on hallucination in place of imagination ?

CONFUSION ? Decor ? Meaning ? Memory ? Body ? Space ? Self ? Rhetoric ? Reality ?

But after examination you find out it's true and say of course that was it all the time, where pure patented mystique fulfills its indispensable acts. That explains everything.

Bruce Andrews

LOUIS ZUKOFSKY

The first (& for a long time the only) to read Pound & Williams with what we wld recognize as modern eye & ear. Ear tuned tautly toward a double function: *intrinsic*, language as he found it (i.e., parole); *extrinsic*, musical composition, determining wholeness, aesthetic consistency, perfect rest. But for whom language began with sight (thus *Bottom* — love : reason :: eye : mind — in wch love contains all the significations Benjamin, so like LZ, gave the term *aura*). In his writing, language (L) synthesizes polar impulses rising dialectically from an equally problematic material base:

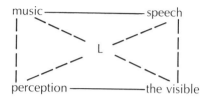

Not the tongue his parents spoke, it always carries some trace of Other (hence *Catullus*), tending toward objectification. Each line &/or stanza a study in balance, silence (peace) proposed as maximum stress in all directions, thus active. This never-to-be resolvd equilibrium of the spoken within the written within the spoken, etc., is for him the motivating center of craft (the final 28 lines of *"A" 23*, last words, escort the reader thru the alphabet, letters are presences).

"A living calendar . . . : music, thought, drama, story, poem" (*23*). A characteristic distinction: the title is *"A"*, not *A*. Its open-ended interconnectedness in *1-6* marks the debt to *The Cantos*, but from *7* (w/ wch he chose to represent himself in the Objectivist issue of *Poetry*, 2/31) forward, a new conceptualization as to the function of part-to-whole relations in the formation of a longpoem starts to emerge: each moment is a totalization, complete to itself, capable of entering into larger structures as a relational fact. This integrity of units is radically unlike *Maximus* or *Passages*, tho it includes (requires!) the capacity to incorporate a piece in open form (*"A" 12* his *Paterson*) — this empowers Zukofsky, & he alone, to complete such a work.

April 5, 1928: St. Matthew's Passion is performed at Carnegie Hall & Connie Mack's Athletics, about to start a season of baseball, introduce a new uniform, replacing their elephant logo with a large letter *A*. These events are reported on facing pages in the Friday *New York Times*.

Ron Silliman

"A"-24

The difficulties "A"-24 imposes on its performers and audience are enormous. They stem directly from Zukofsky's poetics: "An integral / Lower limit speech / Upper limit music." The words function two ways at once: as phonemes, and as syntax, meaning, story.

The structure of the piece insists on language's double ply. There's music playing, Handel's [Bach, Z's expected choice, wd have been too 'good', too complicated & distracting?], sturdy, straight-forward rhythm, clear never quite to the point of obviousness, the vertical architecture (harmonies) and the horizontal (melody, counterpoint) always hearable. 4 voices (Thought, Drama, Story, Poem) are scored into this steady pulse as precisely as if the piece were a quintet for strings and keyboard. Phonetically, the words are treated as music.

But, quoting Act I, Scene I, "Blest / Infinite things / So many / Which confuse imagination / Thru its weakness / To the ear / Noises. / Or harmony / Delights / Men to madness / " (Spinoza), the syntactic side gets stretched. It's often difficult to speak the meanings vividly due to the number of rests scored into each vocal line. And when the musical rhythm is quick enough to allow the line to near speech, the listener has the problem of the vertical overlay of the other 3 voices. [Occasionally (end of first scene) different voices splice without much overlay to sound *one* multi-syntactic phrase/sentence (a bit like Webern), but it's an exception. Not the point of the piece.]

The theory of language approaching music should allow for an approachable 'verbal harmony'. But the analogy misleads. Discounting externals (timbre, octave spacing, etc.) music (standard Western for the moment, the kind Z seemed mainly concerned with) works with a vocabulary of 12 tones, units. English uses, say, 300 phonemes, and they aren't the point, but rather the 500,000 words that are elusively pinned to them. Not to mention syntax/sentences.

Language doesn't occur in time the way music does. Music is strictly sequence, absolutely dependent on time. Language merely uses time to embody itself in a string of phonemes, the meaning occurring both during the sounds, and after they have vanished. In music, a vertical cross-section is unambiguous at every point. The units are instantly 'transparent', so to speak. A g sounds like a g, always, thus allowing

Louis Zukofsky's "A"-24 was performed by Kit Robinson (Thought), Steve Benson and Carla Harryman (Drama; Cousin, Father, Attendant D, Doctor, Son—Steve; Nurse, Girl, Attendant R, Mother, Aunt—Carla), Lyn Hejinian (Story), Barrett Watten (Poem), and Bob Perelman (piano, should have been harpsichord) in April 1978 at the Grand Piano, San Francisco, and later elsewhere in California.

Bach to write such complicated single voices and put as many as 6 of them together into such exciting and 'inevitable' harmonic order, an ability Zukofsky loved him for.

But language doesn't work that way. A phoneme doesn't sound like a word, a verb won't necessarily reveal itself as such until some, or many, more phonemes have sounded. Phonemes, the units of 'verbal music', aren't transparent, can't be superimposed without ambiguity. What the ear tends to do on first hearing "A"-24 is switch rapidly from voice to voice. The quality of all 4 modes of Zukofsky's writing is immediately and ubiquitously apparent, his 'sincerity' [see "An Objective", II], his care in choosing and joining words.

But to fully appreciate the rhymes, harmonies, congruences takes repeated hearings, reading each part separately, joining them to their original contexts. "A"-24 echoes minutely and vastly. There are immediately hearable phonetic rhymes, syntactic rhymes (e.g. pp. 167–8, Thought: "in case he should attempt an escape"; Drama: "but now I go"; Poem: "not many of us will get out of it alive."), but many more echoes, repetitions, allusions that are widely separated. The most compelling congruences are the largest. In the last section, Fugues: Thought: Henry Adams' life/writing; Story: a particular instance of Z's life/writing a single sentence; Drama: Z's dramatization of himself as a young man; Poem: nature as creator/created. Plus Adams' marriage/Z's marriage/ the Son's romance with the Girl, etc., etc., *etc.*

Ultimately, hearing "A"-24 will lead to the totality of Zukofsky's work. As he said, a poet writes one work all his life. "A"-24 really is "Celia's L.Z. Masque," a most accurate portrait of him. The scoring and text selection were hers. (I assume the "idea" of the piece was both of theirs.)

Clearly, everybody hears all the *sound* of the piece. But Zukofsky is trying to hook up the physical instantaneous unconscious undistortable act of hearing with the fullest possible range of thought (all of a life). Performing and hearing "A"-24 presupposes a thorough knowledge of Z's work, an ecstatically dilated time sense in which every syllable continues sounding until they all have resolved each other, and an eternity in which the whole work is present in any of its sounds. A properly ambitious conclusion to "A".

Bob Perelman

"THINK SUN AND SEE SHADOW"

naked sitting and lying awake

dear eyes all eyes

destined actual infinitely initial

rove into the blue initial

an earth of three trees

rendered his requiem alive

blessed ardent Celia happy

an era any time of year

an inequality wind flower

— (4's & 5's from) Louis Zukofsky

Robert Grenier

L.Z.

All men write poetry, but few are poets. Children know that we may see poetry with our ears: ABCD goldfish? MNO goldfish! OSMR goldfish. And that it is our first delight in words that they hopscotch sequential noise— A poet, we say, has vision. Louis Zukofsky's vision came from excision of all but ears to the language itself, letter by letter: A. Like Nature, he was bent on ever more intricate goldfish. "Homer's Argos hearing / Handel's Largo as / The car goes". It is needless to state that this is first a telescope, before it is a poem. Behind the wheel, fiddling the syllables, the finest ears in the business is heading somewhere 100,000 years an hour (or so). Do you not hear them thunder?

Ronald Johnson